Han Unbound

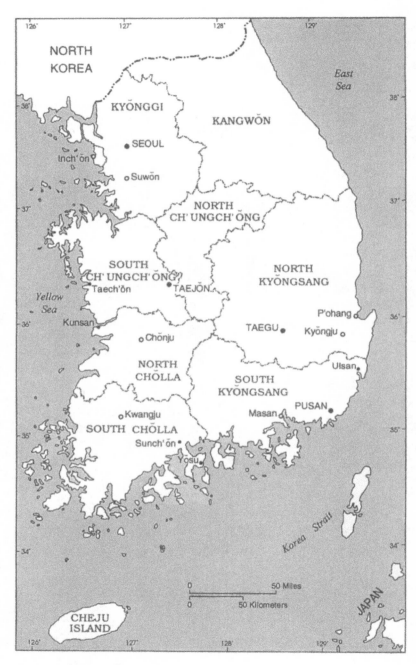

Present-day South Korea

HAN UNBOUND

*The Political Economy
of South Korea*

JOHN LIE

*Stanford University Press
Stanford, California*

Stanford University Press
Stanford, California

© 1998 by the Board of Trustees of the
Leland Stanford Junior University

Printed in the United States of America

Book epigraph: Jorge Luis Borges, from "Epilogue,"
Oct. 31, 1960, in *Dreamtigers*, part II,
trans. Harold Morland (© 1964).
Courtesy of the University of Texas Press.

CIP data are at the end of the book

for Nancy Abelmann

Preface

Decolonization after the Second World War created the Third World and development studies. Ambitious theories promised to provide the key to understanding development. Time and again, however, the fanfare that accompanied a new theoretical breakthrough was silenced by a growing chorus of empirical refutations. Scholars sang a requiem to the once-promising ideal of modernization and development.

Indeed, poverty and famine, dictatorship and disaster, illiteracy and powerlessness characterize too many areas of the world. The gap between the rich First World and the poor Third World appears to be widening (World Bank 1990: 7; Maddison 1995: 22). According to *Human Development Report 1994*, "A fifth of the developing world's population goes hungry every night, a quarter lacks access to even a basic necessity like safe drinking water, and a third lives in a state of abject poverty—at such a margin of human existence that words simply fail to describe it" (UNDP 1994: 2). Some speak now, not of a Third World, but of a Fourth, the world of desperation and despair.

It is against this backdrop that South Korean development emerges as a significant topic. The case of South Korea is especially poignant because, as Irma Adelman (1980: 224) noted, it "was considered to be a bottomless pit" in the early 1960s. Yet the basket case of the 1960s turned out to be a rare showcase by the 1980s. The

British Marxist Perry Anderson (1996: 28) observed after his visit to Seoul: "What a Londoner notices first is the ways in which the city [Seoul] is more advanced than his own." Indeed, South Korean prosperity and democratization have been the envy of other developing countries. For many scholars and policymakers, South Korea is a model to which other Third World countries should aspire.

Nonetheless, it is misleading to stress only the positive aspects of South Korean development. As late as 1986, South Korean manufacturing employees worked the longest hours in the world, their wages were lower than those of their counterparts in Brazil, Mexico, Hong Kong, and Singapore, and their industrial accident rate was one of the highest in the world (Lie 1992a). Urbanites encountered bleak housing conditions, farmers faced rising debts, nature was devastated. The authoritarian regime wreaked havoc on the body politic by muffling dissident voices and egregiously abusing the human rights of its citizens. As one sociologist queried: "Is it proper to speak about development if it creates as politically repulsive a society as South Korea?" (Hall 1986: 240). One may very well question the values that uncritically celebrate the South Korean miracle—those that valorize, for example, the concrete pavement and the smoke stacks that denoted progress at the expense of beautiful mountains and clean air. The dark side of the South Korean "miracle" should be illuminated not only to balance the chimerical scale of historical justice but also to understand its crucial and constitutive part in the drama of development.

In *Han Unbound* I attempt to make sense of the transmogrification of South Korea from a poor, agrarian country into an increasingly rich and industrializing nation-state. I present the trajectory of South Korean development from the Korean War to the 1988 Seoul Olympics, focusing on rapid industrialization and authoritarian politics. In advancing my analytical framework, I criticize previous efforts to explain South Korean development. Most of them are, as I note throughout this book, retrospective constructs that elide shifting contexts and contingencies. There was nothing obvious or predictable about the path of South Korean development. It is a singular story that cannot be explained by any general theory of national development and offers no simple model for other developing countries.

*

I originally became interested in the social sciences in order to understand Third World development. I had hoped to help redress gross social injustices—poverty, famine, pestilence, human rights abuse, and so on—that I read about in libraries and observed during my travels. However, I soon became skeptical about my role as an uninvited outsider. I feared that I would merely be a "rural development tourist" (Chambers 1983: 10–12) or a "disaster tourist" (De Waal 1989: 21–23). Indeed, much development work and research seems to be more part of the problem than any sort of path to a solution. Frequently ignorant of the languages, cultures, and political economies of the countries they study, many policymakers and scholars often only make worse what they had hoped to improve (Colson 1982: 23–24).

What is to be done? For myself, I thought that a small but necessary task was to criticize wrong ideas and to propose better frameworks. When a series of circumstances led me to spend over a year (1988–89) in Seoul, I began to write about South Korean development. After producing a series of uncharitable reviews of books on South Korean development (e.g. Lie 1990b, 1991d), I concluded that an overview of South Korean development would not only be useful to interested readers but might also satisfy my erstwhile critical conscience. The result is this book.

Let me briefly gloss my title. "Han" refers both to South Korea (*Han'guk*) and to the cultural expression of *ressentiment* (*han*). I wanted to capture the ambivalence of development—both its triumphs and tragedies. The celebratory chants about the miracle on the Han (the major river through Seoul) should not silence the plaintive wails of long-suffering farmers and workers. Although this book is not quite a "lyrical drama," I had also hoped to capture some of the poetry—the cries of joy and sorrow—of the South Korean national epic.

As to its "political economy" this book is a direct descendant of the work of Adam Smith, Karl Marx, Max Weber, and Barrington Moore Jr. The classic question of power and wealth and the concern with big structures and large processes are critical for understanding the origins and consequences of modernity. Like them I insist that one cannot adequately understand or explain economic institutions and processes independently of the political, or political institutions and processes independently of the economic. And sociology is, in my view, inseparable from political economy; to sever it from political and economic contexts is to render it trivial.

"South Korea" defines not only a bounded territory but a time period as well—the Republic of Korea was founded in 1948. I analyze South Korea as a "national economy," which is "a political space, transformed by the state as a result of the necessities and innovations of economic life, into a coherent, unified economic space whose combined activities may tend in the same direction" (Braudel 1977: 99).

Throughout the book, I use "development" as a descriptive term in the sense that both W. Arthur Lewis (1955: 9) and Paul Baran (1957: 1) used it to analyze economic growth. Like them, I consider not merely economic factors but social and political ones as well. I realize that development has been used in a myriad of ways and that it remains, like most social scientific terms, an essentially contested concept, "which inevitably involve[s] endless disputes about [its] proper uses on the part of [its] users" (Gallie 1964: 158). Nonetheless, I thought that it best conveyed the nature and scope of my inquiry.

Studying the political economy of development necessarily takes me to the terrain of history. However, I eschew the term "history" because this study departs from a conventional chronological narrative that history evokes for some people, and because I am not an academic historian who perforce engages in archival research. But disciplinary distinctions, whether between the study of politics and of economics, or between history and sociology, are ultimately irrelevant. In the spirit of classical political economy, this study belongs squarely within the singular discipline of the human science.

At least since the *Methodenstreit* of the late nineteenth century, scholars have quarreled about the primacy of explanation (*erklären*) or of understanding (*verstehen*) (Apel 1984: 11–28). The scientific impulse beckons social scientists to seek generalizations and abstract formulations, while the hermeneutic urge calls them to stress cultural and historical particularities. It is problematic to choose between the desert of abstruse formalism and statistical analyses or the jungle of historical uniqueness and ethnographic concreteness. At one level, the two poles are complementary; the great works of Adam Smith, Karl Marx, or Max Weber incorporate both impulses. At another level, Michael Polanyi (1959: 13) was right to insist that "understanding" (what he called "tacit knowledge") "is in fact the dominant principle of all knowledge, and that its rejection would, therefore, automatically involve the rejection of all knowledge whatever." At the same time, he urged that the task of science was to strive toward more abstract knowledge— "explanation." In other words, without some knowledge of the on-the-ground, descriptive, or historical and cultural particulars—in short, without understanding—we cannot explain. Hence, in order to "explain" South Korean development, I devote considerable energy to conveying an "understanding" of it.

Another way of articulating my point is that social scientists should transcend the sterile dichotomies of form versus substance, nomothetic versus idiographic, theoretical versus descriptive, or global versus local. In warning against the twin dangers of "grand theory" and "abstracted empiricism," C. Wright Mills (1959: 6) issued an unforgettable injunction for sociologists "to grasp history and biography and the relations between the two within society. That is its task and its promise." We need to see the general in the particular, just as much as we need to view and contextualize the particular in the general.

The explanatory strategy I employ in this book is "structural sequence analysis." I analyze a series of necessary but insufficient conditions of South Korean development. The logic of necessary but insufficient causes highlights both the structured contexts and the contingencies that unfold in irreversible time. Development is, in my view, as much about avoiding pitfalls as it is about getting things right. It is a path-dependent process from which we can neither derive deterministic schemes nor expunge contingencies.

In analyzing South Korean development as a sequence of structural opportunities and constraints, I do not merely highlight structural variables or preconditions. State-centric theorists, for example, stress the role of the state. Although the state is undoubtedly important, it may well be corrupt and hence impede development, as I argue in Chapter 2. The state should be analyzed in its concrete context, that confluence of internal and external forces which has shaped it. Rather than analyzing abstract variables, I seek to delineate causal relations that occur in concrete contexts and in sequence. In narrating the ways in which South Korea avoided getting things irrevocably wrong and got things right, I take seriously the relevant contexts and contingencies.

In the very late twentieth century large questions are unpopular in many centers of learning. A common scholarly strategy is to delineate a carefully chosen area of inquiry, review the relevant literature, perhaps hazard a hypothesis or two, demonstrate logical and methodological rigor, analyze and present empirical findings, and thereby ensure respectability. I eschew this straight and narrow path. However worthy individual articles and monographs are, there are still large questions that need to be asked; perhaps they are unanswerable, perhaps it is not yet time to answer them (perhaps we must wait for the patient accumulation of facts). To the first objection, I have no riposte save this book. To the second, my reply is that smaller questions and answers are parasitic on larger questions and answers. Quite often, hard-nosed empiricists ask obsolete questions and produce irrelevant answers. In the absence of macroscopic views and concerns, there is the ever-present danger of that sort of abstracted empiricism which obscures even the obvious. As Peter Worsley (1970: x) mercilessly put it, "In the United States the sociologist has been described as a man who spends $50,000 to find the way to a whorehouse."

This book is a synthetic work and I have used a variety of sources. In particular, I worked for a large corporation and taught at a university in Seoul in the late 1980s. I lived in several distinct neighborhoods of Seoul and traveled throughout the peninsula. An adequate sociological understanding—and hence explanation—requires, I think, a certain cultural immersion that militates against the practice of "airport sociology" (Worsley 1970: xii). The ethnographic and interview data supplement documentary sources, such as government publications and contemporary reportage.

I use statistical figures cautiously as illustrations. As a self-proclaimed architect of the First Five-Year Economic Development Plan and a later economic minister told me, "You can't trust the numbers. I know because I wrote some of [the government publications]" (see also Eberstadt 1995b: 5–10; cf. Hill 1986: 33). The illustrative character of statistics is also mandated by my emphasis on unraveling qualitative changes. As Barrington Moore Jr. (1966: 519–20) wrote: "The distinctions in these forms and patterns [of social relations] do not seem to me reducible to any quantitative differences; they are incommensurable. Yet it is precisely such differences that matter most to human beings."

It is not that I celebrate the death of the author, but I feel affinity with Claude Lévi-Strauss's confession that "I never had, and still do not have, the perception of feeling my personal identity. I appear to myself as the place where something is going on, but there is no 'I', no 'me.' Each of us is a kind of crossroads where things happen. The crossroads is purely passive; something happens there." This intellectual product is indelibly marked by a particular milieu. Although I cannot possibly thank everyone, let me acknowledge some of them.

Citations—even as they blight the text—are my minimal recognition of and salutation to past writers (I write, therefore I cite). My anxiety of influence should not hide that I stand, if precariously, atop the tomes that I have read. I have, however, tried to minimize the number of citations and footnotes. I did not want this book to be a pallid imitation of Vladimir Nabokov's *Pale Fire*; any good modernist should know that extensive footnotes are for poems, not for serious works of scholarship.

I feel at times that I was, as James Boswell said of Samuel Johnson, "born to grapple with whole libraries." My bibliomania has been well served at several libraries; my thanks to all who helped me get, as well as to reshelve, countless books. I also benefited from (even as my bank account teetered close to zero) my innumerable visits to that haven of civilization, bookstores.

Nancy Abelmann, Chang Yunshik, Megan Greene, Han Do Hyun, David Hopping, Perry Mehrling, Judith Pintar, Mike Shin, Alvin So, Son Wonje, and David Wank kindly commented on drafts of this book. Miwako Kuno, Soo-Jung Lee, and Shiuan-yi Wang helped me get the references right. Jane Domier did the map; Aya Ezama helped me with the index. To them, my heartfelt thanks.

Muriel Bell at Stanford University Press has been unfailingly encouraging. I am extremely grateful for her support and patience over the past several years. I wish also to thank Jan Spauschus Johnson, a responsive and responsible editor, and Andrew Lewis, a superb and scrupulous copy editor. Roger Janelli and Hagen Koo, as the readers for the Press, offered very helpful comments.

In the late 1980s, when I was shuttling back and forth between South Korea and the United States, several friends offered unmatched hospitality and irreplaceable company. In particular, I wish to thank Judy and Perry Mehrling and Leslie Salzinger, as well as my sister Mahee Lie, in the United States. In South Korea, Kim Jung Sun, Koo Hye Young, Park Hae Jung, and my parents, Harry and Jane Lie, made my stay more bearable. I should also like to acknowledge my uncle Lee Woo Chang and my grandfather Lee Kap Chu, who redeemed South Korea for me during my childhood.

Finally, many thanks to Nancy Abelmann and her family, especially Rena and Walter Abelmann. If Nancy had her way, this book would never have come to be, but this book might never have been without her.

J.L.

Contents

A Note to the Reader

All translations are mine unless otherwise indicated. In transliterating Korean names and words, I use the McCune-Reischauer system, excluding places and names well known to North American readers (e.g., "Seoul" instead of "Sŏul"; "Rhee Syngman" instead of "Yi Sŭng-man"). As the Rhee Syngman example suggests, I follow the received Korean practice of placing surnames first. Exceptions are made for those who write primarily in Western languages.

All references to "Korea" are to pre-Division Korea, "South Korea" to the Republic of Korea, and "North Korea" to the People's Democratic Republic of Korea.

Abbreviations

I use the following abbreviations in the text:

ACHR	Asian Coalition for Housing Rights
CIA	Central Intelligence Agency
CISJD	Christian Institute for the Study of Justice and Development
CTCCA	Commission on Theological Concerns of the Christian Conference of Asia
DRP	Democratic Republican Party
ECCKP	Emergency Christian Conference on Korean Problems
EPB	Economic Planning Board
FAO	Food and Agriculture Organization of the United Nations
FKTU	Federation of Korean Trade Unions
HMY	Han'guk Minjungsa Yŏn'guhoe
HKMY	Han'guk Konghae Munje Yŏn'guso
HSHC	Han'guk Sahoehakhoe, and Han'guk Chŏngch'ihakhoe
HSSY	Han'guk Sanŏp Sahoe Yŏn'guhoe
HSYH	Han'guk Sahoekwahak Yŏn'gu Hyobŭihoe
HTH	Haksul Tanch'e Hyŏbŭihoe
ISI	import substitution industrialization
KCIA	Korean Central Intelligence Agency
KDI	Korea Development Institute
MCI	Ministry of Culture and Information

Abbreviations

MPI	Ministry of Public Information
NCY	Nara Chŏngch'aek Yŏn'guhoe
NSK	Nomura Sōgō Kenkyūsho
OAC	Office of Administrative Coordination for the Prime Minister
OEAR	Office of Economic Analysis and Reporting
OP	Office of the President
OPI	Office of Public Information
POSCO	Pohang Iron and Steel Company
ROK	Republic of Korea
SCNR	Supreme Council for National Reconstruction
SSS	Sŏuldae Sahoehakkwa Sahoe Paljŏn Yŏn'guhoe
THM	Tto Hana ŭi Munhwa
UNDP	United Nations Development Programme
YHSY	Yŏsŏng Han'guk Sahoe Yŏn'guhoe

A man sets himself the task of portraying the world.
Through the years he peoples a space with images of
provinces, kingdoms, mountains, bays, ships, islands, fishes,
rooms, instruments, stars, horses, and people.
Shortly before his death, he discovers that that patient
labyrinth of lines traces the image of his face.

—Jorge Luis Borges, *Dreamtigers*

Prelude

I was born in South Korea in 1959. Although my family soon moved to Japan, we returned almost annually to see my maternal grandparents in Seoul and my paternal grandparents in Taech'ŏn (in the South Ch'ungch'ŏng Province). Seoul in the early 1960s was my childhood conception of backwardness. While I marveled at traffic jams in Tokyo, I was horrified by the oxcarts tottering along on Seoul's dusty roads. Tokyo seemed indisputably modern, with its international-style high-rises, electronic toys, flush toilets, air conditioners, and refrigerators. Seoul, in contrast, appeared unmodern with its Japanese colonial-period architecture, wooden toys, non-flush toilets without toilet paper, and, at best, electric fans and ice blocks. Tokyo was dynamic—new buildings popping up everywhere, store shelves overflowing with new products; Seoul was stationary, trapped in tradition. In Tokyo, I gorged on caramels and chocolates sold in tidy stores; in Seoul, I gagged on grilled grasshoppers peddled on the street. Going to restaurants in South Korea, I was incredulous that rice—by then produced in great abundance in Japan—couldn't be served on certain days because of government restrictions.

Seoul, however, was light-years ahead of Taech'ŏn, a small provincial town near the sea (and not far, incidentally, from the villages studied by the American anthropologist Vincent Brandt [1971]). Nature overwhelmed my senses: endless rice paddies, uncultivated land and forested hills, rivers, streams, and beaches. The quietness of the night was heightened by insect noises and the starry heaven above. To my urbanized, modern consumer self, however, Taech'ŏn was peripheral to everything that made life worthwhile. Indeed, my father's occasional threat to banish me to Taech'ŏn was enough to make me the most dutiful of sons. In Taech'ŏn the only signs of civilization were the bottles of Coca Cola and the bars of Hershey's chocolate my paternal grandfather bought on the black market. I found respite by introducing baseball to the cottars' children; we transformed pebble fields into a baseball diamond.

My memories of the backwardness of South Korea in the 1960s had faded by the late 1980s when I taught at Yonsei University in Seoul. The national hype over the 1988 Seoul Olympics struck a teary chord for older people—"I used to beg for chocolate from GIs; now Americans will come to Korea and they will be impressed by our amazing progress"—while younger people, such as my predominantly urban, middle-class students, took the material plenty for granted. Most of them could hardly believe that the government had once restricted restaurants from serving rice or that south of the Han River, which had become a thriving center of conspicuous consumption by the late 1980s, had been a swamp until the 1970s.

The transformations were political and cultural as well as material. In 1974 South Korea was under the iron grip of President Park Chung Hee. The Korean Central Intelligence Agency (KCIA, often referred to by the location of its headquarters, Namsan, a mountain in central Seoul) was ubiquitous; even café conversations were self-censored for fear of KCIA informants. The specter of the North and the threat of war were everywhere; South Korea was a heavily policed and militarized society. Posters listing emergency phone numbers and enormous rewards for information on North Korean spies were as numerous as telephone poles. One of my Korean American acquaintances was interrogated by the police because he didn't know the correct price of a pack of cigarettes. According to the propaganda instilled in the population, not knowing the prices of common consumer goods was a tell-tale sign of a North Korean spy. The rhythm of daily life was, moreover, monitored by anticommunist discipline. Nightly curfews forced urbanites to scurry back to their homes by midnight. Monthly sirens wailed as the city came to a halt to practice civil defense against an imagined North Korean attack. Repression penetrated everyday life.

In the late 1980s, South Korea experienced a level of political mobilization rare in world history. Students, later joined by middle-class citizens, filled the streets regularly, demanding democracy and engaging in combat with the riot police. Between rock throwing and political sloganeering, radical political culture dominated college life; many students read leftist tracts, sang protest songs, and drank and debated all night. Industrial workers, more dramatically, engaged in a crescendo of strikes and lockouts. As if to prove the class struggle thesis touted by radical students, labor militancy incorporated an ever larger number of workers. Office workers and even the employees of elite financial firms began to strike. For students of social change, it was bliss to be alive in Seoul in the late 1980s.

Change was rapid and compressed. Returning to Seoul a few years later, I was surprised to discover that the revolutionary fervor of students had dissipated. When Marx had been censored, students devoured mimeographed copies, often in a foreign language; now that his writings were readily available in Korean, there was hardly a readership left. While scattered strikes and student demonstrations continued into the 1990s, the mass mobilization that gripped South Korea in the late 1980s had virtually disappeared.

Cultural changes were equally profound. In the 1960s, with the exception of the areas around the U.S. military bases, such as Walker Hill and its casinos or It'aewŏn with its bars and shops, one of the few leisure and consumption centers was Myŏng-dong (literally, the "bright area"), the Ginza of Seoul. Yet compared to Ginza, Myŏng-dong was but an overgrown main street. Movies were strictly limited to domestic films and Hollywood B movies. Foreigners, especially non-Asians, were rare outside U.S. military bases. Intense curiosity greeted foreign businessmen and diplomats, as well as American anthropologists and Peace Corps volunteers.

By the 1980s, the once-brilliant Myŏng-dong had become a squalor in comparison to Kangnam (a rich enclave south of the

Han River), particularly Apkujŏng-dong. In the late 1980s, I strolled through Myŏng-dong for nostalgia's sake, looking for dark cafés, hole-in-the-wall noodle restaurants, and other remnants of the 1960s. In Apkujŏng-dong, I encountered upper-middle-class housewives sporting *haute couture* and affluent youths leading lives of invidious distinction and dissolution. Clean and well-lit coffee shops had replaced the dark and dingy cafés; McDonald's and Pizza Hut, the noodle shops and cheap eateries. With internationalization—more South Koreans were venturing abroad and more foreigners were visiting South Korea—foreigners were greeted not with curiosity but with nonchalance.

What makes these changes and contrasts all the more striking is that they occurred during a mere generation. The pace of change matched Alvin Toffler's *Future Shock* (1970). From the material culture and the built environment to interpersonal relations and intimate thoughts, South Korea had been transformed in a mere three decades.

My personal impressions are far from unique; the anthropologist Choong Soon Kim (1992: xiv) writes:

> I was still unable to comprehend Korean progress until I witnessed the scene myself in 1981, when I returned to Korea for the first time since leaving for graduate school in 1965. Experiencing so suddenly the results of years of economic development and industrialization, I felt a case of "future shock." The entire country seemed to vibrate with economic progress. . . . I remember that near the end of World War II . . . most Korean school children were unable to wear decent shoes because materials for shoes had been confiscated by the Japanese for war supplies. Ironically, in 1986, Korea was the world's largest exporter of shoes.

Although it is easy to sensationalize the changes and to downplay the continuities, it would be foolhardy to deny the economic, social, and political transformation of South Korea from the early 1960s to the late 1980s. This, then, is the subject of this book: South Korean development.

CHAPTER ONE

Liberation, War, and Land Reform

The *yangban* (the landed gentry) dominated Chosŏn Dynasty Korea (1392–1910) and retained their local power during the Japanese colonial period (1910–45). At the founding of South Korea in 1948, the same social stratum dominated the countryside as they had for half a millennium. Their fundamental source of power was land ownership. In *yangban* political economy, monopoly over land ensured dominance in other spheres of social life. The post-Liberation land reform, however, was the crucial structural transformation that destroyed their power base and made later development possible.

The U.S. Military Government in South Korea

After the end of the Second World War, the United States replaced Japan as the dominant power in the southern half of the Korean peninsula. The division of Korea into a Soviet-backed North and the U.S.-backed South was cemented by the Cold War (Conde 1967, 2: 426–55). South Korea became a test case of U.S. containment policy (Leffler 1992: 167; S. H. Lee 1995). As part of its geopolitical and ideological struggle against the Soviet Union, the United States suppressed the indigenous and popular People's Republic and people's committees that had sprung up across much of the countryside after Liberation (C. Mitchell 1951: 14–15; Henderson 1968: 115–19) and supported Rhee Syngman when South Korea became independent in 1948 (G. McCune 1950: 48–49; Scalapino and Lee 1972: 312).

In spite of its near omnipotence, the United States never attained, or even sought to emulate, the sort of colonial presence that the Japanese had had. U.S. soldiers did not replace the colonial police force; U.S. bureaucrats and officials did not administer Korean institutions. Furthermore, Americans in general remained ignorant about South Korea. The journalist Richard Lauterbach (1947: 14) confessed: "And like most Americans, I had the scantiest kind of information about Korea and most of it turned out to be shockingly inaccurate." He was not alone. E. Grant Meade (1951: 51) wrote of his own experience in South Korea: "I received nine months of instruction at two military schools . . . during this entire period [I] heard a single one-hour lecture on Korea." With its heavy reliance on English-speaking Koreans, the U.S. military government was dubbed "the interpreters' government" (Lauterbach 1947: 224).

The paramount U.S. concern was to stop communism. Despite Rhee's imperfections as a leader, the United States could not find a credible alternative who was not tainted by a leftist past (G. McCune 1950: 245). Not only was he "modern"—he had a Ph.D. from Princeton and an Austrian wife and could speak English—his nationalist credentials were impeccable. His ardent anticommunism calmed the South Korean elite, and his ruthless maneuvers eliminated his rivals. U.S. support for Rhee strengthened as his policy became resolutely anticommunist. The last years of Chiang Kai-shek's regime in China were a potent reminder to U.S. policymakers about the importance of political stability. As far as the United States was concerned, Rhee's faults were merely peccadilloes that were more than excused by his politics. The tragedy of post–World War II U.S. foreign policy was that despite its professed Wilsonian idealism, the United States was often perfectly willing to support corrupt and reactionary dictators.

The United States granted political autonomy to Rhee and focused instead on military affairs and economic reconstruction. In so doing, the United States not only retained the colonial-period state bureaucracy and the police force but also rehabilitated known Japanese collaborators (Gayn 1948: 353; Henderson 1991: 134–36). E. Grant Meade (1951: 235) summarized:

> By suppressing the People's Republic and by identifying themselves with a minority group, the Americans distressed and antagonized the people; by providing a highly centralized government, they classified themselves with the Japanese; by arrogance and a patronizing attitude, they insulted and disillusioned those who had long held Americans in esteem; by failure to recognize Korean goals, and the intensity of the people with respect to them, American prestige suffered severely in the eyes of the Koreans.

The U.S. intervention in Korea squelched an indigenous effort at self-government and ultimately dashed the hope for a unified Korea. As Cornelius Osgood (1951: 324), one of the few ethnographers of post-Liberation, prewar Korea wrote: "The inevitable conclusion must be drawn that, for better or for worse, the Koreans as a whole would have preferred to determine the course of events by themselves."

Struggles over Land

The Japanese never challenged *yangban* domination of the countryside (see Appendix). By 1945, there was hardly a cohesive elite opposition within Korea; indeed, many former nationalists were actively urging collaboration. Although the extent of pro-Japanese sentiment and action remains a contested topic in the 1990s, it seems undeniable that the *yangban* had become part and parcel of Japanese rule. "Kapitan Ri," a story by Chŏn Kwangyong (1993), is a paradigmatic portrait of a collaborator, Yi Inguk, M.D. Dr. Yi's linguistic skill allows him to surf smoothly through first, the Japanese, then the Russian, and, finally, the American occupations. He reflects on his sycophantic life: "I've lived among those warty Japanese, made it out of the grasp of those brutish Russians, and now the Yankees—could they be much different? Revolutions may come and the nation change hands, but the way out has never been blocked for Yi Inguk" (K. Chŏn 1993: 83). His self-advancement, to be sure, occurs at the expense of others; for example, he refuses to treat a Korean nationalist for fear of the Japanese authorities. Dr. Yi exemplifies an elite that was widely perceived to be corrupt and unprincipled.[*]

The end of Japanese colonial rule unleashed a series of peasant uprisings that sought land reform, lower taxation, and peasant autonomy. Peasant unrest threatened the newly installed Rhee government. With its redistributive land program, the left—a menagerie ranging from nationalists to communists—remained popular even after the collapse of the People's Republic (G. McCune 1950: 90). Political violence between the Liberation and the Korean War claimed over 100,000 South Korean lives (Merrill 1983: 136). The most momentous of the peasant rebellions were the 1946 Chejudo Rebellion and the 1948 Yŏsu Rebellion (Merrill 1989). The U.S. military played an important part in suppressing them (Cumings 1990a: chap. 8).

The animating concern for most peasants was the land question. Choe Chong-hui vividly captures the post-Liberation contest over land in his 1946 story, "The Ritual at the Well." Watching villagers squabble, the narrator reflects:

> There is no good reason for the two mothers to fight. . . . The one responsible for your starving is . . . Landlord Ch'oe. For decades you worked like slaves on the land from which you got your food. Although the coming of liberation made your situation better the landlords found things difficult. They felt threatened by their former servants and sold the very land upon which you had slaved so long and hard. Then they went to Seoul where they backed the men in politics. . . . Right now these very people are using the money which you earned by your sweat and blood in anyway they wish, foolishly and recklessly. How do they use it? These big, rich landowners like Mr. Ch'oe use the money for themselves; backing those who will set up a new government that will take good care of them. Everything is being turned upside down. (Choe 1983: 89–90)

The struggle over land was the struggle over Korea's future.

---

[*]The South Korean case finds a ready parallel elsewhere. "Quoc Khoi carries the history of Vietnam on the tip of his tongue. As foreign powers have come and gone, Mr. Khoi, who is now in his 50's, has learned French, then Japanese, then English, then Russian. Vietnam is on its own now, and Mr. Khoi is again riding the linguistic wave of history: He is making his living teaching English" (Mydans 1995: E16).

LURCHING TOWARD LAND REFORM

The U.S. military government in South Korea squelched leftists and supported landlords, collaborators, and capitalists. In so doing, the United States at first maintained the prevailing power relations in the countryside. However, in the North Kim Il Sung was gaining legitimacy for his rule by purging landlords and redistributing land (Sakurai 1976: chap. 6). The widely reported 1946 North Korean land reform threatened the U.S.-backed southern government's popularity (C. Mitchell 1951: 17). The U.S. occupation force decided to support land redistribution measures in the South as well, in part to undermine the appeal of communism (C. Mitchell 1951: 23). The U.S. State Department called for a land reform that would "reflect the wishes of the Koreans and their desire to replace wide-spread tenancy with full ownership of the land by the individual farmer" (Meade 1951: 207).

In 1946 the U.S. military government created the New Korea Company from the notorious Oriental Development Company, a much-maligned instrument of Japanese colonial rule. The military government envisioned a "Homestead Act" for South Korea (G. McCune 1950: 129), but the U.S.-engineered land redistribution project was too understaffed and too poorly planned to have much effect. "For too long a time the American personnel charged with the responsibilities of the New Korea Company consisted of one major and one captain in Seoul, with a field staff of one enlisted man in each province" (Lauterbach 1947: 223; cf. C. Mitchell 1949). Furthermore, given that "three fourths of the tenanted land had been owned by Korean landlords . . . the American occupation forces did not have the authority or the desire to expropriate private land" (C. Mitchell 1951: 20). Thus, as late as the beginning of the Korean War, the U.S.-backed land reform had made little headway (Gragert 1994: 161).

Nonetheless, the broad-based popular support for land reform virtually eliminated vocal opposition to it in South Korea (G. McCune 1950: 133–34). Land reform was in the air; even right-wing political parties proposed land reform measures of their own (Sakurai 1976: 28–37). Facing external pressures and internal clamoring, the National Assembly of South Korea passed a land redistribution law in 1949 that capped parcels of land at 7.5 acres and contained provisions for compensating the dispossessed landlords (for the text, see J. Cho 1964: appendix B).

Rhee, however, had little enthusiasm for land redistribution, and most landlords opposed it in practice (Zeon 1973: 119–20). The Rhee government sabotaged the implementation of land reform measures (C. Mitchell 1951: 29). Some landlords exploited the situation by forcing tenants to buy land at inflated prices (K. Pak 1956: 62; Kuramochi 1985: 3–4). In "The Ritual at the Well," the landlord Mr. Ch'oe, like his real-life counterparts, sells his land at a profit and throws his support behind the right-wing, landlord-dominated government.

The 1949 land reform law was not fully implemented (Cumings 1990a: 471–72) until the Korean War.

THE KOREAN WAR

As Paul Fussell (1991: 651) remarks, the Korean War "generated virtually no literature, perhaps the reason it seems to be, as Clay Blair has called it, The Forgotten War." In spite of its murky place in American popular memory, the Korean War was a signal event in the Cold War (Kolko 1994: 409–11; Walker 1994: 82). It institutionalized the Cold War division and confirmed continued U.S. military presence in South Korea in particular and around the globe in general (Kolko 1988: 48–52; McCormick 1989: 99–106). Although scholars battle on over the origins and meanings of the Cold War, there is little doubt that the United States sought to maintain its geopolitical presence and to promote its interests (Leffler 1994: 120). In the mid-1990s, the Korean War was still the most researched and debated topic in modern Korean history (see, e.g., Cumings 1981, 1990a; Matray 1991; Goncharov, Lewis, and Xue 1993; Stueck 1995; Wada 1995).

The war devastated Korea. According to Jon Halliday and Bruce Cumings (1988: 200), over three million Koreans died, or close to 10 percent of the population (other estimates are much lower, see Wada 1995: 320–29). The alternating offensives by North and South dislocated people (Nathan Associates 1954: 22; Chŏn Kwang-hŭi 1992) and destroyed property (Yi Tae-gŭn 1987: 96–113; Yi Hŭng-t'ak 1992). Both sides perpetrated atrocities (Cumings

1990a: 697–707), which laid the groundwork for hatred between the two Koreas.

The Korean War profoundly shaped South Korean political and popular discourses. Its devastation is the source of the particularly urgent character of South Korean anticommunism. The dislike of North Korea, communism, and indeed politics altogether became a powerful undercurrent in South Korea. Furthermore, wartime destruction lies at the heart of the egalitarian ideology that runs through post–Korean War South Korea. The common rhetorical refrain that "we were all poor once" has a material base in the wartorn South Korea of 1953 (Abelmann 1993b). It is difficult to make sense of South Korea without understanding the impact of the Korean War.

LAND REFORM

The most lasting structural consequence of the Korean War was land reform. The absence of solid records and the confusion of wartime made the execution of the 1949 law ambiguous and uncertain (Sakurai 1976: 113–16; Kuramochi 1985: 6–7). The North Korean military, as it swept through the South in its initial drive to unify the country, liberated land for peasants. In effect, former tenant farmers exercised squatters' rights over the land they had been working (Cumings 1990a: 677–80). The resurgence of local people's committees in some instances facilitated land transfer. The actual threat of a communist regime, moreover, contributed to "breaking the back of landlord obstructionism" (Cumings 1990a: 677). The U.S. response to the North Korean liberation was to enforce preexisting land reform legislation. The United States goaded the Rhee government into pursuing land reform in the countryside in 1952, when the war was stalemated at the 38th parallel. Land reform generated support for the Rhee regime and thereby contributed to averting South Korea's defeat (Zeon 1973: 277).

Land reform radically reshaped the South Korean countryside. With land ownership capped at 3 *chŏngbo* (7.5 acres), large landlords virtually disappeared. One-third of farmland changed hands, which affected two-thirds of farming households (Morrow and Sherper 1970: 1–2). In 1944, the richest 3 percent of farming households owned 64 percent of all the farmland; by 1956, the top 6 percent owned only 18 percent (J. Cho 1964: 94). Tenancy dropped from 49 percent to 7 percent of all farming households (Morrow and Sherper 1970: 38). This compared favorably with the widely praised Japanese land reform effort, in which the tenancy rate dropped from 45 percent in 1945 to 9 percent in 1955 (Hayami and Yamada 1991: 84). Many peasants achieved their age-old dream of owning the land they tilled (K. Pak 1956: 133; Y. J. Park 1974: 199). By the mid-1950s the fundamental continuity of traditional Korean social structure had ended.

The Significance of Land Reform

Many accounts of South Korean development ignore land reform (e.g. World Bank 1993). Furthermore, critics from the right and the left converge in concluding that land reform was ineffective (Bauer 1976: 210; Chŏng and Mun 1990: 30–32). Some scholars minimize its significance by pointing out that inefficient smallholding persisted (e.g. Y. Koh 1962: 436, and P. Moon 1982: 206). Land reform, however, generally improves agricultural productivity (King 1977: 62–64). Unlike absentee landlords, small-scale cultivators, especially those who employ family labor, tend to improve their land, to cultivate it more intensively, and increase its yield (Dumont 1965: 238–40; Y. Cho 1963: 106–8; Griffin 1974: 222–29). In South Korea, agricultural productivity improved steadily, if not spectacularly, in the post–Korean War period (Y. J. Park 1974: 255–56; Ban, Moon, and Perkins 1980: 291–93).

Land reform is, above all, an effective solution to rural poverty. Not only does it enhance aggregate productivity, but it also ensures wide distribution of produce (Ahluwalia 1974: 19–21; Bell and Duloy 1974: 116–22; Otsuka 1993). The distribution of land rights is crucial in averting widespread want and famine (Agarwal 1994: 468–78). Indeed, post–land reform South Korea never approached the dire straits that plague many Third World countries (Ban, Moon, and Perkins 1980: 305–6). Land reform guaranteed at least a minimal entitlement for the vast majority of the population (cf. Sen 1981) and prevented a host of afflictions that faced and still face other developing countries.

The resolution of the land question is also important in industrialization. It is not an accident that a structural feature shared by the successful Asian industrializing economies—Japan, South Korea, and Taiwan—is the experience of land reform. To be sure, this generalization, like all generalizations about development, must be properly contextualized to take account of different conditions of agrarian life (de Janvry 1981: 108–40; Berry 1993: 132–34). Nonetheless, the transition to an industrial order requires some resolution of the land question. Given the preponderant power of agrarian elites, however, land transfer needs to be rapid and radical to be effective (Tai 1974: chap. 2). It requires in most instances a major domestic crisis or an external intervention. In the case of South Korea, the Korean War provided the crisis and the United States the intervention.

In the absence of land reform, agrarian elites reproduce the status quo by preserving their source of privilege. They maintain their landholding, squelch peasant clamoring, and often resist nascent industrializing efforts (W. Lewis 1978: 24). There are few incentives for agrarian elites to invest economic surplus in manufacturing when they can simply consume it or turn it into rentier capital. Extreme inequality within a nation-state is, in other words, detrimental for dynamic development. Agrarian elites constitute a reactionary force, whether in pre–Second World War Germany or Japan or in most contemporary Central American countries (see, respectively, Gerschenkron 1943: 173–84; Norman 1940: chap. 5; LaFeber 1993). Agrarian elites' wealth and power ensure their disproportionate political and military power; the state and the military, in turn, promote their interests. Agrarian elite power must be tempered and eventually broken for industrialization to proceed.

At the same time, without large-scale land redistribution, the peasant clamoring for land becomes a permanent political condition (cf. de Janvry 1981: chap. 6). The absence of land reform has led to repeated struggles between military-backed landlord regimes and land-hungry peasants in many Third World countries (Furtado 1976: 251–54; Prosterman and Riedinger 1987: chap. 1). Peasant struggles over land are often waged in the name of communism, which have prompted U.S. military interventions to sustain the status quo, particularly in Central and South America (e.g. LaFeber 1993). Without a large-scale land reform, South Korea may well have faced repeated peasant uprisings against agrarian elite regimes bent on preserving their power.

Consider a counterexample to the South Korean case. The Philippines is, like South Korea, a postcolonial society with strong ties to the United States (Constantino 1975: chaps. 16–17). Although the United States recommended land reform, especially in the 1950 Bell Report, the Filipino government, not unlike the Rhee regime, resisted it (Kolko 1988: 63–66). The state squelched the Hukbalahap movement, guerrilla insurgents in central Luzon (Kerkvliet 1977: chap. 5). The absence of an effective land reform, however, made the peasant clamoring for land a permanent feature of Filipino political life (Kerkvliet 1990: chaps. 2, 5). The 1955 Magsaysay and the 1963 Makayapal land reform laws were ineffective (Tai 1974: chap. 6). Without a major impetus such as the Korean War, agrarian elites persevered and dominated Filipino society. Mounting urban and rural dissent eventually culminated in the imposition of martial law in 1972 by Ferdinand Marcos. Anticommunist U.S. policy supported Marcos's regime, which suppressed dissent and promoted elite interests (Bonner 1987).

The strong landlord class, in tandem with the state, promoted export-oriented agriculture while impeding industrialization. The surplus generated by exports was usurped by agrarian elites and political officials, who did not reinvest it in industrial or infrastructural development (Hawes 1987). The majority of the rural population slipped below the poverty level and the Philippines became one of the poorest nations in Asia (Johansen 1993: 39). Agrarian elite rule, in other words, perpetuated political unrest, promoted authoritarian politics, supported agrarian interests, and limited industrializing efforts.

Requiem for Rural Life

Cornelius Osgood (1951: 6), writing about late 1940s South Korea, could confidently declare: "Certainly if one does not know the village, one cannot begin to comprehend Korean culture." He was absolutely right—the vast majority of South Koreans lived in the countryside. Rural South Korea continues to be important in the 1990s because most South Koreans spent their childhoods in their *kohyang*, their (rural) ancestral villages (Goldberg 1979). The significance of rural origins should not, however, elide the more profound transformation: the end of agrarian society.

Land reform transformed rural social structure. When large landholding disappeared, the countryside became a sea of small landholders. The cultivated area per household was roughly 1 hectare throughout the post–land reform 1950s and 1960s (B. Suh 1972: 24). Hierarchical landlord-tenant relations declined in significance; status subordination gave way to egalitarianism and independence.

The demise of an agrarian elite is inevitable when an agricultural society transforms itself into an industrial one (cf. Habakkuk 1994: chap. 8). The post-Liberation land reform destroyed the *yangban*'s power base. Although their personal prestige and cultural capital survived, they lost their fundamental source of wealth and influence. The 1949 Land Reform Law proved to be a powerful curb on landholding as a source of political and economic dominance. The erosion of their economic base diminished their influence over village life (Pak and Gamble 1975: 101–15). My paternal grandfather, who had been a landlord in the South Ch'ungch'ŏng Province, once took me on a hike through our ancestral mountains. Reaching a plateau and a vast vista of rice paddies, he lamented that all the land once used to be his, but now it belonged to the farmers we could see toiling like ants below us. This sentiment is not unlike that expressed by Don Fabrizio in *The Leopard*, which chronicles the decline of the Sicilian landed aristocracy: "We were the Leopards, the Lions; those who'll take our place will be little jackals, hyenas; and the whole lot of us, Leopards, jackals, and sheep, we'll all go on thinking ourselves the salt of the earth" (Di Lampedusa 1960: 214).

The transition from agrarian to industrial society transformed agrarian culture. In England, for example, the process was protracted. In the nineteenth century, "the great majority of land purchases [resulted] from the social aspirations of the purchasers for landed status" (F. Thompson 1994: 140; see also Scott 1982: chaps. 3–5). In South Korea, however, the desire for landed status virtually vanished. Not only was there a legal limit on land ownership, but the impact of colonial modernity, the devastation of the Korean War, and the rejection of tradition devalued land as a source of prestige and power. The *yangban* and their descendants could no longer rely on landholding to ensure their privileged position. Once land ceased to be the primary source of social power, landlords and their offspring looked beyond their villages. Many left their ancestral land for urban destinations. In the story "The Heir," the young protagonist is promised by his grandfather that "everything in here is yours" (K. Sŏ 1990: 183). But he gives up the trappings of *yangban* privilege and escapes from his grandfather. *Yangban* domination rapidly became a memory in many villages of the post–land reform era. Quite simply, the *yangban* disappeared from the countryside.

Status based on land gave way to class distinctions. As my maternal grandfather was wont to say: "Land is meaningless; you can't carry it around with you." Education, and increasingly business, became the royal road to prestige (H.-B. Lee 1968: 53). My paternal grandfather, for example, invested heavily in his two sons' education, eventually sending them both to the United States to earn doctorates. However, he came to lament that they had not made more money. Although state bureaucrats and professors remained respected, commerce, once despised, became perhaps the most prestigious and certainly the most lucrative career. The very fabric of *yangban* culture had unraveled.

After land reform, peasants became farmers. Because the vast majority of former tenants had become small landholders, they no longer faced landlords and moneylenders but the government and the market. Agrarian surplus was no longer monopolized by landlords but disposed individually. Commodification of agrarian life became an irreversible and accelerated process (Y. Chang 1989: 238–39). Although peasants-turned-farmers faced new problems (Klein 1958: 192–93), the principal condition of peasant-based revolution vanished in South Korea. It also marked the end of an ecologically sustainable rice economy (Bray 1994: xvi–xviii). Furthermore, as the young women and men moved to the cities to work in industry, many villages became the province of the elderly. Development not only depopulated the South Korean countryside, it also transformed and ultimately devalued rural life. It is misleading to identify post-Liberation South Korean villages with any notion of an unchanging rural tradition. External forces impinged constantly even in the remotest villages. The very existence of rural out-migration ensured that news of urban life would reach the countryside through family networks (Sorensen 1988: 36–37). The penetration of mass schooling and mass media, furthermore, integrated villages into national life (McGinn et al. 1980: 241; Turner et al. 1993: 174–79). Most villagers valorized urban life and experienced low self-esteem as they became aware of urban condescension and their "objectively lower quality of rural life" (Keim 1979: 116). Family members and friends in cities provided a visceral metric for the underdevelopment of the countryside.

In a sociological portrait of 1950s South Korea, village and farm life would perforce take a central place. The drama of development, however, inevitably shifted the focus to cities and industries, and peasants and farmers disappeared rapidly from the stage. John Berger's (1979: 211) eulogy of the peasantry is appropriate for the South Korean experience:

> Nobody can reasonably argue for the preservation and maintenance of the traditional peasant way of life. To do so is to argue that peasants should continue to be exploited, and that they should lead lives in which the burden of physical work is often devastating and always oppressive. As soon as one accepts that peasants are a class of survivors . . . any idealisation of their way of life becomes impossible. In a just world such a class would no longer exist.

The disappearance of the peasantry is a world-historical transformation that characterizes the twentieth century. As Eric Hobsbawm (1994: 284) writes: "The most dramatic and far-reaching social change of the second half of this century, and the one which cuts us off forever from the world of the past, is the death of the peasantry" (see also Ladurie 1979: 144–47). In South Korea, this disappearance was rapid and compressed.

*

The crucial change that severed contemporary South Korean political economy from traditional Korea was land reform. The post-Liberation land reform undermined the base of *yangban* power—land ownership—and unleashed a structural transformation that opened up the possibility of later development. Land reform is thus a necessary, if insufficient, condition for development.

CHAPTER TWO

The Triple Alliance
and the Politics of Corruption

Land reform did not lead inexorably to development. From 1953 to 1961 the South Korean economy grew slowly; the average per capita GNP was less than $100 in 1961. Few people, therefore, look for the sources of later dynamism in this period. As Kyung Cho Chung (1956: 225) wrote in the mid-1950s: "[South Korea] faces grave economic difficulties. The limitations imposed by the Japanese have been succeeded by the division of the country, the general destruction incurred by the Korean War, and the attendant dislocation of the population, which has further disorganized the economy." In *This Kind of War* T. R. Fehrenbach (1963: 37) prognosticated that "by themselves, the two halves [of Korea] might possibly build a viable economy by the year 2000, certainly not sooner."

The received wisdom on the 1950s is that U.S. aid prevented the collapse of the South Korean economy. The wartorn and impoverished country would have been, in this vision, wracked by poverty and famines. Edward Mason and his colleagues (1980: 203–4) make exactly that argument in their canonical text, *The Economic and Social Modernization of the Republic of Korea*:

> The massive inflow of foreign assistance before and during the Korean War was essential to the survival of South Korea as an independent country. Continuation of a high level of economic assistance for the decade after the war probably spelled the dif-

ference between some (1.5 percent per annum) and no growth in per capita income. Without this growth, the economic condition of the population would have remained desperate, political cohesion would have deteriorated, and the foundations for subsequent high growth would not have been forged. Thus, aid played a critical role for the two decades from the mid-1940s to the mid-1960s.

There is a widespread consensus on the dire straits of the post–Korean War period and the crucial role of U.S. aid in sustaining the economy (e.g. Kim and Roemer 1981: 58; Cathie 1989: 120; and Haggard and Moon 1993: 60–62).

It is true that South Korea did not have a dynamic economy in the 1950s, but the received view exaggerates both the desperation of South Korea and the benevolence of the United States. The conditions in South Korea after the 1949–52 land reform were more propitious for development than they were in most developing economies. Furthermore, U.S. support of that development was ambiguous. Influenced by the prevailing development discourse, the United States projected an agrarian future for South Korea; preoccupied with the Cold War, the United States used its aid and support to sustain Rhee Syngman's corrupt rule. The fundamental obstacle to South Korean development in the 1950s was the triple alliance of the United States (and its aid), Rhee (and the state), and the dependent capitalists. The 1960 Student Revolution dissolved this alliance and opened the door for dynamic development.

The Continuing Benefits of Land Reform

The economic situation of 1950s South Korea looked bleak to outside observers. E. J. Kahn (1961: 49–50) described impoverished Seoulites as follows: "[They] live in miserable jerry-built shacks, and few of them have been able to find jobs. Beggars, some apparently only two or three years old, are commonplace, along with venders who squat for hours on the sidewalks, offering passersby cigarettes, chewing gum, combs, cheap jewelry, toys, whistles, abaci, and live dogs. The dogs bark constantly; they sound hungry, too." Pessimistic observation was not confined to Western journalists; a South Korean academic recalled that "when I returned to [South] Korea from the United States in 1960 . . . I was really stunned by the extreme poverty still prevailing through the country" (S.-c. Hong 1985: 113).

South Korea was obviously poor compared to the United States, but the South Korean economy in the late 1950s was far from desperate. Signs of recovery were conspicuous (Ministry of Reconstruction 1958, 1959). Even without U.S. aid, South Korea was at little risk of famine, unlike pre–land reform Korea had been, or much of the rest of the Third World still was. Most farming households had some land of their own, and now that they no longer had to pay rent, that was enough to ensure their survival.

The legacy of land reform was propitious in other ways as well. Consider overpopulation. It does not take a convinced Malthusian to predict the consequences of high fertility, which declined gradually in the European demographic transition (Chesnais 1992: 29–46). South Korea, in contrast, seemed to offer a classic instance of the Malthusian nightmare. A U.S. official in South Korea told E. J. Kahn (1961: 55) that "if these Koreans don't stop overbreeding, we may have the choice of supporting them forever, watching them starve to death, or washing our hands of the problem" (see also Nathan Associates 1954: 33, and Y. Chang 1967: 366–68). Yet the Malthusian nightmare was averted in South Korea. Between 1960 and 1989, the total fertility rate dropped from 6.0 children per woman to 1.6 (E. S. Kim 1993: 254). According to Peter Donaldson (1990: 133), "The decline in population growth in Korea was one of the fastest in history."

Economic security—a result of the land reform—was a major cause of declining fertility. In many developing countries, a high fertility rate is correlated with economic insecurity (S. Kuznets 1973: 46–47). In South Korea, land redistribution assured minimal livelihood for the vast majority of the predominantly rural population. The South Korean case, along with all successful economies, suggests that overpopulation is more of a consequence, rather than a cause, of poverty. It seems that there is no surer way to cap runaway fertility growth than to spread wealth across the populace.

Demographic accidents and family planning also helped prevent overpopulation. The baby boom struck South Korea roughly a decade later than it did most of the world—largely because of the Korean War (Kim, Ross, and Worth 1972: 1962). Rural out-migration, mandatory military conscription, and Western cultural influences were three social and cultural changes that postponed marriage age and lowered fertility (Kwon 1977: 263–67).

The widespread equation of family planning with the United States rendered low fertility as a mark of modernity (Donaldson 1990: 150). The state aggressively disseminated contraceptive devices and made abortion widely available (E. S. Kim 1993: 268). It also encouraged overseas emigration, which averaged about 30,000 annually to the United States alone in the 1970s (Abelmann and Lie 1995: 75–77).

A similar story can be told about urbanization. Hyper-urbanization, like overpopulation, is a serious problem in many Third World countries (cf. Bairoch 1988: 509). Indeed, South Korea urbanized rapidly (Mills and Song 1979: 25). The expansion of megalopolis is not, however, in and of itself a developmental catastrophe (Preston 1988: 26). London, New York, and Tokyo expanded as the economies of their respective countries grew. Despite the severe malfunctions that occur in many large Third World cities, a megalopolis does not necessarily impede dynamic development. Rather, as Michael Lipton (1977) has suggested, it is the pervasive urban bias in development that perpetuates rural poverty. And although state policies in South Korea were inimical to farmers, they were largely insulated from the threat of famine by the land reform.

Thus in South Korea famine, widespread rural poverty, and overpopulation were largely averted. These benefits of land reform do not, of course, make development inevitable, but they did make it possible.

U.S. Policy Toward South Korea, 1953–1961

Working initially through the United Nations Korean Reconstruction Agency, the United States ultimately acted unilaterally on South Korean affairs (Lyons 1961: 4). The United States sought to reconstruct the South Korean economy, primarily to ensure its political stability. The United States envisioned an agrarian economy for South Korea and offered political support to Rhee.

ECONOMIC RECONSTRUCTION THROUGH U.S. AID

Foreign aid was the preferred method of international development agencies and First World governments for spurring Third World development. U.S. foreign policy in the 1950s was inextricably intertwined with aid (Packenham 1973: 178–91; Pastor 1980: 268–80; Wood 1986: 122–30). Critics of U.S. (and First World) aid attribute less than savory motives to aid givers. There is little doubt that geopolitical interests and the desire to promote American values motivated U.S. aid to South Korea in particular and other Third World countries in general. In the 1950s the arguments for anticommunism and for South Korean aid went hand in hand. Eugene J. Taylor (1953: 10), writing in the *New York Times Magazine*, observed that "[South] Korea's social-economic reconstruction [was] a project . . . important to the West's primary objective of preventing the spread of Communist aggression." This argument for protecting and supporting South Korea remained popular throughout the 1950s and beyond (e.g. J.D. 1957: 274). The post–Korean War reconstruction of South Korea was a continuation of the war against international communism by other means.

At the same time, the United States envisioned a traditional, agrarian economy for South Korea. U.S. advisers emphasized agriculture because they were skeptical about South Korea's ability to industrialize. This bias is particularly clear in the Robert Nathan Associates' 1952 report on the program of economic reconstruction. Advocating a massive infusion of aid, the Report recommended agricultural development: "It is clear that agriculture will continue to be the most important field of economic activity in [South] Korea for many years to come" (Nathan Associates 1952: 13; see also FAO 1954: 5). In a similar vein, Shannon McCune (1956: 114) wrote: "Any future economy for [South] Korea should be built on a sound, expanding, agricultural base" (see also Lautensach 1950: 116–17, and Zanzi 1954: 43–44).

Consistent with its vision of South Korea as an agrarian economy, the United States did not encourage industrialization. After Liberation, the United States retained the Japanese-owned factories and facilities as vested property (Cumings 1981: 352). The

1952 coordination agreement between the United States and South Korea made South Korea dependent on U.S. imports. This policy only hurt South Korean industrialization (Michell 1989: 160).

Given that small industries were thriving in South Korea in the late 1950s (Y. Lim 1981: 49), industrialization in conjunction with a strong agricultural sector would not have been an inconceivable scenario (see Weems 1960: 45–46). Development consultants, writing three decades later, noted: "[South] Korea has little comparative advantage in many aspects of agricultural production" (Steinberg et al. 1984: 3). The economist Joan Robinson's (1964: 116) observation is apt here: "There is nothing very much for economic theory to say to the planner, except: Do not listen to those who say you want this rather than that—agriculture, not industry; exports, not home production; light industry, not heavy. You always want both."

Why was the United States unwilling to promote South Korean industrialization? Because they perceived the South Korean situation as desperate, policymakers doubted the very possibility of industrialization (J. Lewis 1955: 2; cf. Satterwhite 1994: 191). John Caldwell (1952: 109) expressed this sense of desperation in a gruesome image: "[South] Korea was like a decapitated human being whose body still sought to function even though separated from head and brain, as a hen is sometimes able to walk for a few moments after the ax has fallen." U.S. officers distrusted South Korean business people and government officials (Henning 1952: 372) and retained control of the former Japanese factories in order to protect them from corrupt South Koreans (Oliver 1993: 172).

Furthermore, U.S. advisers followed the received wisdom in promoting agricultural development. According to a dogma of development discourse, an economy was first expected to attain agricultural sufficiency, which would then, and only then, lead to industrialization (e.g. Johnston and Kilby 1975: chap. 2, and W. Lewis 1978: 75). According to the 1952 Nathan Report, "The process of industrialization requires time. A predominantly agricultural economy cannot hope to emerge as a highly developed manufacturing economy within a few years" (Nathan Associates 1952: 132). Nathan Associates (1954: 96) identified "expanded rice production" as "the largest bolster to exports."

UNEASY POLITICAL SUPPORT FOR RHEE

The paramount importance of anticommunism led the United States to prize stability over its distaste for autocratic rule. The Korean War ensured not only continued U.S. military presence in South Korea but continued U.S. support for Rhee.

Rhee's *raison d'être* was reunification. A 1955 government publication stated: "Out of a long and tragic experience with Communism, we of Korea believe there is no middle ground, no possibility of coexistence, no road of modus vivendi" (OPI 1955: 1). Rhee repeatedly clashed with the United States over his desire to unify Korea by military means (S. Han 1985: 146–47). His despotic rule was, moreover, distasteful to many Americans; contemporary U.S. journalism is full of critical reports. Frank Gibney (1954: 27) wrote: "In his conduct of domestic affairs he is, without question, a dictator, seldom reluctant to use police intimidation and force to suppress the political freedoms whose theory he defends." In a "profile of a despot," Mark Gayn (1954: 214) noted: "It is easy to dismiss [Rhee] as a despot, a demagogue, and a dangerous bluffer. He is all of these things, and some that are even less attractive." Negative assessments were not restricted to the press: "The CIA thought Rhee 'senile,' also 'indomitably strong-willed and obstinate,' while in the British embassy he was regarded as 'a dangerous fascist, or lunatic'" (Lone and McCormack 1993: 104).

By preaching anticommunism, however, Rhee wrested reluctant but reliable support from the United States. During the Cold War, the United States repeatedly propped up unsavory regimes, ranging from the Shah in Iran to Marcos in the Philippines and, of course, Park Chung Hee in South Korea (Kolko 1988). U.S. policy ensured Rhee's autonomy, the willingness of South Korean bureaucrats, police officers, and others who had earlier collaborated with Japanese rule to execute his commands ensured his authority (Yun Kyŏng-ch'ŏl 1986: 78–81).

Rhee was certainly no puppet of the United States. His nationalist credentials gave him a solid base of support; he was probably one of the few nationally known figures in a predominantly rural country. Farmers gave him credit for the land reform that he had in fact opposed. And despite opposition to his autocratic rule in the cities and among the intellectuals, he was a legitimate leader in the years immediately following the Korean War. However, under his rule the political situation in South Korea deteriorated slowly toward despotism.

The Triple Alliance:
The United States, Rhee, and Dependent Capitalists

After Liberation and land reform, U.S. aid replaced land as a power base. It was U.S. aid that facilitated a parasitic relationship between state bureaucrats and dependent capitalists. The president and his coterie emerged as the nexus between the bountiful United States and those South Korean capitalists who were to reap monopoly profits from processing and distributing U.S. aid materials. There was thus a hierarchical power structure in South Korea with the United States at the apex, Rhee and the subservient state bureaucracy in the middle, and dependent capitalists at the bottom. This triple alliance dominated the post–Korean War South Korean political economy.

THE TRIPLE ALLIANCE

In his influential study of Brazilian development, Peter Evans proposed a model of triple alliance among international capital, a strong state, and elite local capital. In its pursuit of capital accumulation, the state forges an alliance with multinationals and domestic firms to spur industrialization (Evans 1979: 275–90). The 1950s South Korean triple alliance featured a similar set of actors but the outcome was not development, dependent or otherwise, primarily because the state was not developmentalist. Rhee was simply not interested in industrialization, capital accumulation, and infrastructural development (cf. K. Koh 1963: chap. 5). In this vacuum, the triple alliance created and sustained a structure of corruption.

Against the triple alliance, the rest of the country posed virtually no opposition. The farmers had realized their age-old dream of cultivating their own land and as a group had few grievances and little interest in collective action. The industrial working class was very small. In fact, the greatest threat to Rhee was the vocal opposition of an urban minority—students and the middle class. This urban opposition, however, was stifled by a combination of state repression and patrimonial rule.

Under the triple alliance the economy was static. The processing and circulation of U.S. aid materials provided little stimulation. There were few incentives for business to invest in risky endeavors, when real estate and finance provided lucrative means to reinvest profit. Large corporations exhibited little dynamism in the 1950s.

THE STATE OF CORRUPTION AND THE CORRUPTION OF THE STATE

The state plays a fundamental role in national development. As Lloyd Reynolds (1983: 976) concludes: "The single most important explanatory variable [in economic development] is political organization and the administrative competence of government." Although it would be difficult to prove that the state is *the* most important variable, it is safe to conclude that a corrupt state impedes development. Any viable industrial economy requires the basic infrastructures of nationwide transportation and communication systems, widespread literacy, adequate health care, and a functioning financial system, all of which require a state that is capable of raising and properly investing revenue.

Development is as much about avoiding pitfalls and eliminating barriers as it is about getting things right. As I argued in Chapter 1, the absence of an effective land reform poses a major obstacle to development in many countries. Rural poverty and political instability are symptomatic of societies with a large number of landless peasants. In such societies, states do not invest in infrastructures; more often than not, they siphon off surplus and even pervert productive initiatives. The confluence of a powerful agrarian elite and a corrupt state is a powerful obstacle to economic dynamism—Zaire under Mobutu and the Philippines under Marcos are but two examples in a depressingly long list (MacGaffey 1991; Bonner 1987). As Keith Hart (1982: 87) summarizes: "Embezzlement at the top, black markets, smuggling, and tax evasion—all of these reflect the weakness of the state apparatus and reduce effective government revenues" (see also Sandbrook and Barker 1985). The lack of revenue, in turn, prevents the development of infra-structures. And the vicious cycle perpetuates itself.

The interplay of corruption and despotism leads to the corro-sion of state capacity. The Congo offers an instructive example. Between 1960 (the year of independence) and 1987, the state bu-reaucracy grew from 3,000 to 73,000 persons. "By the end of the 1960s this relatively immense and useless civil and military ser-vice was eating up around three-fourths of the national budget, and its members enjoyed a far higher standard of living than most Congolese" (Davidson 1992: 235). Little more than racketeers, such state elites absorb foreign aid and extract domestic surplus to become a cancerous growth in the body politic.

The corrupt state, furthermore, acts as an "integral state" that "seeks to achieve unrestricted domination over civil society" (C. Young 1994: 288). In addition to outright plunder, corrupt state elite manipulate their economies in order to retain power and to enrich themselves while justifying their rule by invoking the ide-ology of national development. The end result of privileging elite interests and sustaining the status quo is economic stagnation (cf. Boone 1992: 254).

AID AND ITS DISCONTENTS

Critics have assailed the deleterious consequences of U.S. (and First World) aid. Graham Hancock (1989) labels international aid personnel as "lords of poverty." Indeed, World Bank projects, IMF-imposed austerity measures, and other First World aid come with considerable ideological baggage and often benefit international fi-nance and multinational corporations at the expense of those it is supposed to be helping (Payer 1974: chap. 2; 1982: chap. 3). Aid may create dependence, impede domestic development, and sus-tain the existing international political economic order (Jalée 1968: chap. 4; Hayter 1971: 9). In addition, foreign aid often imposes First World values and neglects local realities (Paddock and Pad-dock 1973: 299–300; Colson 1982: 3).

My principal concern here is, however, how foreign aid func-tions as a crucial resource for the corrupt elite. Given the state-state relationship presumed in foreign aid, the nature of the receiving state determines the efficacy of aid. In a corrupt regime, aid fattens the leader's personal coffers, may be used to quell domestic dissent, and perpetuates autocratic rule (cf. Ferguson 1990: 254–56). Its reform depends on external or internal forces. Aid may dry up, or a countervailing domestic force may extirpate the corrupt elite. In the case of South Korea, as we will see, the April Student Revolution unhinged the triple alliance and the politics of corruption.

U.S. aid to South Korea was well-intended and reflected a faith that South Korea might one day become like the United States (Packenham 1973: 20). The U.S. largesse—whether grain distributed under the P.L. 480 food aid program or chewing gum dispersed by GIs—left an indelible impression on many South Koreans.[*] Already admired for its part in the Liberation and the Korean War, the United States came to stand for all things good and modern. Indeed, until the 1980s the vast majority of South Koreans regarded the United States as the greatest country in the world (Abelmann and Lie 1995: 61–64).

The United States committed a great deal of money, products, and produce to South Korea in the 1950s (E. Park 1985: 109–10). From 1953 to 1961, South Korea received $2.3 billion in aid, with 85 percent coming from the United States; in fact, foreign aid financed two-thirds of total South Korean imports (S. Park 1969: 32). In the late 1950s U.S. economic aid to South Korea accounted for over 10 percent of the South Korean GNP (Kang Haeng-u 1986: chap. 2).

---

[*]Graham Hancock argues that food aid frequently hurts the Third World and attributes a less than salutary motive for aid: "Administering America's huge 'Food for Peace' programme under Public Law 480, the US Agency for International Development operates on the streetwise principles that those who accept free handouts today will become paying customers tomorrow" (Hancock 1989: 168). He continues: "As well as creating expensive addictions to non-indigenous cereals, and discouraging export-production of items like corn and rice in which the USA is expanding its own trade, P.L. 480 has frequently served as a major disincentive to the efforts of local farmers to grow food even for domestic consumption" (169). The case of South Korea supports his argument. The South Korean import of U.S. food products was $2.1 billion in 1981 alone, more that the total of U.S. food aid to South Korea between 1955 and 1959 (168). Furthermore, P.L. 480 food aid enabled the South Korean government to maintain low grain prices, which contributed to agricultural underdevelopment.

Nonetheless, a fundamental flaw of U.S. aid was its shortsightedness. In South Korea, U.S. aid inhibited domestic industrial production because much of it was in the form of produce and finished products, rather than infrastructures and industries (U. Chung 1982: 178–79). The United States contributed less than one-fourth of South Korea's capital-related aid. The vast majority of U.S. aid—and all P.L. 480 aid—was consumable, such as agricultural produce and other commodities. Ignorant of the proverbial injunction to give fishing poles, rather than fish, to people in need, the United States, in short, opted for temporary measures.

I am not arguing that all aid renders the recipient dependent and corrupt. All aid is not alike. Some projects, such as the Small Business Revolving Loan Fund, were successful in initiating enterprises that manufactured chemical, paper, soap, and other low-technology goods in 1950s South Korea (Reeve 1963: 116). Aid oriented toward grassroots productive investment is more likely to be successful than commodities or grants given to state elites. Context is crucial in determining the efficacy of aid efforts. In the case of 1950s South Korea, the context was at best problematic.

AUTOCRACY AND PATRIMONIALISM

Rhee exercised personal dominion over the national elite through his control of the repressive institutions, important bureaucratic posts, and major economic decisions. The resource that allowed him to act autocratically was U.S. aid.

Rhee controlled the military and the police—the institutional legacy of Japanese colonial repression (Cumings 1990b: 41). By cultivating key officers, he ensured the personal loyalty of these two major organs of state control (J. Oh 1968: 28–29). The National Security Law justified politically motivated arrests. By 1950, nearly 80 percent of the 60,000 people in prison in South Korea were charged with violations of the Security Law (Eckert et al. 1990: 349). In rural areas, the police were particularly powerful in shaping the political process; they "suppressed all anti-Rhee activity, demanded that Liberal partisans be allowed to address religious or educational gatherings, levied a one-tenth rice tax for party support, and supervised the balloting" (Crofts 1960: 547–48). Anticommunist youth groups and goon squads squelched dissent (Y. J. Lee 1990: 151). The road to despotism was paved by "para-nazi methods" (Reeve 1963: 69).

Rhee also systematically filled key bureaucratic positions with his allies. The patronage system under his control became a defining characteristic of the 1950s South Korean state. As Chi-Young Pak (1980: 57) wrote: "Politics and government were the main source of personal advancement and disadvantage in [South] Korea. Therefore, if one loses politics, he loses all." In effect, the state became Rhee's private domain and personalism was the dominant principle of recruitment and promotion in his bureaucracies. He dictated all the important bureaucratic and military appointments. "Any cabinet minister who had shown any indication that he was politically unreliable from Rhee's standpoint was immediately dismissed. Similarly, any minister who would not readily agree with Rhee at cabinet meetings or in private was abruptly removed" (J. Oh 1968: 26).

Patrimonialism is a common feature in many societies. The sovereign employs kinship and other personal ties to ensure loyalty in exchange for key government positions (cf. Weber 1978: 1010–15). Patrimonialism in fact manifests itself in advanced industrial societies as well, such as the United States, where an incoming president may make a series of appointments based on personal ties. Although an ideological opposition to nepotism may exist, important posts are given to favored and trusted personnel. F. M. Cornford (1994: 109), in a very different context, presents the impeccable logic of distributing jobs on the basis of personal networks:

> The most important branch of political activity is, of course, closely connected with *jobs*. These fall into two classes, My Jobs and Your Jobs. My Jobs are public-spirited proposals, which happen (much to my regret) to involve the advancement of a personal friend, or (still more to my regret) of myself. Your Jobs are insidious intrigues for the advancement of yourself and your friends, speciously disguised as public-spirited proposals.

The pull toward patrimonialism and personalism is powerful at all times and across all cultures (cf. Sandbrook 1993: 29–34). In advanced industrial societies, however, the sheer size of the state apparatus, the exercise of meritocracy at lower levels (which are more visible to the public), and the entrenched system of elite circulation through regular elections temper the power and limit the extent of patrimonialism (Theobald 1990: 64–75).

In the case of 1950s South Korea, the state as an institutional presence was still small (C.-H. Cho 1972: 93). The college-educated elite was a small group (in the late 1950s, college students constituted only 6 percent of the college-aged South Koreans) (McGinn et al. 1980: 47). The small and intimate circle of elites in the mid-1950s had not expanded much beyond that which Gregory Henderson (1989: 175) describes in his study of 1948 Seoul: "Pre–[Korean] war Seoul combined incomparable intimacy and excitement. . . . When a car went down the street . . . you leaned out of a third story and said, 'Oh, there goes Mr Lee. He's going to visit Governor Koo.' You knew everyone who owned a car in Seoul in 1948 and you usually knew where he was going." The bureaucratic centralization in Seoul, accelerated during Japanese colonial rule, created a tight nexus of national elites (Choi Jang Jip 1993b: 264). My father, who worked in the state bureaucracy in the late 1950s, was acquainted with many elite bureaucrats and politicians, some of whom went on to become cabinet ministers. When we watched TV news on new cabinet appointments in the late 1980s, he claimed to know most of them.

Patrimonialism and corruption were two sides of the same coin. The dynamic of graft reverberated down the bureaucratic hierarchy and penetrated the country. Personal favors shaped bureaucratic conduct (Bark 1967: 62–63). "Official corruption in South Korea is on a fabulous scale, and it reaches both high and low levels. Among the beneficiaries are the rural police, who often collected and pocket 'taxes,' and members of Rhee's own political machine, who exact 'voluntary assessments'" (Gayn 1954: 215). From electric power to the Parent-Teachers' Association, the "voluntary payment system" became the means to ensure not only favors but basic services (Reeve 1963: 98). The significance of smuggling and black-market activities cannot be underestimated either; the post–military coup government's desire to eliminate them attest to their ubiquity (Reeve 1963: 98–99).

Graft was a matter of necessity for state bureaucrats because their pay was abysmal. Official remuneration satisfied only the ascetic: "It was next to impossible for the ordinary official to live on his pay" (Reeve 1963: 96). In the mid-1950s, an average government employee earned less than an average worker (Chao 1956: 66). For the bureaucratic elites lacking a sound financial base, bribes were the only way to achieve promotion, power, and even mere survival. Ever escalating gifts shaped promotion and undermined the putatively meritocratic system; the ineptitude and the venality of the state in turn contributed to the discontent of the educated populace.

DEPENDENT CAPITALISTS: THE 'YANGBAN CHAEBŎL'

Dependent capitalists constituted the weakest partner in the triple alliance. The lucky ones received monopolistic privileges and systematically benefited from state policies and initiatives. They hailed from the same elite background as the political leaders; they were, in essence, *yangban chaebŏl.* *

State patronage was the single most important determinant of corporate growth (Kong 1992: 39–52). In the post–Korean War years, the state controlled U.S. aid, dispersed resources, and erected bureaucratic barriers (K.-D. Kim 1979: 68–70). In particular, state distribution of sugar, flour, and cotton—the three "whites" that were essential consumer commodities in postwar South Korea—paved the royal road to business success. U.S. aid, in other words, undergirded corporate growth.

Tight webs bound state bureaucrats and dependent capitalists (K.-D. Kim 1979: 67–70). Business leaders, in turn, returned the favor in the form of kickbacks. In short, state elites and dependent capitalists created a racket out of the distribution of U.S. aid. The close relationship with the state was critical not only for plant purchases and acquisitions but also to ensure a continuous supply of raw materials. The problem was acute for smaller manufacturers. One businessman told *Newsweek* (May 16, 1960: 58): "Just by

---

* *Chaebŏl*—which is written with the same Chinese characters as the Japanese *zaibatsu*—has no legal or formal definition (M. Kang 1996: 10–12). Any large and diversified conglomerate can plausibly claim to be a *chaebŏl*. Family ownership is another common characteristic.

saving what I used to have to give the Liberals in bribes . . . I can re-equip my plant within a year."

Consider some examples of *yangban chaebŏl*. Kim Sŏng-su's Kyŏngsŏng Spinning was one of the largest colonial-period Korean-owned enterprises. His brother, Kim Yŏn-su took over the enterprise, which prospered from state patronage and guaranteed access to cotton sent from the United States. State support was also crucial for the Kim family's Samyang sugar refinery. Taking over a Japanese-owned plant, Samyang received the capital he needed to purchase equipment from U.S. loans and his sugar from P.L. 480 aid (McNamara 1990: 131–32). The career of Pak Hŭng-sik, a colonial-period Japanese collaborator and entrepreneur, illustrates the same mechanism at work. He received Teikoku Hemp Spinning Company's Inch'ŏn plant and a UN grant of $850,000 to purchase equipment in 1955. The company also benefited from favorable government loans (McNamara 1990: 131). South Korea's most successful *chaebŏl* in the early 1990s was Samsung; the founder Lee Byung-chull had his first major success in Cheil Sugar, which became South Korea's largest sugar refiner in the 1950s. State patronage was crucial in obtaining loans and raw materials from the United States, which propelled Samsung to diversify and to become a leading *chaebŏl* (Clifford 1994: 316–19).

In summary, the triple alliance among the United States, Rhee's state, and dependent capitalists was connected by aid and graft. U.S. support was crucial for Rhee's autocratic rule, and U.S. aid contributed to corporate and bureaucratic parasitism. South Korean enterprises established personal links to the president in order to gain access to precious commodities provided by U.S. aid as well as to retain monopolistic privileges *vis-à-vis* competitors. The structure of corruption ultimately robbed South Korea of potentially innovative improvements and beneficial competition. Surplus, rather than being productively invested, accumulated among the political and business elites. The South Korean economy was stagnant.

The April 1960 Student Revolution

Even after the destruction of *yangban* power, the traditional elite managed to dominate South Korean political economy, albeit with

U.S. support. It was the 1960 Student Revolution that shattered the triple alliance and cleared the ground for later development.

DOMESTIC POLITICS, 1952–1960

After the purge of leftists, Rhee's chief rival was the Democratic Party. The political conflict of the 1950s pitted one elite faction against another. Rhee's Liberal Party and the opposition Democratic Party both drew most of their members from the same privileged *yangban* background; over 40 percent of the 1948 National Assembly hailed from the landlord class (J. Oh 1968: 13). Rhee's Liberal Party was essentially nothing more than his personal networks (H.-B. Lee 1968: 71–76). The Democratic Party's base was the landed class and former Japanese collaborators who had thrived as bureaucrats and business people in the latter part of the colonial period.

Rhee had won the 1952 presidential election in a landslide, garnering over 70 percent of the vote. However, his creeping senility, the blatant corruption of his rule, and the stagnant economy eroded his electoral share to 56 percent by 1956. The opposition Democratic Party campaigned under the slogan: "We can't make a living; so let's change" (J. Oh 1968: 51). Rhee's handpicked vice-presidential candidate, Yi Ki-bung, lost to Chang Myŏn of the Democratic Party in the 1956 election.

The 1950s witnessed growing tension between the president and the National Assembly (C. Pak 1980: chap. 6). The National Assembly sought to oust Rhee time and again; the Democratic Party repeatedly challenged his presidential power. Rhee's response was to deploy a panoply of political tools. The 1948 National Security Law justified repressive measures (Pak Wŏn-sun 1989), and Rhee used the police and goon squads to harass opposition politicians (Gayn 1954: 216). The closing of newspapers was common; one editor was executed for his antigovernment journalism (J. A. Kim 1975: 159–60). The list of outright political abuses would fill a long history book.

One of the most violent conflicts was the 1958 crisis over revisions to the National Security Law (Macdonald 1992: 195–99). The mounting tension led to a sit-down protest by the opposition party. The proposed revision to the National Security Law defined all transgressions against Rhee as acts of communist sabotage and treason; the 1948 Constitution, with its liberal promises, became not merely *de facto* but *de jure* defunct (J. Oh 1968: 55–58). The inefficacy of the rule of law in South Korea was to continue through the 1980s; as D. K. Yoon (1990: 217) commented: "Law in Korea has been long on justifying government powers and short on checking their abuse."

Convinced of his mandate, Rhee tightened his grip on power even as his mental faculties and popular support eroded. When a trusted adviser, Robert Oliver, suggested to Rhee that he should retire at 85, he replied: "There is nothing I would like better, . . . but who would carry on the fight? . . . I must stay in, I owe it to my people" (Q. Y. Kim 1983: 33).

Rhee's corrupt rule spawned a culture of despair by the late 1950s. Perhaps the best-known fictional work from this period, Yi Pŏm-sŏn's "A Stray Bullet," published in 1959, captures the pervasive sense of hopelessness. The protagonist, a struggling but sincere clerk, is surrounded by social ills: a mother who is mad, a sister who is a prostitute, a brother who is a thief, and a wife who dies in childbirth. He personifies anomie, haunted by the mad mother's incantatory urge: "Let's go!" At the end of the story, he is in a taxi cab but is unable to decide where to go; he says to himself: "I've too many roles to fulfill. As a son, a husband, father, older brother, a clerk in an accountant's office. It's all too much. Yes, maybe you're right—a stray bullet, let loose by the creator. It's true, I don't know where I'm headed. But I know I must go, now, somewhere" (P. Yi 1973: 154). Personal and social ills crash in on him as the story ends with him spitting blood and staining his white shirt.

'SA-IL-GU'

Rhee's prospects for preserving his power seemed bright in the first months of 1960. It was almost as if he had Heaven's mandate to rule. His challenger in 1960, Cho Pyŏng-ok [Chough Pyong Ok], died suddenly before the election, as in fact had Sin Ik-hŭi [Patrick Henry Shinicky] in the 1956 election (the other candidate in that election, Cho Pong-am, was later convicted of communist conspiracy and executed) (S. Han 1972: 46–49). The only threat to his victory was his own mortality.

The March 1960 election had, however, also pitted vice-presidential candidates Yi Ki-bung and Chang Myŏn against each other. Chang had once been, like former presidential candidates Cho and Sin, a follower of Rhee. Unlike Chang, and others, who had broken with Rhee over political differences, Yi had remained steadfastly loyal. Yi's degenerative disease, however, made him an easy target of mockery; he had lost to Chang in the 1956 vice-presidential election. When the 1960 election results revealed a landslide victory for Yi, a major demonstration occurred in Masan. To informed South Koreans, Yi's victory was inconceivable; the election had clearly been rigged (Yun Kyŏng-ch'ŏl 1986: 173–82).

The disturbance in Masan at first seemed isolated. But when a young demonstrator's corpse was accidentally discovered and the public learned that he had died from the police's teargas shell, South Koreans in various cities demonstrated. In addition to university and high school students, the moderate forces also began to openly express their discontent (Pak Se-gil 1989: 73–97).

The largest demonstration occurred in Seoul on April 19, 1960—immortalized in South Korean political memory as *sa-il-gu* (4-1-9, or April 19th; many key events in modern Korean history are expressed as integer chains denoting the date). The police shot many demonstrators, killing 186 and wounding 1,600 (Q. Y. Kim 1983: 5). The violence shocked the literate population and prompted a major demonstration by university professors on April 25th.

Demonstrations were, however, necessary but insufficient to topple Rhee's regime. What made his departure all but inevitable was the erosion of his crucial support. The military and the police remained neutral, while U.S. backing, which had never been more than tepid, evaporated (J. Oh 1968: 63–64). Rhee's rule collapsed. He resigned on April 26th and fled to Hawaii where he died in 1965.

Rhee's hold on power had seemed robust. Why was it, in retrospect, so fragile? He had relied on repression, an uneasy alliance with the United States, and a compliant polity. The repressive state apparatus—the police and the military—constituted the single largest organizational actor and, in the absence of serious opposition, the ruling force. Politics was played on an urban surface against the backdrop of a largely rural country. Because no serious challenge existed, the cloak of democracy obscured the reality of autocracy.

Japanese colonial rule had greatly strengthened the state apparatus at the expense of local governments, while eliminating or weakening independent organizations. The Korean War had destroyed inchoate peasant organizations; land reform had eradicated the traditional ruling class and eliminated farmers' fundamental source of discontent. Farmers remained a potentially powerful but unorganized social force. The urban opposition was not well organized. After an intense period of political activity in the late 1940s, the Korean War and Rhee's rule discouraged political organization. Many middle-class privileges, such as universal suffrage, were given by the U.S.-dictated constitution. Because of the combination of repression and rights, 1950s South Korea had few autonomous political organizations. In this context, the stirring of students and the educated middle class was felt as a titanic disturbance at the center.

Rhee's downfall is in large part a story of hubris and personal weakness. His biographer, Richard Allen (1960: 240), wrote: "Wielding the power that he did, Rhee might have been the Kemal Atatürk of [South] Korea. But he had no program for his country apart from his preoccupation with unification." Driven by a singular desire to unify Korea, a national hero had become an ineffectual and irrelevant head of a corroding, corrupt regime.

The impact of what came to be known in South Korean political history as the April Student Revolution was profound. Most reports, within and without South Korea, simply saw the fall of a corrupt ruler and the triumph of democracy.* In South Korea, it not only denoted the victory of democracy and the human spirit but also became a powerful political myth (Q. Y. Kim 1983: 2). *Sa-*

---

*See Min 1993. *Life* commented: "The triumph of democracy in Korea was a triumph of youth and was fittingly celebrated even by those almost too young to understand what a great thing had been done" (May 9, 1960: 30). The article went on to remark: "The events were capped by a tragedy that seemed senselessly bizarre to the Western mind but was a peculiarly fitting kind of justice to the Oriental" (May 9, 1960: 30). The tragedy referred to was the collective suicide of the vice-presidential candidate Yi Ki-bung and his family; what was a Shakespearean drama became transmuted into an inscrutable Oriental plot.

il-gu emerged as a defining moment in modern Korean history equal in significance to *Sam-il* (the March First 1919 uprising against Japanese colonial rule) and *Yuk-i-o* (June 25, 1950, the beginning of the Korean War). Two widely used texts on Korean history end their narratives with the April Student Revolution. "It showed that Korean democracy was alive and healthy, and none doubted that it would continue to grow and prosper (W. Han 1974: 509); "The April Revolution, therefore, held out bright prospects for the development of democracy in Korea" (K. Lee 1984: 385). Student demonstrations became institutionalized in South Korean politics, an object of fear for the powers that be and a mobilizing myth for generations of students. [*]

The Rise of Modern Ideals

The April Student Revolution demonstrated the power of the urban middle class. By 1960, nearly 30 percent of South Koreans lived in cities with over 50,000 people, while 70 percent of the people were literate (Eckert et al. 1990: 353). Along with the steady growth of the urban population and the educated middle class had come cultural changes. In particular, two ideals became salient by the late 1950s: egalitarianism and materialism. These modern values motivated the movement to topple Rhee.

Consider egalitarianism. Chosŏn Dynasty Korea was extremely stratified. The *yangban* elite lorded over peasants and slaves. Osgood's (1951: 44) description of a stratified village provides a glimpse of the pre–land reform era: "The [*yangban*] did no work, wore horsehair hats, and lived off the labor of their tenants or each other. Their local power was great and sometimes absolute and they acted as intermediaries between the commoners and the government. Needless to say they held the important political offices and operated a system of nepotism which was classic in its proportions." The dominance of the agrarian elite persisted through-

---

[*] See, e.g., Sin Yong-ha 1990: 325–34. The sanctification of the student movement is by no means unique to South Korea. Adam Gopnik (1995: 68) writes of France: "In fact, the phrase 'student movement' has in France much the same magic that the phrase 'family farm' has in America, conjuring up an idealized past, even for people who never took part in a student movement or lived on a family farm."

out the colonial period. There were, to be sure, cooperative practices and egalitarian sentiments that animated peasants in
pre–twentieth century Korea; they can be found in nearly every
civilization (S.-b. Han 1993: 286–88). However, as Bruce Cumings
(1981: 282) observed: "Few nations in 1945 could surpass Korea in
inequitable land relationships."

Largely due to land reform, however, South Korea emerged from
the post–Korean War period as a relatively egalitarian country. The
twin effects of the post-Liberation land reform and rural exodus
fostered egalitarianism in many villages. The devastation of the
Korean War only accentuated the pervasive sense of egalitarian origins, assiduously fostered by nationalism that stressed homogeneity (and hence equality) of South Koreans.

An egalitarian sentiment became a noted characteristic of
South Korea (Brandt 1991: 85). One expression was the desire for
democracy and participation. Its pervasiveness can be gleaned
from the prominent dissident politician Kim Dae Jung (1987: 325),
who wrote: "Democracy is the founding principle of our country."
It is not merely in obeisance to the United States that successive
South Korean presidents employed the rhetoric of democracy to
vindicate their rule.

Along with egalitarianism, the diffused desire for the effects and
attributes of modernity became pervasive in the 1950s. Although
no one starved to death, the common greeting in South Korea until
the 1960s was "Have you eaten today?" In this context, material
longings loomed large, and America came to stand for plenty and
modernity *tout court*.

The embodiment of the United States in GIs and the impressive material culture they brought with them was crucial. The
contact between U.S. military personnel and South Koreans
reached its height among Katusas (Korean Army Troops with the
U.S. Army) and military base town prostitutes. General Mark
Clark's (1954: 171) statement is suggestive: "The ROK [Republic
of Korea] saw the wonderful equipment our industry produces for
our American Army. He saw mechanical hole diggers for telephone poles. He saw bulldozers. He saw helicopters carry supplies
atop mountains that ROK bearers would take many hours to
climb. He saw hot food and ice cream delivered in giant tins to

Americans in the frontline bunkers. He soon wanted all these things." The shock of material plenty in wartorn South Korea is palpable in many accounts. Beyond GIs and their goods, Western influence spread steadily through South Korea. John Lewis (1955: 25) wrote of "a new phalanx of western civilians" who "speeded up the Westernization of material wants, extending this phenomenon even into the countryside . . . —until the Sears and Roebuck catalogue became, almost literally, the most popular book in the country."

Hollywood movies—another America—captivated and cultivated new South Korean sensibilities. Chang Key Young, deputy prime minister in the late 1960s, told *Time* (March 10, 1967: 41): "When we hammered in the spikes for a new railroad recently, I was reminded of American cowboy movies and the winning of the West." My father loved Westerns and named my brother after one of his favorite directors. Beyond the ethos that the movies projected, their lasting impressions were in the display of American might—big houses and big cars, sumptuous feasts and extravagant parties. American movies and television shows were effective missionaries for the cult of consumer culture (Twitchell 1992: 145–47). Few South Koreans in the 1950s escaped the sweet lure of material plenty represented in Hollywood films, which supplemented the gum and chocolates that American soldiers dispensed with such abandon. Imported luxury goods became the most visceral marker of modernity and prestige. They proved irresistible, despite the protests of intellectuals, to most people in the Third World (cf. Colson and Scudder 1988: 118–19).

Materialism also manifested itself in the overweening ambition of younger South Koreans. Julien Sorel—the exemplary upstart— declared in *The Red and the Black*: "I've got more intelligence than they have; I can pick the right uniform for my century" (Stendhal 1991: 336). That is in fact what many South Koreans attempted to do; they sought careers in the military, the bureaucracy, and corporations. South Korea became, in other words, a nation of Julien Sorels. When my father initially came to the United States in 1952, he named himself after the U.S. president (Harry, after Truman) and what he took to be the president of the world, the Secretary-General of the United Nations (Lie, after Trygve). A

Paris correspondent of a major South Korean newspaper expressed his shock when a child working at a *patisserie* said that he would like to be a baker when he grew up, just like his father. The reporter mused that South Korean children would undoubtedly have answered the question by saying the president of South Korea or of a large company. High aspirations and vaunted ambition came to characterize South Koreans. The "can do" spirit (*hamyŏn toenda*)—or what W. Arthur Lewis (1955: chap. 2) called "the will to economize"—became a powerful impulse in South Korean life.

In summary, the growth of the urban middle class was accompanied by a cultural change that championed modern values. Egalitarianism became meaningful as the desire for democracy and political participation spread. The desire for modernity and material goods stimulated the urge for economic growth. Both these emerging values militated against the continuation of Rhee's rule and underlay the cultural discontent of the younger educated South Koreans around 1960 (cf. M. G. Lee 1982: 98–101), which brought down the structure of corruption built around the triple alliance among the United States and its foreign aid, Rhee and the state, and dependent capitalists and opened the door for dynamic development in the 1960s.

CHAPTER THREE

Muddling Toward a Take-Off

Most accounts of South Korean development depict the 1960s as a watershed decade. Park Chung Hee (1971: 114) himself noted: "In the 1960's Korea changed from a premodern, underdeveloped society to a modern, productive, constantly growing society." A quasi-official South Korean publication proclaimed: "It was the Third Republic that made the 1960's the decade of development, inspired the will to develop, and marked a turning point in the history of modernization in Korea" (KDI 1975: 16). And, as the economist Byung-Nak Song (1990: v) argued: "All these changes resulted from the success of [South] Korea's export-oriented growth strategy." In this line of reasoning, Park's leadership in the 1960s catapulted the country into the trajectory of export-oriented industrialization, beginning a 30-year odyssey from poverty to wealth (see, e.g., Chapin 1969: 563; Cole and Lyman 1971: 3; and Wade and Kim 1978: 23).

This triumphalist narrative presumes three major propositions: first, that Park's leadership was strong and effective; second, that the First Five-Year Economic Plan advocated export-oriented industrialization; and, third, that economic growth began in accord with the plan. The received view is a retrospective construct that highlights the role of the state and of internal factors in accounting for development and elides the effect of social forces and external factors. I contend that Park's rule was fragile, the initial economic

strategy was nationalistic and pursued import-substitution industrialization, and economic growth occurred in spite, or at least independently, of the plan.

The growth of light industrialization depended on the Normalization Treaty with Japan in 1965 and the growing U.S. involvement in Vietnam, both of which integrated the South Korean economy into the expanding Japanese and U.S. economies. The confluence of contingent and external forces created a growth-oriented
milieu in the mid-1960s. Export-oriented industrialization was not
planned; opportunities came and were seized.

Military Rule, 1961–1971

The plotters of the 1961 military coup envisioned a revolutionary overhaul of South Korea. Their dominant ideals were egalitarianism and economic growth. Park Chung Hee, however, set aside
these ideals in his quest for personal power and political legitimacy.

THE CHANG INTERREGNUM

Rhee's departure marked the end of an era. The Liberal Party
collapsed, and Hŏ Chŏng headed an interim government. In the
July 1960 election, Chang Myŏn [John Chang], the former vice
president, was victorious. A Catholic from a privileged background
educated in the United States, Chang presented the modern, moderate face of South Korea. He advocated "Economic Development
First" (J. A. Kim 1975: 209–16) and sought to punish corrupt bureaucrats and business people (Yun Kyŏng-ch'ŏl 1986: 209–14). The
initial promise of his rule, however, was betrayed in less than ten
months. By the time of the military coup, many people who had
envisioned a bright future had lost hope that South Korea was
ready for democracy.

Chang lacked internal or external support. His own Democratic
Party, torn by internal conflict, eventually split into two parties
(J. Oh 1968: 80–82). Not only had he alienated the police and the
military, but he also faced an ideologically polarized polity (Yun
Kyŏng-ch'ŏl 1986: 216–18). The urban middle class—the force that
toppled Rhee—was never content with his rule. The heightened

expectation of a new era only made the politically active population eager for even more change; in addition to political reforms and economic growth, some citizens advocated national unification and supported leftist political parties (Yun Kyŏng-ch'ŏl 1986: 221–26).

Park Chung Hee and a group of other graduates of the Korean Military Academy were planning a coup in February 1960 but were interrupted by the April Student Revolution (J. Oh 1968: 100). Chang's declaration that he intended to cut the military by a third and the resurgence of the political left made Park and his coterie eager to seize state power. On May 16, 1961, 1,600 soldiers marched to the presidential palace and overthrew the government without bloodshed (J. Oh 1968: 105). The Chang regime simply collapsed, without any significant show of resistance (see S. Han 1974: 176; cf. Luttwak 1968: 36–37).

THE 1961 MILITARY COUP

Military coups are common in developing societies. Between 1945 and 1985, there were 183 successful and 174 unsuccessful coups in the Third World (David 1987: 1–2). The confluence of external and internal threats contributes to the expansion of Third World militaries. The beneficiary of financial, technological, and organizational support from external powers, the military often becomes the most modernized organization in a developing nation-state. The Cold War ensured that superpowers would offer military aid to friendly regimes, especially to countries in contested areas (David 1987: 66–68). Furthermore, in many countries internal threats from political rivals or peasant rebellions heighten the military's "super-police" function (Janowitz 1964: 33).

In the case of South Korea, the omnipresent threat of North Korea offered a compelling rationale for expanding the military. By 1960 Rhee and the United States had transformed the South Korean military into the largest and the best-organized institution in the entire country. A minuscule force in 1948, the South Korean military had over 600,000 active troops by 1954 (S. J. Kim 1971: 40). Accounting for over half the national budget (indeed, in the fiscal year 1953–54, nearly 80 percent), it was the fourth largest in the world in terms of the number of soldiers in 1960 (Lovell 1975: 165–69). Rhee dreamed of using his army to reunify the peninsula and found it quite useful for domestic social control. The United States nurtured the South Korean military force in order to reduce its own deployment (Lovell 1975: 165).

Thus in retrospect, the 1961 military coup in South Korea seems to have been unavoidable (see, e.g., Lovell 1970: 144). Indeed, American political scientists suggest that militaries replace only unstable regimes (Perlmutter 1977: 98). This thesis is an *ex post facto* construct based on a circular argument, given that these same political scientists define an unstable regime as one that was toppled by a coup. What is more important, in the case of South Korea this argument ignores the question of why the military grew so dramatically and the crucial role of the United States in the process. Behind both factors loomed the specter of communism.

It is by no means foreordained that a country's largest institution should rule. In the immediate aftermath of Rhee's ouster, for example, the military strong man "Tiger" Song told a *Time* reporter: "If the military take over, our democracy will go and our fight against Communism in vain" (May 9, 1960: 25). The U.S. military sought to instill the virtues of civilian democracy in its South Korean trainees: "The growth of the Korean armed forces had been closely supervised and scrupulously guided by the American advisers" (S. Han 1974: 47). What prompted U.S.-trained officers to breach the democratic dogma and to seize state power?

The young military officers around Park saw themselves as the last hope of a country on the brink of collapse. They were alarmed by the threat from North Korea, continuing corruption, political instability, and the stagnant economy (Yun Kyŏng-ch'ŏl 1986: 227–28; cf. Stepan 1978: 129–30). The examples of Nasser's Egypt (1956), Ne Win's Burma (1958), and other military coups were undoubtedly not far from their minds. The Japanese military influence was also crucial. Park himself was trained in the Japanese Imperial Army with its close military-civilian ties (S. J. Kim 1971: 48–49). The prewar Japanese military had played an intrusive role in politics; Tōjō Hideki was but one example of a military officer who engaged in civilian politics (Huntington 1957: 134–38). Despite his public denunciations of Japan, Park remained deeply influenced by its prewar military ethos (Masumi 1993: 315–16).

There was also discontent within the South Korean military. Its upper echelon was deeply implicated in Rhee's corrupt rule and riven by internal conflicts generated in part by Rhee, who sought to divide and conquer the top leadership (S. J. Kim 1971: 56–59). Furthermore, young and ambitious officers had little hope of advancement, since the top posts were filled by relatively youthful generals (J. Sohn 1968: 108). Younger officers considered the corruption and the stagnation of the status quo ample reasons to rebel.

The class dimension of the coup cannot be ignored. Many military officers, like Park, hailed from humble social backgrounds (H.-B. Lee 1968: 146). Their quest for personal ambition coincided with their desire for national greatness. As we will see, Park's desire to eliminate special privileges and to stress egalitarianism marked a politics informed by his non-elite origins.

None of the foregoing, however, can explain why the coup was successful. As I mentioned earlier, nearly half of the coups attempted in the Third World between 1945 and 1985 failed. It is important that in South Korea the coup was not opposed. The majority of the South Koreans in the countryside remained politically inactive. Although many middle-class citizens championed liberal political values, they represented a narrow social base. Furthermore, the political unrest during the Chang regime raised concerns that civil disturbance would create an opportunity for a North Korean invasion (Okai 1976: 39–44). In general, the restoration of order and the suppression of civil disturbance offer powerful rationales for military intervention (Huntington 1968: 216–17). In the case of South Korea, the fear of North Korea rendered those justifications all the more potent (N.-Y. Park 1961: 365).

The rise of the military regime and the urgency of anticommunism cannot be separated. Anticommunism has been a powerful ideological current in twentieth-century Korea. During the colonial period, Japan transmitted both procommunism and anticommunism. While some students, intellectuals, and labor leaders came under the sway of Marxism and other leftist thoughts while studying in Japan and reading Marxist works in Japanese translation, the Japanese authorities inculcated anticommunism in South Korean police and military officers, bureaucrats, and intellectuals (Han Kye-ok 1988: 56–62; Ishizaka 1993). The strength of anticommunism reflects in part the appeal of communism. The People's Republic that emerged after Liberation was predominantly left-leaning, as were the local peoples' committees. Together, they marked the leftist, in some cases communist, origins of South Korea that were violently suppressed by the U.S. military government and the Rhee regime. Furthermore, the devastation of the Korean War, as I have suggested, shaped the visceral character of South Korean anticommunism. Virtually no one was spared the death of a close family member or friend. The war was inscribed not only in many injured bodies but in the physical destruction that remained years after the final shot sounded. The stress on destruction and dislocation—in the official South Korean version, the alpha and the omega of the Korean War—captures only part of the picture, but the specter of communism found embodiment in the war and its scars. Thus the brief resurgence of leftist parties after the Student Revolution led some South Koreans to support the coup despite their antimilitary sentiments.

As I have emphasized repeatedly, anticommunism colored U.S. policy toward South Korea. Although the United States remained skeptical about Park and pressured him to hold a democratic election, it did not strongly oppose the coup in the light of North Korean threat. Just as the United States had long tolerated Rhee's corrupt and autocratic rule, it was also to support, however tepidly, Park's military rule (Macdonald 1992: 213–17). The primary U.S. concern remained anticommunism; the substantive political constitution of South Korea was, at best, of secondary interest. As *Time* reported the U.S. reaction to Chang's ouster: "The junta felt justifiably confident that General Magruder [U.S. military commander in South Korea] would not . . . contest the coup" (May 26, 1961: 21). Magruder, in fact, defended Chang's civilian regime, but James A. Van Fleet, "the father of the ROK army," reportedly called the coup "the finest thing that has happened to Korea in a thousand years" (*Time*, July 28, 1961: 25).

THE INITIAL PHASE OF MILITARY RULE

The military junta established an emergency government, elevating Chang To-yŏng, the army chief of staff, to leadership in part to assuage American anxieties. The United States came to accept the *fait accompli*, optimistically believing in the junta's promise to return power to civilians after it had restored order (J. Oh 1968: 109–17).

Declaring itself the Supreme Council for National Reconstruction (SCNR), the military junta proclaimed the Law Regarding Extraordinary Measures for National Reconstruction on June 6, 1961 (for the text, see S. J. Kim 1971: 179–84). The six "revolutionary pledges" were to oppose communism, support the United States, reunify the country, "eliminate corruption and eradicate other social evils," eradicate poverty (to create a "self-sustaining economy"), and "return to our proper military duties" after other pledges had been accomplished. The pledges to oppose communism and eliminate corruption were particularly important (Secretariat SCNR 1961: 9–16).

The ideology of the junta was a paradigmatic instance of the professional military ideology of developing countries. According to Morris Janowitz (1964: 63–66), four tenets are crucial: (1) "a strong sense of nationalism"; (2) "a strong 'puritanical' outlook and an emphasis on anticorruption and antidecadence"; (3) "the acceptance of collective public enterprise as a basis for achieving social, political, and economic change"; and (4) "an 'anti-politics' outlook of the military." Fervent nationalism and strident puritanism were particularly evident during the initial phase of South Korean military rule.

Outbursts of puritanical zeal are common in postrevolutionary societies. Radical measures not only impose a vision of a pure and principled new society (which is invoked to justify the seizure of political power) but also eliminate dissent and instill discipline in the body politic. A similar spirit of austerity had pervaded the April Student Revolution and the Chang regime. During the Chang interregnum, the call for "Fresh Tide Society" resulted in movements to abandon Western suits, chauffeured vehicles, expensive restaurants, and Western imports such as coffee (N.-Y.

Park 1961: 345). To be sure, this phenomenon is not unique to South Korean political culture; Richard Hofstadter (1955: 15) writes of the "failings of American political culture": "The most prominent and pervasive failing is a certain proneness to fits of moral crusading that would be fatal if they were not sooner or later tempered with a measure of apathy and of common sense."

The SCNR squelched opposition by imposing its puritanical vision on what it considered unruly society. Beginning with a large-scale arrest of urban "hoodlums" and "beggars," the SCNR passed a spate of measures, to include rationing rice at restaurants and outlawing smuggling, black marketing, and usury (S. J. Kim 1971: 105–6). A nightly curfew was imposed. People in Seoul donned austerity suits and dresses to reflect the spirit of anti-luxury. Park stated that "the sight of luxury goods arouses wanton desires in the mind of the people. Burn them" (*Time*, March 9, 1962: 35). He objected to everything from "failure to pay taxes to being late in appointments. . . . Both men and women were urged to greet each other with the words, 'Let us reconstruct'" (N.-Y. Park 1961: 348). The promise of a new society also proposed a vision of a "new man"; consider its articulation in a 1961 government publication:

> After sweeping his yard and eating [a] wholesome breakfast, he puts on simple but clean trousers and [a] short-sleeved shirt. He is really glad he no longer has to wear [a] necktie and thick suit in this hot weather. Then he takes a bus or a street car without being ashamed—most decent people take them now. . . . At noon, he eats from his lunch box, which he carried according to the logicality of living the Revolution has taught him. He admits without shame that Korean cigarettes are as good as any foreign made ones. He has realized that coffee is not indispensable like he once believed from his morbid vanity (Lovell 1970: 176).

In the initial phase of military rule, austerity and purity superseded affluence and cosmopolitanism.

PARK CHUNG HEE

Park quickly emerged as the most powerful figure in the junta by skillfully manipulating alliances and ruthlessly purging his rivals. His initial prey was Chang To-yŏng, the symbolic head of the coup. Charged with counterrevolutionary activities and sentenced to death, U.S. pressures commuted his sentence and Chang eventually became a professor at an American university (Oliver 1993: 277). To shore up U.S. support for the coup Park replaced Chang with General Tiger Song (J. Oh 1968: 126–27) but soon purged him too. Overall, Park dismissed two thousand senior military officers (Henderson 1968: 356–57). Park brooked no threats to his power, removing one trusted colleague after another. Only a third of the original SCNR members remained by December 1963 (Lovell 1970: 180).

Park was barely 43 when he became the effective leader of South Korea. He had grown up in a poor farming household in North Kyŏngsang Province. After a hapless tenure as an elementary school teacher, he joined the Japanese Army. After the Liberation, Park was implicated in the communist-backed 1948 Yŏsu Rebellion and sentenced to death (C. S. Lee 1985: 63). After he was rehabilitated, he entered the Korean Military Academy and after graduation rose through the military hierarchy (Yang 1981: chap. 6).

Park advocated "Koreanizing democracy" or "Administrative Democracy," which was modeled on Sukarno's idea of "Guided Democracy" (C. H. Park 1962: 207–10). Park said: "There are two kinds of democracy. One pursues complete freedom. The other one is guided democracy. The latter will suit South Korea" (*Newsweek*, January 1, 1962: 22). He also stated that to believe that democracy would arise from "past confusion" was tantamount to believing that "a rose could blossom in a garbage can" (*Time*, May 25, 1962: 38).

Park's intended goals for the military revolution were egalitarianism and materialism, which were also the guiding ideals behind the April Student Revolution. He stressed equality as the prerequisite of democracy and insisted on eradicating "privilege consciousness," which included "wealth consciousness," "rank consciousness," "academic snobbery," and "family complex" (C. H. Park 1962: 6–7). He wrote that "there is no room in our society for privilege consciousness or class superiority" (C. H. Park 1962: 9). In other words, in the society he envisioned there were to be no divisions based on class, status, education, or family background (C. H. Park 1962: 174–75).

Park also sought to pursue material goals. His stated desire was "to eliminate poverty and hunger from this land and to realize economic equality both in name and in fact" (C. H. Park 1962: 21). He later wrote of the First Five-Year Economic Development Plan that "the most important purpose of this plan was to remove all forms of corruption, iniquities, and social evils that prevented social and economic development of Korea" (C. H. Park 1970: 65). His two primary goals were to improve rural life (C. H. Park 1962: 232–36) and to establish a "self-sufficient" or "independent" economy (C. H. Park 1962: 119, 1970: 29).

Park's actions ultimately revolved around his desire to stay in power. As he once said: "The only criterion in making the decision is the circumstances. Neither popularity nor honor should play a part in one's decision-making" (Yang 1981: 260). Indeed, by elevating power over principle and clinging to it tenaciously, he mirrored his adversary to the north, Kim Il Sung.[*]

STRONG MEASURES, FRAGILE RULE

The 1961 military coup consolidated a major elite transition initiated by the end of *yangban* rule and deepened by the April Student Revolution. The *yangban* elite, who had lost their land a mere decade earlier, were finally forced to cede their hold on political power as well. Youthful, non-*yangban* military officers were now in charge, not the aging *yangban* elite. In effect, a new power network had emerged (Hattori 1992: 158–79). But the new elite was far from secure. Their immediate task was to find a way to turn might into right, naked power into legitimate authority. Only economic growth could justify military rule.

The First Five-Year Economic Development Plan expressed the junta's desire to reform the South Korean economy. It opened with the following sentence: "The social phenomenon which in the past most vividly attested to the corruption and inefficiency of the past regimes was the demoralization of the national economy"

---

[*]A U.S. official, in an interview with Mark Clifford (1994: 82), stated: "Once I met Lee Hu Rak [KCIA chief]. . . . I tried to raise a neutral topic. 'You recently went to North Korea,' I said. 'How did that make you feel?' 'Very strong,' he said, referring to the North Koreans, gesturing with his thumb up. 'One-man rule. Quite a guy.' It was an admiring reaction toward Kim Il Sung."

(ROK 1962: 9). In the body of the plan the junta blamed corruption and the illicit accumulation of wealth for the stagnation of the South Korean economy (ROK 1962: 12–13). A spate of measures followed: the anti-*chaebŏl* law and the announcement of the economic growth plan in February 1962, the establishment of governmental control over the financial sector in May 1962, and the currency reforms of June 1962 were all attempts to eradicate the structure of corruption and to promote economic nationalism (B. K. Kim 1965: 44–49).

True to its desire to extirpate corruption, the SCNR fired nearly one-sixth of South Korea's 240,000 civil servants (J. Oh 1968: 124) and arrested leading South Korean businessmen on charges of illicit profiteering (Yun Kyŏng-ch'ŏl 1986: 240–48). In effect, the junta demonstrated its supremacy over the state bureaucracy and dependent capitalists. By dismissing 35,000 civil servants, the coup effected a generational shift in the state bureaucracy (Taniura 1989: 8–9). The younger bureaucrats, the beneficiaries of this unprecedented opportunity for advancement, repaid the junta with their loyalty.

The SCNR sought to secure and to strengthen state power in other ways. In addition to restructuring the military hierarchy and the police force, Kim Jong-Pil organized the KCIA, which was modeled after its namesake in the United States (J. A. Kim 1975: 234–35). Beginning as a corps of 3,000 officers dedicated to military rule, the KCIA had 370,000 employees by the late 1960s (S. J. Kim 1971: 111–12).

The military junta was, however, not permitted to stay in power as a *military* junta (H.-B. Lee 1968: 174–75). In the face of pressure from the United States and at home, the SCNR disbanded and military leaders donned civilian clothes (Macdonald 1992: 219–22). The junta could not afford to jeopardize continued U.S. support. In the early 1960s U.S. military aid accounted for over 70 percent of South Korean defense expenditures (Eckert et al. 1990: 361). Bowing to U.S. demands that he establish an electoral democracy, Park, with the aid of Kim Jong-Pil's "brain trust," organized the Democratic Republican Party (DRP), which "was to be highly structured along a hierarchical, single command system" (C.I.E. Kim 1971: 371–75).

Nonetheless, the DRP could not ensure an easy electoral victory for Park. In October 1963, Park won the presidential election by just over one percent of the vote. He won only 43 percent of the vote overall; a united opposition would have defeated him (J. A. Kim 1975: 252–54). In the following National Assembly election, DRP members gained only 34 percent of the votes, although the electoral system allowed them to control over 60 percent of the actual seats (J. Oh 1968: 164–71). The thin margins of victory are all the more remarkable given Park's advantage in political organization and funding (K. B. Kim 1971: 155–69) and widespread electoral frauds and irregularities (Axelbank 1967: 10). An anthropologist in the late 1960s noted "the cynical brutality with which local elections are 'supervised' by the police" (Brandt 1971: 14). In spite of Park's electoral victory, his rule was far from secure.

Park needed to enhance his popularity. His control of the institutions of repression was not enough. Like many other military regimes in the Third World, Park's government depended on rural support (R. Wade 1982: 18), but unlike them Park also needed the support of the growing urban middle class. In order to guarantee widespread support, he needed to eliminate corruption, to fight communism, to foment nationalism, and to pursue egalitarian and material ideals. The urban middle class demanded material prosperity and political participation. He answered their desire for prosperity by championing economic growth. He justified the authoritarianism of his rule by invoking the specter of North Korea. Thus economic growth and anticommunism became the twin ideological pillars of his fragile hold on power.

The First Five-Year Economic Plan: Image and Reality

National plans were part and parcel of development discourse in the 1950s. The pervasive desire for an economic plan was not only a reflection of the state of development discourse but also an expression of diffused yearnings for economic growth and the popular perception of the duty of governments to fulfill these yearnings. In the mid-1960s, Albert Waterston (1965: 28) wrote in his widely used textbook *Development Planning*: "Today, the national plan appears to have joined the national anthem and the national flag as a symbol of sovereignty and modernity. But it is only within the last decade . . . that the diffusion of development planning became world-wide" (see also W. Lewis 1966: 13, 1969: 121). Planning in the Third World became, in A. F. Robertson's (1984: 26) words, "both inevitable and necessary." Indeed, as Waterston puts it, "whether or not [Western aid-providers] have favored planning for their own economies, they have accepted planning in recipient countries and often insisted on the formulation of plans before they extended aid to less developed countries" (Waterston 1965: 36).

In the 1950s, most developing countries advocated an import-substitution industrialization strategy (ISI)—the manufacture at home of what had been imported before. Economists believed that expanding the domestic industrial base was the shortest route to development (Nurkse 1962: 314–22). An export-oriented industrialization strategy entails stimulating domestic industrial production by meeting external demands. In practice, however, the two had to go hand in hand. ISI requires foreign exchange to purchase capital goods and raw materials. As Hal Lary (1968: 13) pointed out: "If the less developed countries are to earn foreign exchange in amounts commensurate with their needs, they will have to achieve a rapid increase in their exports of manufactures to the developed countries." Export-oriented industrialization, in turn, depends almost inevitably on a prior base of industrialization (often due to ISI), as well as on domestic demand for manufactured products.

Park's five-year plan was by no means the first economic plan in South Korea's history (Satterwhite 1994). Rhee's economic advisers had formulated a three-year plan (1960–62), but his government was overthrown by the April Student Revolution before it was implemented (Oregon Advisory Group in Korea 1961: 13–23). Similarly, the Chang Myŏn regime had a five-year plan (1962–66), but that government was overthrown by the military before it could even be started (Wolf 1962: 23–24).

The received view that South Korean planners pursued an export-oriented industrialization strategy is a retrospective construct; Park's plan, which was closely modeled on the Chang plan (J. W. Lee 1966: 12), did not initially advocate export-oriented industrialization. His principal goal was to "establish a self-reliant economy" (C. H. Park 1962: 119, 1970: 65–66; see also Chŏng 1988). The First Five-Year Plan projected the export of agricultural produce and raw materials (specifically rice, pork, and laver) and some minerals (tungsten, iron, and graphite) but not industrial products: "Exports will consist of such primary products as pigs, rice, seaweed, fresh fish, frozen marine products, and dried cuttlefish" (ROK 1962: 39). The provisions for industrialization were in keeping with the prevailing wisdom of development economics—ISI. The Plan called for "guided capitalism" (ROK 1962: 28); in a Marxist language, it declared that "an increasingly larger portion of the expanding gross national product will be invested in the expansion of the means of production" (ROK 1962: 24). In particular, it stressed energy production and infrastructural development, advocating growth of "import-substitute industries [such] as cement, chemical fertilizer, and synthetic fibers" (ROK 1962: 25).

In spite of the Plan, the South Korean economy did little more than sputter along. GNP and export growth fell short of the planners' expectations; the popular perception was that the economy was in the doldrums (J. S. Kim 1975: 258). By 1964, the ambitious goals of the Plan had to be revised downward (P. Kuznets 1977: 202–3). A 1965 publication from the Ministry of Public Information attempted to gloss over these difficulties: "In carrying out the long-term economic development plan, the first of its kind in Korean history, many obstacles had to be overcome, and valuable experience had been gained. . . . The fundamental problems of the Korean economy [include] land resources, energy resources, the national defense burden, agricultural problems, and mobilization of domestic capital" (MPI 1965: 6, 20). The economy, in other words, seemed stagnant.

Observers in the United States were not impressed by the situation of the South Korean economy in the mid-1960s. James Morley (1965: 51) wrote the following assessment of the competence of Park's regime:

> Regrettably, however, the military life did not train these men in the political arts, nor did it give them broad knowledge and skill in economic affairs. They have not themselves known how to get the country on its feet, and by their authoritarianism they

have temporarily at least frustrated the development of an alternative young civilian leadership, either in the government bureaucracy or in the public at large.

In a 1964 survey, over 80 percent of South Korean intellectuals deemed Korean character to be "bad"—reflecting the failure of both democracy and development (S.-c. Hong 1969: 177–78). The future looked bleak for Park's rule and the South Korean economy.

Kim Sŭngok's 1965 story "Seoul: 1964, Winter" exemplifies the frustration and desperation of post-coup South Korea. In the story, two 25-year-olds meet a man whose wife has just died of meningitis. The widower attempts to use up the money he received from the hospital for her body. After a few rounds of drinks, the man throws the money into a fire and later commits suicide. The wealthy graduate student asks the narrator:

"You and I are definitely twenty-five, aren't we[?]"
"I definitely am!"
"I definitely am, too." He nodded once. "It frightens me."
"What does?" I asked.
"That 'something.' That . . . " His voice was like a sigh. "Doesn't it seem we've become old?"
"We're barely twenty-five," I said. (S. Kim 1993: 101)

Such a portrait of tentative and anomic youths, however, was soon to become a thing of the past. The rapid economic growth that was to transform South Korea dates from this period.

External Stimuli: Japan, Vietnam, and the United States

The sources of the transformation of the South Korean economy cannot be found in official economic planning documents or in the wisdom of Park and his advisers but in the resurgence of the Japanese economy and the U.S. intervention in Vietnam. South Korean diaspora networks facilitated the economic integration of South Korea into the expanding Japanese and American economies. Contingent, external factors—not planned, internal ones—proved critical in propelling South Korean light industrialization and export.

BEFORE AND AFTER THE 1965
NORMALIZATION TREATY WITH JAPAN

Rhee's anti-Japanese sentiments, which were in part sincere and in part a ploy to mobilize domestic support, were more virulent than his anticommunism (Cheong 1991: 135–43). His intransigent refusal to conclude a normalization treaty between the two countries hampered the Japanese–South Korean diplomatic and economic relationship at every turn (Reeve 1963: 52–59). Japan and South Korea disagreed on questions of property claims, fishery rights, and the status of Korean residents in Japan (Macdonald 1992: 117–27). In addition, there was widespread fear that the Japanese would colonize South Korea again, this time not politically or militarily but economically (D. Chang 1985: 73–74). Park, for example, warned against "another form of Japanese aggression against [South] Korea" (1962: 163). National pride and anti-Japanese sentiments rendered any normalization problematic (B.-i. Koh 1973: 50–51). Consider Park's cultural polemic:

> The "Japanese Boom" under the Chang Regime numbed the reason of the people: tea-houses in the major cities of Seoul and Pusan vibrated with cheap Japanese music to the exclusion of Korean, more than a hundred institutions teaching the Japanese language sprang up, pornographic Japanese magazines and literature flooded Korea. The Chang Regime soon faced the charge of being a pro-Japanese Cabinet, as our markets were flooded with tax-evading, shoddy Japanese commodities coming in through smuggling routes. "The Japan Wind" under Chang was frowned upon by conscientious people as an anti-national trend. (C. H. Park 1962: 196)

The ritual invocation of anti-Japanese sentiments—inevitably focusing on the colonial period—dominated the post-Liberation South Korean discussion of Japan (Takasaki 1993). Despite expressions of Korean superiority (Tanaka 1988: 128–58), most South Koreans recognized that Japan was years, perhaps decades, ahead of South Korea. The sense of inferiority, combined with anticolonial, nationalist sentiments, undoubtedly motivated many South Koreans to do all they could to catch up (Dore 1990: 359–62). The fear of Japan manifested itself in cultural legislation that banned the showing of Japanese films or the singing of Japanese songs. At the same time, however, colonial nostalgia and Japanese economic might combined to create a powerful countercurrent of pro-Japanese sentiments, especially among the South Korean elite. South Korean business people, in particular, adopted Japanese idioms and mannerisms. Japanese corporate cultural practices could be found in various South Korean settings, from the decor of expensive bars to the nomenclature of the managerial hierarchy. Furthermore, the young and the old (including both Kim Il Sung and Park Chung Hee) furtively delighted in Japanese popular culture.

Despite the prevalence of anti-Japanese sentiments, a treaty with Japan was all but inevitable by the mid-1960s. The United States encouraged it strongly, and South Korean businesses lobbied for it (K. B. Kim 1971: 78–80). Some yearned for reduced Japanese tariffs and hence greater South Korean exports to Japan, while others envisioned gradual transfer of Japanese light industrial production to South Korea (K. B. Kim 1971: 87–90). By the mid-1960s, Japan was well on its way to becoming an economic superpower; it had not only the capital but the technological know-how as well. It is not surprising that Park, despite his anti-Japanese rhetoric, eventually sought help for the South Korean economy in the industrial might of Japan. Japanese businesses also contributed money to Park's party (Clifford 1994: 91). The most pressing reason for a treaty, however, was the regime's economic difficulties, compounded by declining U.S. aid (from $266 million in 1961 to $194 million in 1965) (K. B. Kim 1971: 85). The treaty with Japan promised a quick infusion of cash and credit to the economy, as was revealed in the infamous Kim-Ohira memorandum (Yun Kyŏng-ch'ŏl 1986: 290–92).

Demonstrations against the 1965 Normalization Treaty with Japan began in 1964 (K. B. Kim 1971: 109–16; for the text of the treaty, see Han Kim 1972: 53–54). The first major demonstration on June 3, 1964, named the *yuk-sam* (6-3) generation (Pak Se-gil 1989: 143–53; Pak and Kim 1991: 175–96). The struggle against the Normalization Treaty unleashed not only anti-Japanese sentiments but even stronger antigovernment feelings (Yun Kyŏng-ch'ŏl 1986: 296–303). To stop the mass demonstrations and complete the signing of the Treaty with Korea's former colonial ruler, Park imposed martial law.

The immediate windfall of the 1965 Treaty was an infusion of cash. Japan gave South Korea about $200 million in public loans, $300 million in grants, and another $300 million in commercial credits (Bix 1974: 214). The Treaty also encouraged Japanese investment. Total direct Japanese investment in South Korea was only $1.2 million in 1965, but that figure had risen to $27.1 million by 1969. Equally significant was the diffusion of technological and business expertise from Japan to South Korea.

The incorporation of South Korea into the Japanese economic zone marked the turn in its fortunes. In effect, South Korea became integrated into Japan's growing economic networks and the international division of labor (cf. Fröbel, Heinrichs, and Kreyer 1981: 44–48). The opening of Japanese–South Korean economic relations laid the foundation for South Korean businesses to follow Japanese companies in the product cycle (Kobayashi 1983; Cumings 1984; cf. Mitchell and Ravenhill 1995).

South Korea followed Japan in two ways. In terms of production, Japanese technology and the diffusion of Japanese skills facilitated the development of South Korean enterprises (Hirakawa 1988: 175–76). In particular, Japanese corporations exported older, often pollution-producing, machinery to South Korea (Ozawa 1979: 18–19). Also, in Japan, domestic pressures to eradicate pollution and external demands to restrain exports forced Japanese manufacturers to change their industrial practices. Thus as Japanese corporations turned to less-polluting, higher value-added production, their superseded products and machinery were taken over by South Korean companies. In other words, South Korean enterprises assumed the low-technology, labor-intensive, pollution-producing, and low value-added production that Japanese companies had abandoned (Watanabe 1982: 194–96). South Korea's geographical proximity and cultural similarity to Japan only made the transfer of Japanese production technology to South Korea that much easier (E. Park 1984: 28–29). In short, South Korean industry dressed itself in Japanese corporate hand-me-downs.

Japan was equally important in marketing South Korean exports. Many South Korean products were initially exported to former Japanese markets, especially the United States. From textiles to transistors and black-and-white television sets, South Korean products found ready-made niches in the export market that Japanese businesses had cultivated in the post–World War II period (Borden 1984).

The Japanese colonial legacy facilitated Japanese–South Korean economic relations. Many South Koreans spoke Japanese fluently; some had even attended the same schools or shared other ties with their Japanese counterparts, which eased business dealings considerably (C. S. Lee 1985: 61–62). The founder of Samsung, Lee Byung-chull, for example, was educated in Japan and made frequent and extended visits to Japan in order to see his mistress in Tokyo, to sustain his business contacts, and to observe the Japanese economy firsthand. As the president of Samsung's trading company told an American reporter in the late 1980s: "When [Lee] returned from Japan, he would gather directors of the relevant companies and tell them about his ideas," including Japanese management techniques (Tanzer 1988: 87).

Korean residents in Japan also acted as conduits between the two countries. The Lotte Group is only the most prominent of Korean-Japanese enterprises in South Korea. But there were many more cross-national deals both high tech and low, ranging from steel production to toy manufacturing. The commercial history of South Korea in the 1960s is the story of countless Korean-Japanese business people and South Korean business people criss-crossing the Sea of Japan to close deals. My maternal uncle, for example, used our Tokyo home in the 1960s as a base to conduct export-import deals with Japanese companies. With his excellent command of Japanese, his business prospered rapidly. His example was far from unique.

Reestablishing a diplomatic and economic relationship with Japan in the mid-1960s brought South Korea into the expanding Northeast Asian economic system. Henceforth, the South Korean economy followed the Japanese path. In terms of both production and trade, the relationship with Japan proved to be a crucial spur to the South Korean economy.

SPOILS OF WAR: THE VIETNAM WAR AND SOUTH KOREA

The U.S. intervention in Vietnam* was as significant a factor
as the renewed relationship with Japan for South Korean development. It generated demands for South Korean products and stimulated exports and industrialization.

South Korean soldiers fought in Vietnam from October 1965 to
March 1973. At the peak of the war, from 1966 to 1971, close to
50,000 South Korean soldiers were sent every year, making them
the largest U.S. allied force after the South Vietnamese themselves.
Over the eight years of South Korean involvement, over 300,000
South Korean soldiers fought in Vietnam (S. Han 1978: 893). They
were known for their "courage" and their "brutality." According
to A. Terry Rambo, South Korean soldiers killed "hundreds of
South Vietnamese civilians while on tactical duty in Phuyen
Province" (Lee and Yim 1980: 85). South Korean soldiers and entrepreneurs, riding on the coattails of the United States, were
widely disliked by South Vietnamese (Kim Sun-il 1973: 142–44).

It is clear why the United States encouraged South Korean participation in the war. Although Rhee's offer to send South Korean
soldiers to Laos in 1954 had been refused (Kahin 1986: 54), Park's
similar offer in 1965 was eagerly accepted (Macdonald 1992:

---

*The Vietnam War itself was partly a product of the Korean War, which had
lodged the United States in Asia and confirmed Cold War foreign and military
policy. Further, the lesson of Korea shaped U.S. policymakers' decision to es-
calate U.S. intervention in Vietnam: "Korea served as a classic example of limited war under modern conditions. This later became the *raison d'être* of Mc-
Namara's 'flexible response' strategy to fight a war of national liberation in
Vietnam" (J. Nam 1986: 54). Yet according to General Mark Clark (1954: 2): "I
emphatically disagree with statements of so-called military experts that victory was ours for the taking at any time during my period of command with
the limited forces at our disposal and without widening the scope of the conflict. Korea's mountainous terrain literally soaks up infantry. We never had
enough men, whereas the enemy not only had sufficient manpower to block
our offensives, but could make and hold small gains of his own." Indeed, the
lessons not learned in the Korean hills were repeated with a vengeance in the
Vietnamese jungles. As Yuen Foong Khong (1992: 101) argues: "A fundamental lesson of Korea was . . . that international communism was at work. . . . By
comparing the Vietnam conflict to the Korean War, the analogy also implied
that the political stakes in Vietnam were extremely high" (see also K. Thompson 1981: 197; Kahin 1986: 339–41).

108–10). After the 1964 Gulf of Tonkin incident and the February 1965 aerial bombing of North Vietnam, the United States had intensified its commitment to South Vietnam. But the war, which was never officially declared in the United States, had proven extremely costly in both financial and domestic political terms. South Korean troops were economically and politically attractive for the United States. The monthly pay of an American soldier was over twenty times that of a South Korean soldier (Burchett 1968: 165). More significant, South Korean casualties had virtually no effect on popular support for the war in the United States (Young 1991: 158).

The South Korean decision to send troops to Vietnam was not unanimous. Opposition leaders criticized Park for selling the blood of South Korean youths in order to buy continued U.S. backing for his regime (Kim Sun-il 1973: 138). Park responded by crushing all dissent. Public debate on the Vietnam War was suppressed far longer and more deeply in South Korea than in the United States. Yi Yŏng-hŭi's (1974) book criticizing Park's Vietnam policy was censored and the author was jailed.

What prompted the Park regime to send South Korean troops to Vietnam? An anticommunist war in a divided Asian country was, quite obviously, significant for South Korean leaders (Y. Koo 1975: 224–25). More crucially, South Korea's Vietnam involvement ensured not only continued U.S. military presence in South Korea but continued U.S. support for Park as well. After Park had dispatched his troops to South Korea, "The Johnson administration overcame whatever reservations it still had about [Park regime's] legitimacy and instead began to praise it lavishly for its achievements and governing ability" (S. Han 1978: 907). The Park regime also counted on financial support and economic windfall from the military involvement. U.S. military aid doubled after South Korea committed its soldiers (J.-H. Kim 1970: 123). Park was also acutely aware of the role the Korean War had played in the resurgence of the Japanese economy in the early 1950s (Lee Sookjong 1992). Many South Korean officials and business people were conscious of the historical parallel; as a South Korean told *Newsweek* (February 7, 1966: 37): "In the Korean war, the Japanese made the money while we Koreans did the fighting. . . . Now it is Korea's turn."

The export of South Korean bodies did not begin with Vietnam. In order to acquire foreign exchange and to alleviate unemployment, the state had encouraged South Koreans to work abroad.[*] The 1962–65 effort sent miners and nurses to West Germany, but the total number amounted to only 3,809 (I. Kim 1981: 53–54). In contrast, by the peak years of the war, 1968 and 1969, 16,000 South Korean technicians, business people, and workers, in addition to soldiers, were in Vietnam (Pak Kŭn-ho 1993: 28). The number is all the more remarkable given that there were only 26,000 foreign civilian employees in Vietnam (Kahin 1986: 335).

South Korea probably benefited the most from the U.S. intervention in Indochina (J.-H. Kim 1970: 122). The war-related income accounted for over $200 million in 1969 and 1970 and generated over $1 billion between 1965 and 1972 (constituting 3.5 percent of GNP in 1967) (Pak Kŭn-ho 1993: 29–37). The total military procurement was under $3 million in 1965, but the figure rose to over $57 million by 1970. Products such as food, uniform, shoes, cement, and blankets accounted for 80 percent of military procurements (Pak Kŭn-ho 1993: 23). South Korean businesses were also active in Vietnam, generating $34 million in transportation, $8 million in cleaning, and in total $55 million in 1969; the sum from 1966 to 1972 amounted to $233 million (Pak Kŭn-ho 1993: 27). Remittances of South Korean soldiers, technicians, and workers not only benefited individuals but the government as well. The revenue generated during the Vietnam War in large part financed the construction of the main South Korean artery, the Kyŏngbu Highway connecting Seoul and Pusan, which was built between 1968 and 1970 (Pak Kŭn-ho 1993: 43).

The impact of the income generated by the Vietnam War was significant because it was linked to domestic production and stimulated industrial exports (Naya 1971: 45). For example, the export of South Korean cement to Vietnam amounted to $1.5 million of the total export of $1.6 million in 1967; by 1970, the corresponding figures were $6.1 million and $8.7 million. The South Korean export of fertilizer to Vietnam was $1.2 million in 1968 out of the

---

[*] The state's drive for foreign exchange reserves led to its promotion of prostitution (Lie 1995) and even the "export" of babies (N.-h. Lee 1989; Lewin 1990).

total export of $1.9 million; by 1970, the corresponding figures were $4.7 million and $6.3 million (Pak Kŭn-ho 1993: 22–23). South Korea achieved self-sufficiency in cement, fertilizer, and petroleum products through export to South Vietnam. Thus the goals of the First Five-Year Economic Plan were achieved by the economic boom generated by the war.

The difference between aid and demand that stimulates industrial production is critical. In the former case, as we saw for the Rhee regime, it often results in state-level corruption. The processing of aid materials rarely leads to the development of self-sustaining production. When industrialists engage in production to meet external demands, they reinvest their profits to enhance and improve productive capacity.

The demand generated by the Vietnam War provided a crucial niche for South Korean light industrialization and export in the late 1960s. Here Japanese technical and financial assistance were crucial. Japanese enterprises provided business and technological know-how for South Korean manufacturers (Pak Kŭn-ho 1993: 88). The U.S. war economy, furthermore, generated demand for South Korean light industrial goods, such as plywood, shoes, and textiles. While exports to the United States accounted for 30 percent of the total in 1964, the figure increased to 37 percent in 1966 and 52 percent in 1968, before falling to 34 percent in 1974. In the late 1960s, 40 percent of South Korean exports to the United States was textiles (Pak Kŭn-ho 1993: 51). The political goodwill generated by South Korean military intervention facilitated textile trade agreements (*Department of State Bulletin*, February 22, 1965: 274–78). The impact of the Vietnam War was profound in promoting not only exports but light industrialization *tout court* in the late 1960s South Korea.

The Vietnam War affected South Korean military personnel as well. Two later presidents, Chun Doo Hwan and Roh Tae Woo, both served in Vietnam. Although some veterans pursued successful careers in business or politics after the war, others were less fortunate. Many Vietnam War veterans returned to South Korea physically and psychologically wounded. The daredevil taxi drivers who dominated Seoul streets in the 1970s were said to be disgruntled Vietnam War veterans. In *White Badge*, a soldier reflects

on his sacrifice: "The blood money we had to earn at the price of
our lives fueled the modernization and development of the country. And owing to our contribution, the Republic of Korea, or at
least a higher echelon of it, made a gigantic stride into the world
market. Lives for sale. National mercenaries" (J. Ahn 1989: 40). In
a similar vein, Sergeant An Yong Kyu, the protagonist of *The
Shadow of Arms*, blurts out to an American: "Our land is divided,
like a body severed in two. My real home is in the North, you
know. It was only after I came to Vietnam that I began to see my
homeland objectively" (S. Hwang 1994: 342). His ire extends to a
critique of the United States: "[My] parents' generation was forced
to serve in armies of colonials and many were killed, just like now,
all over Asia and the Pacific in wars fought by the imperialist powers. From that time, you people were already on the scene. Your
government partitioned our country and occupied it" (S. Hwang
1994: 343).

THE INTEGRATION INTO THE U.S. AND JAPANESE ECONOMIES

The 1965 Normalization Treaty and the Vietnam War integrated
the South Korean economy into the expanding U.S. and Japanese
economic spheres. South Korean diaspora networks provided concrete economic ties. Both the American and Japanese economies
were predisposed to promote South Korean manufacturing exports.
Furthermore, there was little competition in the Pacific economy
to take over Japan's niche in the global division of labor.

In economics textbooks, imports and exports are simply trade
across national borders. In this abstract view of the market, it matters little who is exporting or importing. In reality, however, tangible ties between traders and trading organizations sustain the
import-export nexus (cf. Lie 1992b). South Korean immigrants in
the United States provided the crucial link for fledgling South Korean enterprises to export their products, just as much as Korean
residents in Japan were critical in forging economic relations with
Japan.

The wig industry provides a compelling example. Although one
may very well be skeptical about its significance in South Korean
development, it was consistently one of the two or three most im-

portant export items in the late 1960s, accounting for about 10 percent of total exports (S. Koh 1973: 75). At the peak in 1970, South Korean wig exports to the United States amounted to over $80 million (I. Kim 1981: 125). Given the local knowledge necessary to initiate and to sustain the marketing of wigs, Korean Americans played a crucial role in stimulating this export-oriented industry (I. Kim 1981: 121–43). As S. K. Koh (1973: 75) noted: "The imports to the U.S. market [of wigs] was initiated by young Koreans who had come to the U.S."

The trading networks were further embedded in the expanding economies of Japan and the United States. There was a trade triangle that connected South Korea to the two countries. In effect, South Korea imported lower value-added manufacturing facilities, know-how, and product markets from Japan; South Korea in turn exported former Japanese exports to the United States. The preponderant role of the Japanese and American economies cannot be overemphasized. Three-fourths of all South Korean exports in the 1960s were to the United States and Japan (S. H. Kim 1970: 106). Between 1967 and 1974, for example, 70 percent of total Korean trade was with these two countries (W. Hong 1976: 9). This dual dependence was to persist until the late 1980s. In the case of Japan, South Korea followed closely on the heels of Japan's ascent through the product cycle. In the case of the United States, the demands generated by the Vietnam War offered an unprecedented opportunity for South Korean light industry.

Plywood provides a good illustration. Although South Korea did not begin producing plywood until 1959, by 1967 it had become the largest exporter of plywood to the North American market, and by 1970 it controlled over half the market share (G. Lee 1973: 84). Indeed, by 1964 plywood had become South Korea's largest export item; by 1968 South Korea was the largest exporter of plywood in the world (OEAR 1972: 20, 35). The success of this industry can be traced to external and internal factors. In 1957, for example, Japan had accounted for over 80 percent of the plywood imported by the United States (OEAR 1972: 168–69). When Japanese manufacturers moved on to higher value-added production, South Korea filled the niche they vacated. Through the late 1960s over 90 percent of South Korean plywood exports were to the

United States (OEAR 1972: 35–36). The South Korean state also promoted the plywood industry by providing tax relief and preferential interest rates, as well as other incentives (OEAR 1972: 45–49). In particular, it facilitated the import of hardwood, which is a crucial material for plywood production. The other internal factor favorable to development of the plywood industry was the low cost of labor in South Korea. By the late 1960s, the cost of labor in South Korea was half that of Japan and lower than that of the Philippines and Taiwan (G. Lee 1973: 121). Given low technological requirements and the roughly similar raw material and transportation costs, lower wage costs gave South Korean manufacturers a critical edge in their export drive.

Chaebŏl, such as Hyundai and Hanjin, benefited from the Vietnam War boom. However, many of the export-oriented enterprises were far from being large conglomerates, and even Hyundai and Hanjin were not the colossi they were to become in the 1980s. The late 1960s marked an entrepreneurial moment in South Korean business history. Small, entrepreneurial firms were crucial in the production and sale of South Korea's leading export items, such as plywood, textiles, and wigs. The proliferation of enterprises was a source of humor at the time. Companies of two or three employees operating out of small rented rooms were often jokingly referred to as *chaebŏl*. Similarly, it was commonplace to see these employees calling each other President, Director, and so on. As a popular song lyric from 1969 put it:

> While walking down the street, I uttered
> "company president" in a low voice.
> Ten out of ten turned around to answer.
> However, I noticed that one kept on going
> as if he didn't hear me.
> I stopped him and found that he was
> a managing director.
>
>   . . .
>
> Front and rear, company presidents are everywhere.
> However, being a company president is lonesome and
> troublesome (because he is his only employee
> and his conscience bothers him).
>
> (Christie 1972: 216)

External and contingent factors were crucial in integrating South Korea into the expanding U.S. and Japanese economies. In the late 1960s the United States pursued an open trade regime (Block 1977: 10), and U.S. import policy was therefore favorable for South Korean manufactured exports. Then the United States advocated free trade in general. Because South Korea's labor-intensive manufacturing exports constituted only a small part of U.S. trade, they posed little threat to the U.S. economy (Lary 1968: 94). South Korea's favorable political relationships also aided economic dealings with the United States.

By the late 1960s, Japan was in a position to move to higher value-added production (Kobayashi 1983: 7–14). The Japanese state was instrumental in attempting to expand the Japanese sphere of influence and facilitated Japanese-South Korean economic relations (D. Chang 1985: 55–57). In addition, South Korea also had little competition for the slot directly behind Japan in the global division of labor. The niche vacated by the Japanese ascent through the product cycle was virtually earmarked for South Korea. In Asia only Taiwan was capable of mounting comparable industrialization efforts. The industrializing economies of Latin America at the time were focusing on import-substitution and were geared primarily to the North American market (Bulmer-Thomas 1994: 278–87). Most Latin American economies also suffered from governments that were content to promote agriculture and to export raw materials, while the strength of the labor unions in South America hindered the promotion of export-oriented industrialization based on cheap labor.

Japan, the Vietnam War, the United States, and the trading networks transformed the South Korean economy. By the late 1960s, South Korean exports rose and industrialization was proceeding rapidly. Let us compare 1958 and 1969 export statistics. In 1958, only tungsten, iron ore, and fish yielded export values of $1 million or more; the three primary sector commodities, moreover, constituted well over 40 percent of total South Korean export. By 1969, the top three South Korean exports were clothing ($161 million), plywood ($79 million), and wigs ($60 million). These three commodities amounted to close to one-half of the total South Korean export of $622 million (Bartz 1972: 98).

It would be a gross exaggeration to credit the state economic plan for the export growth of the 1960s. Export-oriented industrialization had not been part of the plan; Park's regime had initially sought self-sufficiency and import substitution. Initial spurs to export-oriented industrialization came from outside.

The Park Regime's Economic Orientation

However important external opportunities were, they may well have been squandered had the structure of corruption embodied in the triple alliance sustained itself into the 1960s. The 1965 Normalization Treaty with Japan, for example, could have been delayed. The economic opportunities provided by the Vietnam War might have been missed. The April Student Revolution severed the parasitic bond between the state bureaucracy and the *chaebŏl* and Park's legitimation crisis laid the groundwork for the developmental state.

Park's rule was a constant scramble for both external and internal support. He permitted elections in response to U.S. pressure and sent troops to Vietnam to ensure continued U.S. support. He discarded his anticorruption (and anti–big business) campaigns and negotiated a new relationship with big business in order to promote economic growth (Pak Il 1992: 137–39). Yet the military regime's vision and will are far from adequate to make sense of the trajectory of South Korean political economy in the 1960s. Park's revolution, as limited as it was, would not have even been possible if the social forces competing against him had not been so weak.

Consider the case of Peru under General Juan Velasco Alvarado. After a coup in October 1968, Velasco and the military sought wide-ranging reform. Like Park, Velasco advocated a nationalist and anticommunist platform that called for the creation of the "new Peruvian man" (Lowenthal 1975). It attempted to reform land tenure, labor-management relations, education, and much more. By the mid-1970s, however, the reform campaign was in full retreat. Why did the Peruvian revolution fail? Although it would be easy to celebrate Park's political acumen, a far more significant factor was the well-entrenched and organized resistance to the Peruvian revolution. The Velasco regime faced a powerful agrarian oligarchy that resisted land reform (Harding 1975), while organized parties and trade unions opposed what they perceived to be a bourgeois revolution (Quijano 1971; Becker 1983). In spite of the expansion of state capacity, the Velasco regime was incapable of carrying out reforms without an alliance with existing organizations and social forces (Cotler 1978). Eventually, the ideological polarization among military officers tolled the death knell of the abortive revolution (North and Korovkin 1981: 69).

Park, in contrast, faced neither a powerful landed oligarchy nor well-organized opposition parties or trade unions. There was no one in the public sector in South Korea who could stop Park from seizing the few economic opportunities he had.

CONSOLIDATING THE ECONOMIC BUREAUCRACY

The breakdown of the triple alliance signaled the end of an openly patrimonial bureaucracy. The 1963 National Civil Service Law marked the beginnings of a meritocratic bureaucracy. According to Lee Hahn-Been (1982: 223–24), the South Korean civil bureaucracy switched from a seniority-based to a merit-based promotion system in the course of the 1960s. Although formalism and ritualism continued to characterize many parts of the state bureaucracy (M. K. Kim 1991: 38), a new stratum of modernizing bureaucrats emerged. As I noted, the coup had purged many senior bureaucrats and replaced them with younger technocrats. The social basis of bureaucrats shifted; in 1959, half of them hailed from the landlord class, but by the mid-1960s, only a quarter of them did (Whang 1968: 77–78). University-educated intellectuals and former military officers constituted two new groups (Whang 1968: 153). What united the newcomers was an allegiance to the modernizing regime.

Under Park presidential power over the state bureaucracy was strengthened (B.-K. Kim 1987: 57–58). The system began to operate with an efficiency born of dictatorial fiat. Park expanded the infrastructural capacity of the economic bureaucracy. And most important, the state seized control of finance. The 1962 Bank of Korea Act placed banking under government, not central bank, control. By 1970 the state controlled 96 percent of all financial assets

(Michell 1988: 67; see also Shaw 1973: 210). State control over finance would prove to be significant throughout the era of rapid industrialization.

Tax administration serves as an illustration of the new economic bureaucracy. As Sven Steinmo (1993: 1) pithily summarizes: "Governments need money. Modern governments need lots of money." Under Rhee's rule, tax collection was rife with corruption and marred by inefficiency. According to Gilbert Brown (1973: 65): "The secret of [South] Korea's success in improving its tax administration after 1965 was a strong stand by the President that made the tax office immune from normal political influences." Park installed a powerful military head, who assiduously sought to improve efficiency. By the late 1960s tax collection had become a reliable source of government revenue (C. K. Park 1991: 250–63).

The most important organs in the economic bureaucracy were the Economic Planning Board (EPB) and the Presidential Secretariat (Taniura 1989: 7–9). The EPB was established in 1962 to replace the Economic Development Council. Although continuities in personnel should not be ignored (Satterwhite 1994: 378–82), the qualitative change was in the concentration of economic decision-making power in the EPB (B.-K. Kim 1987: 120–21). Park articulated growth-oriented measures through the EPB. While the EPB functioned as the public face of Park's economic plan, the Secretariat worked closely with the president away from public scrutiny. As a sort of KCIA of the economy, the Secretariat attracted bright, ambitious officials willing to work at Park's behest. Its symbolic power can be gleaned from the fact that many *chaebŏl* owners formed their own, private secretariats to manage their business concerns.

Although the economic bureaucracy was far from autonomous, it would be a mistake to see it merely as an instrument of Park's will and vision. Two factors combined to promote bureaucratic autonomy and decentralized decision-making. First, Korea had long had a tradition of bureaucratic autonomy, owing to the legacy of both the Chosŏn state and Japanese colonial rule. As Tony Michell (1984: 35) puts it: "The [South] Korean official has a degree of independence of decision-making which perhaps only the immigration official has in the British civil service." High-ranking state bureaucrats held considerable prestige and power (Kim and Leipziger 1993: 32–33). Second, the forging of the new economic bureaucracy entailed infrastructural expansion. In other words, the very size and complexity of the state bureaucracy tempered Park's despotic control. Consequently, high-ranking bureaucrats held more autonomy in personnel appointment and promotion, as well as in decision-making, than they had had under Rhee.

INFRASTRUCTURAL DEVELOPMENT AND EXPORT PROMOTION

The Second Five-Year Economic Development Plan was launched amid difficulties. "The First Plan had been discredited, its revision ignored, and the planning staff was not significantly involved in the current major economic policy deliberations" (Cole and Lyman 1971: 218). In fact, the Second Plan was nearly identical to the First; and like the First, its major goal was the establishment of a self-sufficient economy (P. Kuznets 1977: 206).

The state sought to improve the basic infrastructures that make industrialization possible, including electricity, transportation, and communication (Brown 1973: 85–96). Electric power generation, for example, grew more than ten-fold between 1961 and 1971. In the same decade, freight car capacity nearly doubled, while port loading and unloading capacity grew 2.5 times (Hasan 1976: 31). In 1961, 13 percent of the national roads and 5 percent of all roads were paved; by 1975, the corresponding figures were 44 percent and 23 percent (Keidel 1981: 129). National telephone service became effective (Brown 1973: 92–96). Between 1961 and 1972, the number of postal stations doubled, while the number of telephones rose six-fold (Hasan 1976: 33). The state poured the majority of foreign aid and loans into infrastructural development throughout the 1960s (Adachi 1986: 48). State-owned enterprises played a key role in this process (Cole and Lyman 1971: 197).

There was, furthermore, a stirring of official interest in supporting export-oriented industrialization. The first sign of this new emphasis can be seen in the Second Five-Year Economic Development Plan (Adelman 1969). As an official South Korean government publication put it, "A relatively unfavorable endowment in natural resources imposes upon the [South] Korean economy the necessity for being an open economy. It is not possible to maintain a self-supporting open economy based upon industrialization without increasing exports" (ROK 1966: 15). The state instituted tax breaks, liberal credit, and other measures to promote exports (Kawai 1988: 81–84). In 1964, for example, the state devalued currency by half and facilitated exporters by giving credit incentives and granting import licenses (Frank, Kim, and Westphal 1975: 47–50). In addition, it offered tariff exemptions, which included a wastage allowance, on the import of raw materials to exporters (Hasan 1976: 56). It established the Korea Trade Promotion Corporation and strengthened the Korea Traders' Association (Michell 1988: 64–67). In 1970, the state established export-processing zones to attract foreign capital (Pak Il 1992: 79–80). "The administration did not hesitate to make exporting into a national campaign, almost a patriotic duty" (Cole and Lyman 1971: 90). By the late 1960s, then, the state promotion of exports was in place. By preventing a free outflow of foreign exchange earnings and encouraging exports, the Park regime protected South Korea's infant industries and promoted economic growth.

Park's state-building effort not only entrenched the economic bureaucracy but gradually transformed it into a relatively autonomous and efficient institution.

Park promoted economic growth to shore up his support. The rapid expansion of South Korean exports, however, was not the result of his regime's economic planning. The credit lies rather with external forces: the integration into the Japan-centered regional division of labor and the demand generated by the U.S. intervention in Vietnam. Thus it is misleading to argue that Park engineered the 1960s growth spurt. A complex confluence of external and internal factors lies behind the South Korean economic take-off of the 1960s. Yet the economic achievements of the late 1960s should be placed in a proper perspective. The 1968 average per capita GNP for South Korea was $138, $2 less than the Japanese figure in 1951, the year Japan regained its sovereignty. Most economic indices suggested that South Korea lagged behind even North Korea in the late 1960s. Quite clearly, we need to explore farther to make sense of South Korean development.

CHAPTER FOUR

In and Under the Tracks of Development

During the Yusin period (1972–79), the state pursued heavy industrialization, infrastructural development, and export growth. In so doing, it contributed to the rise of the *chaebŏl* and of cheap labor. The rapid export and industrial growth of the 1970s, however, ran on the tracks laid in the late 1960s. South Korean products followed their Japanese counterparts in the product cycle, sustaining the trade triangle among Japan, South Korea, and the United States. What fueled South Korea's economic ascent was cheap labor, which provided the crucial comparative advantage for South Korean labor-intensive manufacturing exports.

Many explanations of South Korean development highlight the state. Perhaps the most ambitious articulation of this view is Alice Amsden's (1989) *Asia's Next Giant* (see also R. Wade 1990; Woo 1991; Kim Sŏk-jun 1992; and Hart-Landsberg 1993). According to Amsden, the absence of a strong state in the 1950s accounts for the stagnation of the South Korean economy, the presence of one from the 1960s explains its growth. She offers a powerful refutation of the *laissez-faire* mythology; whatever the origins of South Korean development, the unfettered operation of the free market is certainly not one of them. Despite successfully demolishing the market myth, Amsden ends up with a myth of the autonomous state (Lie 1991d). I am not denying the paramount and pervasive significance of the state in 1970s South Korea. By stressing state autonomy, however, Amsden slights internal and external factors that shaped state economic policy.

The developmental state was forged in the crucible of the post-Liberation land reform that destroyed the landed gentry, the citizen movement that shattered the triple alliance, and military rule that required development as legitimation. In order to pursue development, however, the state repressed workers, exploited farmers, and silenced citizens. Political authoritarianism and capital accumulation are inseparable themes in the political economy of Yusin-era South Korea, the most triumphant and the most tragic period in the annals of South Korean development.

Legitimation Crisis and Political Authoritarianism

Many narratives of South Korean development feature Park Chung Hee as the charismatic, if ruthless, leader whose vision and will propelled economic growth. When an American journalist asked the founder of Samsung, the premier *chaebŏl* in South Korea in the late 1960s: "Who is responsible for the economic growth of modern Korea?" Lee Byung-chull "replied without hesitation" that it was Park Chung Hee (Sochurek 1969: 320–21; see also C.-y. Kim 1994: 115–23). It would be wrong, however, to attribute to Park powers and abilities rare in world history. Although it is impossible to write about South Korea in the 1970s without mentioning his name, it is crucial to understand the context in which his vision emerged and the constraints under which he operated.

By the 1971 presidential election, Park could boast economic achievements unimaginable in the 1950s. Exports and light industries were thriving, per capita GNP was rising rapidly. And Park could claim the lion's share of credit. Furthermore, he commanded an extensive and well-funded political organization and thereby the ability to manipulate the elections (Kim and Koh 1980: 79–80). Nonetheless, his margin of victory over the 41-year-old Kim Dae Jung was perilously thin. Why was this the case?

Many South Koreans, especially the educated middle class and the civilian bureaucracy, had never fully accepted military rule. In the 1970s, the military permeated South Korean life and invoked the threat of communism to justify its pervasive surveillance of

South Korean civil society. Educated South Koreans desiring to emulate the advanced industrial countries found military rule not only unpalatable but embarrassing. They yearned for modernity, which for them implied democratic, not military, rule.

Furthermore, social discontent, inspired in part by the ideals of egalitarianism and materialism, began to mount in the late 1960s. Students and intellectuals constituted a small but steady opposition to Park's rule. Rapid industrialization also generated a powerful countervailing force. Workers agitated for higher wages and better working conditions. The self-immolation of Chŏn T'ae-il at the Peace Market in 1970 highlighted their plight. The Peace Market was a center of small textile production in Seoul where nearly half of the 27,000 workers were under fifteen years old. Some earned as little as $10 per month while working sixteen hours a day with no days off (H. Sohn 1989: 34). In addition, the bedrock of Park's support—farmers—began to erode as the rising urban-rural gap and the systematic exploitation of the agricultural sector worsened their conditions. Regional disparity also manifested itself by the early 1970s, particularly in the relative impoverishment of the Chŏlla provinces (E. Yu 1990: 26).

Park also faced external challenges. In the context of détente and the imminent U.S. withdrawal from Vietnam, U.S. support for South Korea seemed to be on the wane. The United States withdrew 20,000 soldiers from South Korea in 1970 (Eckert et al. 1990: 364). The U.S. Military Assistance Program to South Korea declined rapidly from nearly $300 million in 1974 to nothing by 1978 (Ha Young-Sun 1984: 118–19).

The U.S. government sought to temper authoritarian rule in South Korea, if only to avoid international embarrassment. The American public held South Korea in low esteem (Watts 1982: 80). As *Time* (June 24, 1974: 46) reported: "As practiced by President Park Chung Hee, 'modern democracy' has become an Orwellian synonym for despotic one-man rule." In this climate, the "Koreagate"—the revelation of South Korean influence-peddling campaign from 1970 to 1976—erupted in 1976, leading to the nadir of U.S. public support for South Korea (Boettcher 1980: 332). As *Fortune* noted in 1977: "To most Americans today, South Korea connotes, not an incredibly successful economy, but a repressive government that has spent fortunes bribing our congressmen" (Rowan 1977: 171).

Furthermore, in the 1970s the threat, both military and political, of North Korea was still very real (Kihl 1984; Clough 1987). In the early 1970s, it was still far from clear that the South Korean model was preferable to that of North Korea. Some Western observers relayed favorable impressions of North Korea (J. Robinson 1965: 541–42; Brun and Hersch 1976: chap. 7). The per capita GNP of South Korea did not surpass the North Korean figure until the mid-1970s (CIA 1978: 6). In the post–oil shock era, the North Korean economy was weakened by its rising external debt and the cost of its mounting military commitment (it spent 15 to 20 percent of its GNP on its military, compared to less than 5 percent for South; 12 percent of North Korean working-age males were in the military, compared to 6 percent for South) (CIA 1978: 6–8). Today no one disputes South Korea's claim of superiority over North Korea; before the mid-1970s the question was still open (J. Ha 1971: 443; Dumont and Mazoyer 1973: chap. 9; E. Hwang 1993: chap. 3).

Park's response to these internal and external challenges was to impose martial law in October 1972. A government publication justifying this action noted: "We cannot rely on others, and that we must therefore solve our own problems by ourselves" (MCI n.d.: 10–11). The Yusin ("Revitalizing") Constitution was promulgated two months later (for the text, see Hinton 1983: 155–75). Under this constitution South Korea was still officially a democracy. In an interview Park told the Korean American journalist Peter Hyun (1974: 591) that "we know that democracy is the sole path to peace and happiness, and that we must preserve it at all costs." Yet in fact the Yusin Constitution gave the president even more power and allowed him to serve an unlimited number of six-year terms. The veneer of democracy did not hide the reality of autocracy. The KCIA became the most powerful state institution (J.-H. Kim 1978: 196); and Yusin South Korea became a human rights disaster area. There was some truth to Kim Dae Jung's allegation that Park was becoming "an Asian version of Hitler" (*Time*, August 20, 1973: 39).

Still, even a dictatorship requires some social support. Leviathan stands, willy nilly, on the precarious foundation of popular opinion. Thus economic growth remained the principal carrot of Park's rule. The dissident poet Kim Chi Ha (1974: 92) coined the following aphorism on this topic: "Development's main purpose; / To rationalize dictatorship." By combining repression with growth, Park attempted to gain domestic legitimacy and simultaneously to empower the nation. The Yusin Constitution and the heavy and chemical industrialization drive were inextricably intertwined.

The State and the Economy

The three main goals of the Third Five-Year Economic Development Plan, which was announced in 1971, were "the dynamic development of the rural economy, a dramatic and sustained increase in exports, and the establishment of heavy and chemical industries" (ROK 1971: 2). In part to mollify rural and regional discontent, the plan emphasized balanced development and even included some social welfare measures (R. Johnson 1972). To counter the threat of U.S. quotas on South Korea's light manufacturing exports and because he desired industrial (and, in particular, defense-related) self-sufficiency, Park proposed the 1973 Heavy and Chemical Industrialization Plan, which targeted six key industries— steel, nonferrous metals, machinery, shipbuilding, electronics, and chemicals (S.-C. Lee 1991: 432–34).[*]

The interdependence of export- and import-orientation should not be overlooked. In the discourse of development economics, import-substitution industrialization and export-oriented industrialization are often viewed as two opposing strategies. Development discourse also tends to reduce and reify the South Korean state's economic policy in the 1970s as export-oriented. As I have

[*]The Fourth Plan envisioned continuities: "[South] Korea must develop an economic structure for self-sustaining growth by promoting industries in which we have a comparative advantage" (ROK 1976: 6). It sought paradoxically to "continue to expand exports" while seeking "to minimize our dependence on the international economy" (ROK 1976: 7–8). The practical resolution was to seek technological efficiency and trade diversity (ROK 1976: 11–12). These documents do not contain, as I suggested in Chapter 3, any blueprints for the course that South Korean development actually followed.

noted, however, development-oriented policymakers often pursue both simultaneously (cf. Hirschman 1958: 124). The Yusin state's focus was clear; 77 percent of total manufacturing investment between 1976 and 1978 was in heavy and chemical industries (Choi Jang Jip 1993a: 37). In order to import the raw materials and machinery needed to establish these industries, the state promoted export-oriented production to bring in the needed foreign exchange reserves.

The state played a powerful role in promoting rapid industrialization in the 1970s. In particular, it performed three crucial tasks. It protected the domestic economy from foreign capital and competition, established public enterprises and offered incentives and sanctions to private firms, and sustained the condition of cheap labor.

DIRECT FOREIGN INVESTMENT AND TRANSNATIONAL CORPORATIONS

Most developing economies seek infrastructural development and heavy industrialization. Nonetheless, most of them lack crucial resources—money, technology, organizational skill, business knowledge, and so on—to effect the changes they desire. Many turn to transnational corporations for assistance. While Third World governments have all the powers of sovereign entities at their disposal—ranging from taxation to nationalization—transnational corporations are usually the stronger partner (Hymer 1979: 72). Most crucially, the executives of the transnational corporations have the final say on whether or not to invest in a given country, and their decisions are, not surprisingly, motivated by self-interest. It is quite often the case that direct foreign investment detracts from or even undermines national development goals. Indeed, there is a correlation between high foreign investment and economic underdevelopment (Bornschier, Chase-Dunn, and Rubinson 1978).

Consider the case of copper in Chile. In the 1970s copper production accounted for nearly 20 percent of the Chilean GDP and 80 percent of its hard currency earnings (Moran 1974: 6); thus foreign control over copper made Chile a dependent economy. From Eduardo Frei's Chileanization to Salvador Allende's nationalization, there was a virtual tug of war between the transnationals and the Chilean state (Moran 1974: chap. 5). The climax of Chile's struggle for regaining economic independence was Allende's effort to nationalize the copper industry. It generated U.S., as well as international and domestic, retaliation, which contributed to a military coup that toppled the Allende regime (Moran 1974: 250–53). One of the goals of General Pinochet's regime was to make Chile "safe" for transnational corporations (Valdés 1989). Although struggles between transnational corporations and Third World governments do not always end so dramatically, their relationship has often been troublesome. The United States frequently intervened militarily whenever a Third World government attempted to nationalize major U.S. corporate holdings (Krasner 1978: chap. 8; Gibbs 1991; Chomsky 1993: chap. 7).

Transnational corporations, to be sure, do not inevitably triumph over Third World countries. There is always some room for negotiation; the state is potentially a powerful actor (Krasner 1985: 179–88). But economic nationalism is no panacea for developmental ills (cf. H. Johnson 1967). The need for capital, technology, and knowledge remains, as does the powerful force of international finance and economy (Biersteker 1987: 298–99).

How did South Korea deal with transnational corporations? In the first place, the transnationals were not the problem in South Korea that they were elsewhere in the Third World. External and internal reasons combined to limit foreign intervention in the domestic economy. To begin with, South Korea is virtually devoid of raw materials, one of the major reasons for direct foreign investment in the Third World. The oft-stated claim that South Korean development occurred despite the absence of raw materials is misleading. The existence of a valuable mineral could have rendered South Korea ripe for exploitation or made it overdependent on a single commodity (cf. Baran 1957: 203–5). South Korea's major resource, cheap labor, was not in great demand in the 1960s, either in nearby Japan or in the United States, which could look for low-paid labor closer to home, in Central and South America.

Furthermore, the state controlled and limited the autonomy of transnational corporations (Rodgers 1993: 354). It screened investment closely and intervened in all facets of cross-border economic transactions (Luedde-Neurath 1988: 85–88). The motive behind state control was, in part, ideological; Park repeatedly stressed the imperative of national autonomy and control in terms not so different from Kim Il Sung's *chuch'e* (self-reliance) philosophy (D.-S. Suh 1988: 302–9; cf. M. Robinson 1993: 184–85). As Park Chung Hee (1979a: 21) put it himself: "Succinctly speaking, *jaju* [*chaju*] means we should be the master of our own house." Thus by the 1970s, when South Korea became more attractive for foreign investors, it had both the ideological commitment and the institutional capacity to preserve its national self-determination. Even then, foreign direct investment in South Korea between 1972 and 1976 amounted to only 2 percent of GNP, compared to over 4 percent in Brazil or Mexico (Westphal, Rhee, and Pursell 1979: 372).

South Korea was also able to acquire capital and technology without resorting to direct foreign investment and corporate control (Mardon 1990: 119). South Korea was extremely important to both the United States and Japan for geopolitical and economic reasons alike. It was a key "border state" in the Cold War and an essential, if junior partner in the western Pacific economic region. Thus both nations had strong incentives to support South Korean industrialization (Kobayashi 1983: 7–8).

For capital, South Korea could rely on foreign loans, rather than direct foreign investment (E. M. Kim 1989–90: 41–42). The state became the fundamental source of capital and credit.[*] It was the ultimate guarantor of foreign loans, which it channeled to favored corporations to relieve their debt burdens (Cole and Park 1983: 162–68). It established a range of financial institutions to facilitate

[*]To be sure, the state financial monopoly coexisted with the vast informal capital market. Many corporations relied on informal, curbside loans. Generated through lending networks (*kye*) and private savings, the informal curbside loan market was estimated to amount to 80 percent of the money supply in 1972 (W. Kim 1991: 168). A 1981 survey revealed that nearly two-thirds of all loans were generated from the informal market (Watanabe 1986: 161; cf. Nam and Lee 1995: 33–34). Although the state could not completely control the informal market, the 1972 Presidential Emergency Decree for Economic Stability and Growth provided relief for corporations suffering from high interest rates charged by curbside lenders (Choi Jang Jip 1993a: 30–31). As one corporate executive stated: "We had no other solution except to declare bankruptcy. Everyone was in despair. Suddenly we received news about the decree. Everyone screamed 'Hurrah! We are saved!' and we all cried with tears" (Ogle 1990: 43).

capital accumulation and credit allocation (Cole and Park 1983: 65–67). Between 1964 and 1971 public loans amounted to $1.6 billion, which accounted for the bulk of the $2.3 billion net capital inflows. Between 1972 and 1976, the comparable figures were $3.1 billion and $3.7 billion (Westphal, Rhee, and Pursell 1979: 370).

To gain access to modern technology, South Korea relied on licensing agreements, especially with the United States and Japan (Kim Yŏng-ho 1988: chaps. 6–7). Over 80 percent of South Korea's technology transfer involved these two countries (Hattori 1988: 211). As Ezra Vogel (1991: 8) observes: "It was above all the Cold War that led the preeminent industrial power, the United States, to allow and even encourage technology to flow to its allies." The operations of the product cycle transferred obsolete Japanese technology to South Korea (B. Koo 1985: 205–8). In particular, the 1970 establishment of the Masan Free Export Zone created a niche for low-technology transfers from Japan (Kobayashi 1983: 100–104; Bloom 1992: 50–51). Japanese investment and technology were important, for example, in textile production (O. Lee 1990: 89–92). There was also a steady stream of Japanese engineers who moonlighted for South Korean corporations. When Japanese engineers were unavailable, South Koreans relied on Japanese-language manuals (Watanabe 1986: 75–76). In addition, the state and corporations began to send South Koreans to the United States and Japan to acquire scientific and technological knowledge. The state also promoted domestic research, establishing for example the Korea Institute of Science and Technology.

STATE CAPITALISM AND INFANT INDUSTRY PROTECTION

The neoclassical economic dogma stipulates the superiority of free trade. In this line of reasoning, protectionism is unwarranted; free trade ultimately benefits everyone (Bhagwati 1988: 24–33; cf. J. Robinson 1974). But the interpenetration of political and economic relations invalidates this model at the international level (Hirschman 1980: 78). Dependency theorists argue that the free trade regime can systematically worsen a country's terms of trade; a poor agrarian country, for example, would be worse off trading against an industrial country (Emmanuel 1972: xii–xx). Given the declining terms of trade and waning economic independence, pro-

tectionist measures are often necessary in order to promote indigenous industrialization.

The father of the infant industry protection argument was
Friedrich List. He criticized the advocates of free trade—"the popular school"—for ignoring the salience of national boundaries (List
1966: 126). He insisted that a nation must impose protectionist
measures, such as tariffs, if it is to industrialize: "A nation acts
foolishly if it sacrifices its manufacturing power to foreign competition by commercial treaties, and thereby binds itself to remain
for all future time dependent on the low standpoint of merely agricultural industry" (List 1966: 324). Only when a nation-state has
achieved industrialization should it trade freely with industrialized countries (List 1983: 178, 189). By emphasizing the interpenetration of politics and economics, List makes a compelling case
for infant industry protection (List 1966: 140; cf. League of Nations
1945: 33–34).

The pervasive importance of the state in promoting economic
growth has been proven time and again. The economic historian
Paul Bairoch (1993: xiv) writes: "Excluding England, which became liberal only a century and a half after the Industrial Revolution, European liberal policy lasted only two decades and coincided
with—indeed led to—the most negative economic period of the
nineteenth century. (Incidentally, the United States did not share
this brief interlude of free trade and this was that country's best
economic period of the nineteenth century.)" He goes on to decry
the negative impact of compulsory liberalism in the Third World.
Conversely: "In all cases protectionism led to, or at least was con-
comitant with, industrialization and economic development"
(Bairoch 1993: 54).

The South Korean state used a variety of measures to promote
exports and to control imports. It instituted special measures for
each targeted industry, such as the 1967 provision for machinery,
1969 for electronics, and 1970 for shipping. It provided capital and
credit, facilitated import of raw materials, and offered tax incentives and export subsidies to favored corporations (Frank, Kim, and
Westphal 1975: 63–67; Kim, Shim, and Kim 1995). It assigned export quotas to firms, rewarded high achievers, and sanctioned poor
performers. It also sought to overcome emerging protectionist

measures in the United States and Japan and to bargain with these two nations for an optimum trade environment (Yoffie 1983: 206–12).

The state's export policies were necessary in part to promote the development of domestic production. In order to ensure export, the state granted import licenses—whether to acquire technologically sophisticated machinery or raw materials—only to firms that met their export quotas (P. Kuznets 1977: 159). In effect, corporations found it necessary to export in order to import. Thus, the Park regime averted the rentier-profit-seeking behavior of corporations during the Rhee years.

The state also erected numerous protectionist barriers to shield domestic industry from being overwhelmed by foreign competition. Richard Luedde-Neurath (1986: 131–32) identifies several distinct barriers to free trade: trader licensing, quantitative controls, measures to restrict automatically approved import items, restriction of foreign exchange allocation, the necessity of ministerial approval, the need for advanced deposits, and, finally, the customs office. "If the [South] Korean authorities wish to prevent the inflow of certain items, they have at their disposal an arsenal of tools to stall them, regardless of what the rules may say on their importability" (Luedde-Neurath 1986: 132).

The South Korean state's import control went far beyond infant industry protection; it actively curbed the import of consumer goods to protect South Korea's foreign exchange reserves. From luxury items to cigarettes, outright ban or heavy duties greeted foreign goods (Jones and SaKong 1980: 115–19). Foreign corporations found that they were unable to compete with domestic producers in the South Korean consumer market (H.-C. Lim 1985: 118). Indeed, what was most remarkable for many foreign visitors to South Korea in the 1970s was the virtual absence of foreign cigarettes and cars. It was only in the 1980s that transnational corporations were finally able to challenge the protected South Korean market (Barnet and Cavanagh 1994: 200–204).

In spite of the reality of trade protection, South Korea claimed to be a market economy with few trade restrictions. Neoclassical economists, such as Jagdish Bhagwati (1988: 93), have largely endorsed this view. However, in the experience of most foreign business people operating in South Korea, the facts of the matter were far from the *laissez-faire* ideal. The rhetoric of free trade masqueraded the reality of protectionism.

THE GLOBAL ECONOMY

The dynamic of expanding foreign investment contributed to a shift in world industry structure. Deindustrialization in the advanced industrial countries occurred in tandem with industrialization in the newly industrialized economies. South Korea's export expansion, as I have stressed, followed the Japanese path; South Korean exports filled the niches abandoned by Japanese corporations that had moved to higher value-added production. The international division of labor therefore allowed South Korea to ride on the coattails of Japanese economic dynamism and to sustain a trade triangle with Japan and the United States. South Korean domestic production grew to accommodate the demand from the United States and Japan—South Korea's two most important trade partners. The liberal international trade regime remained intact and the Pacific economy continued to expand throughout the 1970s (Van der Weer 1986: 345–58), and South Korea was one of the major beneficiaries.

South Korean exports followed the trajectory of Japanese exports. As Japanese manufacturers shifted to higher value-added production, they left vacant niches in global demand, particularly in the United States. Technological diffusion from Japan promoted South Korean production. Furthermore, the Korean diaspora networks facilitated trade relations and the flow of commodities and business information. Park's extensive connections to Japanese political and business elite also aided economic relations between the two countries (McCormack 1978b: 181–82). South Korea may have been dependent on Japan, but—paraphrasing Joan Robinson—it was better than not having anyone to be dependent on.

At the same time, there were few competitors. Most developing economies, wracked by peasant rebellions and focusing on primary sector exports, were unable to engage in export-oriented light industrialization. Many of them had followed the prevailing developmental discourse and concentrated on import-substitution industrialization (cf. Aggarwal 1985: 6–7). Even when some did pursue export-orientation—an Egyptian parliamentarian famously exclaimed in the mid-1970s: "Export or die!" (Richards and Waterbury 1990: 28)—other factors impeded export-led industrialization (Richards and Waterbury 1990: 214–18). Communist bloc countries, for example, faced political obstacles to trade. By following in Japan's footsteps, South Korea was almost guaranteed success.

The footwear industry provides an illustration. As Japanese labor costs increased, Nike and other shoe manufacturers began to rely on South Korean production (Korzeniewicz 1994: 256). South Korea could offer low labor costs, sufficiently high levels of technology and skills (which were not available in Thailand and other Southeast Asian countries with comparable labor costs) (Korzeniewicz 1994: 257), cost-effective mass-production capability (Gereffi and Korzeniewicz 1990: 59), and an emphasis on export-oriented production. No other developing country could offer a similar combination of advantages.

External and contingent factors were also important. The 1973 oil shock, following OPEC's four-fold increase in crude oil price, was a boon for South Korean exports. This is paradoxical given South Korea's reliance on foreign oil. The state pursued an aggressive energy conservation policy and promoted alternative fuel sources (Y. H. Kim 1991: 189–93). The oil shock also made Japanese and German light industrial goods less competitive worldwide, since Japan and Germany also depend heavily on foreign oil. When U.S. president Nixon decided to float the dollar, the Bretton Woods system of fixed exchange rates suffered a partial collapse (Odell 1982: 340–42). The Japanese yen and the West German mark rose in value, a reflection of the manufacturing prowess of those two countries. The comparative cost advantage against Japanese, German, and other nations' light industrial products made South Korean products even more attractive in the German, Japanese, and U.S. markets. From 1972 to 1973, South Korean exports to Japan rose three-fold, while exports to Germany doubled.

South Korean exports to cash-rich Middle Eastern countries also grew rapidly in the post–oil shock period. After light manufacturing, South Korea's most lucrative export was its workers. Following the state-organized mercenary venture in Vietnam, the

South Korean state aggressively pursued the export of its citizens to the Middle East (McCormack 1978a: 101–2). "In early 1976 the South Korean government converted several military bases in South Korea into training centres for construction workers financed jointly by the South Korean government and the construction companies" (Disney 1978: 203; see also Westphal et al. 1984: 22–26). The state provided the necessary diplomatic and financial support (C. H. Lee 1991: 532–34). State-initiated and *chaebŏl*-organized Middle East construction projects employed thousands of South Korean workers. Contracts and remittances generated foreign exchange earnings, which were crucial for capital formation and imports. In 1977, for example, South Korean construction contracts with Saudi Arabia amounted to $2.5 billion (J. K. Park 1985: 252–53), while South Korean exports to the Middle East amounted to close to $1 billion (Disney 1978: 200). Hyundai's spectacular growth, for example, owed a great deal to its involvement in Middle East construction projects (Kirk 1994: 81–96). Between 1974 and 1981, Middle East construction amounted to 44 percent of all merchandise exports (C. H. Lee 1991: 527) and at its peak in 1982 constituted 6.6 percent of the South Korean GNP (NSK 1988: 194–95). Like the Vietnam War in the late 1960s, the Middle East construction boom in the mid-1970s provided a major boost to the South Korean economy.

Agents of Industrialization: State-Owned Enterprises and Chaebŏl

It is not surprising that a late-developing country such as South Korea should feature many public corporations. In such countries the state is often the only actor with not only the financial means but also the bureaucratic capacity to operate industrial enterprises. Furthermore, the establishment of industrial infrastructures—ranging from electricity, to transportation, to communication—remains the realm of state action. Under such circumstances private enterprises may get a free ride, but that is no substitute for the capital, technology, and other resources requisite for independent action. Only the state can absorb both the risks and the start-up costs of infrastructural development.

The legacy of state intervention legitimated state-created enterprises in South Korea (Jones 1975: 73). The Rhee regime established state monopolies to raise revenue and foreign exchange (Jones and SaKong 1980: 143–47). In the 1960s, it operated several large companies, including Honam Fertilizer, Taehan Oil, and Korean Air Lines. Neoclassic economic theory and its ideology of laissez-faire had few adherents in the economic bureaucracy.

In the early 1970s, the state intervened extensively in the economy, particularly in capital- and technology-intensive industries (for the list, see Jones 1975: 44–46). State-owned enterprises accounted for about 10 percent of GDP (Jones 1975: 68–69). The extent of state ownership was greatest for capital-intensive industries. Of the eleven most capital-intensive industries, four were nearly completely state-owned, and six others had substantial state involvement. The lone exception was cement, which required relatively low technology and assured high demand that guaranteed profit (Jones and Mason 1982: 39). In 1972, for example, twelve of the sixteen largest South Korean corporations were in the public sector (Jones and Mason 1982: 38). As Leroy Jones and Il SaKong (1980: 164) noted: "Public enterprise has been a 'leading' sector during the period of rapid economic growth. That is, it grew significantly more rapidly than the economy as a whole, and there were identifiable mechanisms linking that growth to other sectors."

The paradigmatic case is Pohang Iron and Steel Company (POSCO), which began production in 1973. The indisputable importance of steel in heavy industrialization requires no discussion; Park showed great personal interest in developing domestic steel production. However, not only was the World Bank against the plan (C.-y. Kim 1994: 53–54), but large conglomerates were hesitant to follow Park's initiative (Rhee 1994: 69–71). Ironically, POSCO came to represent South Korea's dynamic economy and laid the foundation for higher value-added industrial production in the 1980s. The state initiative, however, required external support. U.S. grants and loans amounted to $74 million, but the Japanese contribution was more crucial (C.-y. Kim 1994: 56–57). In particular, Park Tae Joon, the head of POSCO, cultivated Japanese ties to gain credit and technology (Clifford 1994: 71). The Japanese state bureaucrats and corporate executives worked hand in hand with their South Korean counterparts in the Pohang project, as they often did in ventures abroad (Ozawa 1979: 33–39). The Japanese government extended $124 million in loans (D. Chang 1985: 114–15), while Japanese steelmakers offered technology (Amsden 1989: 302–3). Building on the advantage of backwardness—the ability to adopt the latest technology—and relying on cheap labor, POSCO was successful (Clifford 1994: 73–75).

THE LIMITATIONS OF STATE OWNERSHIP

The state actively promoted public ownership. Many large state-owned companies were run by Park's close associates, creating a tight political-military-economic nexus. The head of POSCO was, for example, one of Park's most trusted and experienced associates (Clifford 1994: 68–71). In 1969, 33 out of 42 major publicly founded industrial enterprises were headed by military officers (S. J. Kim 1971: 162). Why didn't the state establish more state-owned and -operated enterprises? There were powerful constraints against extensive state ownership.

First, the Park regime presented itself to the nation as well as to the United State as a capitalist government. The mid-1950s South Korean government publication, for example, stated: "The entire philosophy of the [South] Korean Government is to end the transitory half-socialism just as quickly as possible, and dedicate this country to the free enterprise type of economy that has made the United States the strongest and most powerful country on earth" (OPI 1955: 26). And what could be more communist than state-owned enterprises? Park's earlier communist association rendered his espousal of free enterprises all the more urgent (Jones 1975: 133–39). Successive economic development plans repeatedly discussed capitalism, the free market, and the free enterprise system. The dominant state ideology of anticommunism required South Korea to be capitalist, if only to ensure that it remained as distinct as possible from North Korea.

Second, the state lacked the infrastructural capacity to found and operate many enterprises simultaneously. Given its focus on military security and the dearth of competent managerial personnel, the state needed other agents.

Finally, there was no clear-cut public-private distinction. The pervasive importance of personal networks transcended the simple dichotomy between state-owned and private-owned enterprises. In effect, the same web that bound the top management of POSCO to Park existed between private corporations and Park. State power—especially in the realm of finance—ensured its dominance over all corporations. State-*chaebŏl* relations were not qualitatively distinct from state-state enterprise relations.

THE STATE AND THE 'CHAEBŎL'

To promote rapid industrialization, the state encouraged capital concentration and, in so doing, caused the *chaebŏl* to become a commanding presence in the South Korean economy. While the combined sales of the top ten *chaebŏl* as a percentage of GNP was only 17 percent in 1970, that figure rose dramatically to 48 percent by 1980 (S. K. Kim 1987: 2). Such impressive growth always attracts praise; William Overhold, an American businessman, exclaimed that the *chaebŏl* was "the most efficient economic machine the world has ever seen" (Stephens 1988: 193).

Some writers have stressed the uniqueness of the *chaebŏl* to South Korea, if not to East Asia (e.g. Kirk 1994: 32–35). However, family-owned corporations are prevalent in other countries, developed or not. Consider the Salim Group of Indonesia, which in the early 1990s accounted for 5 percent of that nation's GNP, with 427 companies and 150,000 employees (Abegglen 1994: 164). Others insist that "the success of the [*chaebŏl*] can largely be attributed to aggressive and ambitious entrepreneurship" (S. Koo 1994: 157). In the mid-1980s, the founders of Samsung, Hyundai, and Daewoo wrote bestsellers about their journeys from rags to riches. The retrospective construction of a hero-entrepreneur is well-nigh universal among capitalists. But the individualistic perspective misses the salient characteristic that unifies all the major *chaebŏl*—the preponderant role of the state and social networks. As we have seen, the *chaebŏl* of the 1950s were dependent capitalists, in the 1970s they were still followers rather than leaders, executing industrial policy conceived by the state (E. M. Kim 1988; Amsden 1989).

The state pursued an aggressive policy of corporate welfare and shaped the very possibility of corporate growth. One way was through the use of the "investment license," which granted a corporation monopolistic privilege over a particular commodity. In 1972, for example, each of the ten largest conglomerates had one or more exclusive investment licenses (S. K. Kim 1987: 111–17). The state used its control of capital and credit to shape and promote corporate growth (Rhee 1994: 71–76). By consistently expanding the money supply, which resulted in chronic inflation, it made it easier for the *chaebŏl* to obtain credit and service their debts (Michell 1982: 212). The state employed other means in their corporate favoritism. It sold state-owned enterprises to the major *chaebŏl* (Chŏng Ku-hyŏn 1989: 183–84), which facilitated their acquisition of small- and medium-sized private firms (Koo and Kim 1992: 135–36). International opportunities were channeled through the state. In the very profitable Middle East construction boom of the 1970s, the top ten conglomerates garnered 16 percent of aggregate earnings (S. K. Kim 1987: 196–201).

State control of finance was a powerful way to monitor the *chaebŏl* (Zysman 1983: 285). In times of capital shortage, access to credit made the difference between corporate expansion and stagnation. There was a high correlation between the amount of debt that a corporation could generate and its corporate success (Kuk 1988: 120–21). The *chaebŏl* were heavily leveraged; in times of economic downturn, state support was crucial. One such instance was the August 1972 Presidential Emergency Decree when the state relieved corporate debts (W. Kim 1991: 165–67). Given the corporate dependence on loans, state disfavor could even lead to bankruptcy (Fields 1995: 127–32).

Corporate diversification followed the state-shaped structure of opportunity. The most effective way to accumulate wealth was to expand into as many monopolistic spheres as possible. While only 34 subsidiary companies were founded or incorporated by the top ten conglomerate groups in the 1960s, the number rose to 114 in the 1970s (Kuk 1988: 116). The state offered significant tax and other financial incentives for its targeted import-substitution industries (S. T. Suh 1975: 214). It also designated ten General Trading Companies (in effect, the ten largest *chaebŏl*), which were given special privileges and loans to assist them in conducting foreign investment and trade (Fields 1995: chap. 6).

Corporate growth was shaped by state initiatives. The four crucial modes of rapid growth were (1) assuming control over Japanese-owned plants; (2) processing the "three white's" in the 1950s; (3) taking advantage of the "Vietnam boom"; and (4) following Park's industrialization plan. In all four modes, state support was crucial. It was in the 1970s, however, that the most dramatic growth occurred. Indeed, in 1973, less than 10 percent of the total industrial capital stock was from before the Korean War (W. Hong 1976: 22). Essentially, the successful *chaebŏl* embodied the South Korean economy's rise toward higher value-added production.

The recent provenance of contemporary large conglomerates should be clear from comparing the seven largest *chaebŏl* in 1966 with those in 1985. In 1966, the largest corporations were Samsung, Samsang, Samyang, Kaetong, Tong'a, Lucky, and Taehan; by 1985, they were Samsung (established in 1952), Hyundai (1948), Lucky Goldstar (1947), Daewoo (1967), Sunkyong (1953), and Ssangyong (1948). As the founding years suggest, many *chaebŏl* are no older than South Korea. Samsang, Samyang, Kaetong, Tong'a, and Taehan had by 1985 ceased to be major players. By the mid-1980s, only two major corporations (Ssangyong and Daelim) could be traced to the colonial period. Furthermore, only two of the ten largest corporations in the mid-1980s were targets of the 1961 Illicit Accumulation Law.

Personal networks between Park and entrepreneurs provided access to capital and credit on the one hand and monopolistic privileges on the other hand (K.-D. Kim 1979: 75). As Lee Hahn-Been, former deputy prime minister, explained: "You name one hundred . . . largest or most conspicuous projects or plants in the sixties and seventies. Whatever they may be, the final decisions were made at the top of the regime" (S. K. Kim 1987: 109). The "top of the regime" was, of course, Park Chung Hee. Personal connections to Park provided the privileged path to business success in the 1970s. Beyond Park, ties to relevant officials, whether in the Ministry of Construction or the Ministry of Finance, led to favors and, equally important, prevented bureaucratic obstacles.

In the quest for preferential treatment, family, military, school, and regional networks all favored some individuals over others. Former military and government officials often joined *chaebŏl*

management and forged ties between corporations and the state
(Hattori 1984: 183–84). Regionalism manifested itself: people from
the Kyŏngsang provinces were disproportionately represented
among the military, state, and business elite, while the neighbor-
ing Chŏlla provinces became underdeveloped (Chon 1992: 155–58).
Prized above all was the TK mark (referring to the city of Taegu
and Kyŏngbuk High School), which dominated the political and
business elite. Both Chun Doo Hwan and Roh Tae Woo belong to
this nexus (Seoul Kyŏngje Sinmun 1992: 29–33).

The role of state patronage cannot be overemphasized. Two major corporations, Lotte and Kolon, that did not initially rely on
close state ties, were founded by resident Korean entrepreneurs in
Japan (Mabe 1986: 115–29). More significant, major corporations
that opposed the "top of the regime" often met with disaster. Consider the example of Samhak, a major distillery and one of the
largest conglomerates in the late 1960s. The owner backed Kim
Dae Jung in the 1971 presidential election. Several months later,
Samhak was convicted of tax evasion and forced into bankruptcy
(Shim and Sherry 1995: 71). As the later examples of Yulsan and
Kukje suggest, the state penalized not just poor performers but de-
fiant, independent-minded ones (Clifford 1994: 219–26; C. Nam
1995: 357–58).

In stressing state patronage, I do not mean to dismiss entrepreneurship altogether. There was a cultural and social foundation for
entrepreneurship in the post–Korean War South Korea. The Confucian disdain for commercial activities had declined. The disappearance of the landed oligarchs created a pool of overeducated
elites seeking new sources of wealth and power (Hattori 1988:
153–56). The new structure of business opportunities was seized
by the ambitious, which included not only the scions of the landed
gentry but also those of humbler background intent on raising
themselves by dint of their talent and diligence. There was a meritocratic moment in South Korea from the end of the Korean War
to the consolidation of the *chaebŏl* in the 1970s. Like the fictional
protagonists of the Horatio Alger novels, however, sheer hard work
was not enough. Success came to those who were willing to work
hard and had connections to the powerful that facilitated success.

Chung Ju Yung, the founder of Hyundai, is a good example.

Hailing from a humble social background, his company would have remained modest had he not assiduously cultivated his relationship with Park Chung Hee (Kirk 1994: 59–60). Although founded in 1948 by Chung, Hyundai only began to distinguish itself in the 1960s as a construction company by gaining U.S. military contracts and by undertaking major state projects, including the Kyŏngbu Highway (Hattori 1989: 46–47). Hyundai became heavily involved in Vietnam-related businesses and continued to grow. It also benefited from the Middle East construction boom and under Park's heavy industrialization plan was awarded lucrative contracts in highway construction and in shipbuilding. Hyundai created thirteen companies during the period of the Third Five-Year Plan, following the contours of state economic priorities (Hattori 1989: 47). In all these moments, state patronage was critical. The founder-entrepreneur's close ties to Park led the media to dub Hyundai as the "Yusin *chaebŏl*."

Family ownership and control characterized virtually all *chaebŏl* in the 1970s (Hattori 1988: 92–103). But family ownership and control as a pattern is hardly unique to South Korea. Most firms begin by delegating executive and management responsibility only to trusted personnel, such as family members, kin, school friends, and so on (cf. Hattori 1988: 21–24). Family dominance was common in U.S. businesses; consider the early history of the Rockefellers, the Fords, or the Carnegies. It is usually the pressures of inheritance tax that breaks up family control. South Korean corporations are under no such pressure to loosen family control. As late as 1984, only 2 out of the 50 largest conglomerates were headed by professional managers (Kuk 1988: 128). Family and kinship networks provided the personnel to staff *chaebŏl* expansion. Especially in the 1970s, patrimonial ties marked the corporate hierarchy (Kim and Kim 1989). In addition, former military officers, politicians, and bureaucrats staffed *chaebŏl* managerial hierarchies (Lim and Paek 1987: 26). Donald Christie (1972: 219) writes of the "Korean way" of promotion: "not through hard work, but through conniving and connections." When I worked at a *chaebŏl*-affiliated firm, many mid-level executives constantly complained about the family "mafia" that controlled the corporate group. Against the meritocratic ideology they espoused, family ownership and management was not only repugnant but widely believed to be inefficient as well.

STATE POWER AND DISCIPLINE

I have argued that state patronage was crucial for *chaebŏl* growth in the 1970s. Although corruption and personalism persisted, the state-capital relationship did not degenerate into the stasis that had characterized the 1950s. The state harnessed competition and disciplined large corporations in order to enhance export and economic growth.

Corruption did not disappear in the 1970s. In the mid-1970s, a South Korean social scientist noted: "The rapid expansion of the functional scope of governmental authority has tended to induce corruption at a far greater scale and in an even more pervasive manner than before" (Hahn 1975: 301). From 1975 to 1977, for example, there was a widely publicized anticorruption campaign in the bureaucracy (S. H. Oh 1982). The 1978 Hyundai Scandal—the exchange of luxury apartments for government favors—revealed widespread corporate influence-peddling among the state bureaucrats (K. Nam 1989: 142–43). As late as the late 1980s, corporations were expected to donate large sums of money to the state and state officials (CISJD 1984: 100–132; Sin Tu-bŏm 1993: 146–53). These same state officials also expected similar "donations" from foreign companies trying to do business in South Korea (Clifford 1994: 92–93). Several executives complained to me about the state's demand for large contributions to the 1988 Seoul Olympics. When I worked for a *chaebŏl*, I observed several discreet exchanges of envelopes (containing large sums of cash) between business people and government officials. Quite clearly, money and corporate entertainment greased the link between the state and big business. The widespread public association of the *chaebŏl* with corruption is not a figment of radical South Korean students' imagination. Kim Yŏng-nok's (1973: 232) complaint in the 1960s is paradigmatic: "The vicious circle continues in which the entrepreneur must obtain government support to start a business; to obtain this he begins by buying the goodwill of officials and ends with a substantial 'token' of his appreciation for favors rendered. . . . Entertainment must be offered only at first-rate restaurants." Critical writings on the *chaebŏl* do not merely reflect Confucian disdain for pecuniary pursuits or anticapitalism but express rather a disgust with the pervasive personalistic ties that constituted the political-business nexus (Janelli 1993: 82–88).

Be that as it may, what distinguished the 1970s state-*chaebŏl* relations from the 1950s variety is the imperative of development. The social forces that brought about the end of the triple alliance impelled the new regime to promote growth. Corporations did not receive raw materials to process but rather capital and opportunities to produce commodities. Loans, quite simply, needed to be paid back. It is in this context that the goals of state-led development played a crucial role. Rather than engage in businesses with few linkages, the state's developmental ideology mandated businesses to pursue productive endeavors with many linkages. The state insistently observed the Veblenian distinction between industry and business. The state foreclosed the possibility of rentier profit. Instead, it channeled entrepreneurial drives to industry— manufacturing in general and export-oriented production in particular. To put it another way, positive-sum efforts superseded zero-sum games (Jones and SaKong 1980: 277). State allocation of credit depended on reasonable corporate performance. To succeed in exporting products, conglomerates needed to produce commodities that were competitive in terms of cost and quality. Global competition, in other words, drove corporate performance. Corrupt or not, the changing context ensured that corporations contributed toward the industrialization of South Korea.

Pakistan provides an interesting comparative case. In the late 1960s, 43 families controlled over half of the total assets of nonfinancial firms (White 1974: 58–59). Like South Korea: "The dominant position of the leading industrial families and groups was related to their mastery of the licensing system" (White 1974: 121). In spite of many similarities, what distinguished late 1960s Pakistan from 1970s South Korea was state power over capitalists. In Pakistan, large landlords and large capitalists combined to challenge and to temper state power (White 1974: 155–59). Hence, the state was unable to discipline capital or to pursue export-oriented production.

In summary, the *chaebŏl* became the principal agents of state-led development. Conglomerate growth was part and parcel of state policy. There is considerable truth to Fernand Braudel's (1977: 113) claim that "capitalism has always been monopolistic," requiring state support. In other words: "Capitalism only triumphs when it becomes identified with the state, when it is the state" (Braudel 1977: 64). The South Korean case is clearly no exception.

The Exploitation of Workers

In pursuing rapid industrialization during the 1970s, the South Korean state dominated the population *tout court*. Capital accumulation and labor exploitation went hand in hand. Cheap labor was a necessary, although far from a sufficient, condition for economic and export growth. The state squelched labor organizations, retarded the development of the agricultural sector, and silenced the citizenry. State repression must be seen in its totality; the social foundation of cheap labor entailed nothing less than a powerful and systemic assault on civil society.

STATE LABOR POLICY

Export-oriented industrialization is premised on cheap labor. Given the South Korean dependence on foreign technology and the absence of raw materials, its most valuable asset was its labor force. The ideology of comparative advantage—cheap labor—became widely accepted and was invoked to justify low wages (S.-K. Cho 1987: 228–29). There was in fact a high correlation between export industries and labor intensity (Watanabe 1982: 113–116). Nam Duck Woo, South Korean deputy prime minister in the mid-1970s, said: "There is a criticism that we are exploiting labor with low wages. But in my view, the first stage is getting the economy going; the next stage is to consider [social] welfare. First growth and efficiency, then equity" (*Time*, December 22, 1975: 40). The state seeking growth and legitimacy and the *chaebŏl* pursuing profit and credit combined to sustain the condition of cheap labor.

Most accounts of South Korean development present cheap labor as a quasi-natural condition or as a cultural phenomenon. They assume the existence of plentiful (therefore inexpensive) and

compliant labor (Hasan 1976: 29; Liebau 1987: 66–67). As I elabo-
rate below, the steady oversupply of labor was due in part to agrarian underdevelopment. Furthermore, it is problematic to assume
cultural passivity on the part of South Korean workers (C. S. Kim
1992: 197–98). The history of South Korean labor movements
demonstrates a tradition of activism (Y.-K. Park 1974: 43–52; Kim
Nak-jung 1982: 92–104; D. Chang 1985). Furthermore, South Korean workers manifested a materialistic orientation to their workplace, evincing little corporate loyalty (K.-D. Kim 1979: 19), and a
high degree of class consciousness (K.-D. Kim 1992: 395–423).
Throughout the 1960s and 1970s, the systematic disorganization
of workers, and especially the super-exploitation of female workers, produced and reproduced low-paid labor.

The state was fundamentally antilabor. It deprived workers of
their basic rights in an attempt to control them, and when it
failed, it repressed them. On the surface, however, South Korean
labor legislation—modeled after U.S. labor laws—seemed progressive (Y.-K. Park 1974: 30–42). The South Korean labor law of 1953
emulated the U.S. Wagner Act. The 1963 amendment, albeit more
regressive than the 1953 law, still upheld labor's basic rights (Choi
Jang Jip 1989a: 85–86). Article 1 of the Labor Union Law guaranteed "to workers the autonomous rights of freedom of association,
collective bargaining and collective action aimed at maintaining
and improving their working conditions" (Y. K. Park 1974: 125; for
the text, see 125–37). All labor unions were organized by industry
under an umbrella organization, the Federation of Korean Trade
Unions (FKTU) (Kim Paek-san 1985; Shimizu 1987: pt. 2; Bognanno 1988).

The mounting challenges by workers, exemplified by the 1970
Peace Market suicide of Chŏn T'ae-il, and the mandate of export-
oriented light industrialization (with cheap labor as the chief comparative advantage) prompted the state to harden its line. During
the Yusin period, the South Korean legislation denied labor its basic rights—freedom of association, collective bargaining, and collective action (J. T. Lee 1988: 138). Government agencies dictated
settlements, and no genuine process to resolve labor-management
disputes existed (Bognanno 1987: 179–80). The state also weakened the right to collective action; the 1969–70 legislation banned

strikes for foreign companies and the 1972 Special Law Concerning National Defense and Security prohibited strikes for workers in virtually all the heavy industries (Liebau 1987: 75–76). Workers were, in effect, stripped of their rights (Im Chong-nyŏl 1985).

The state and private capital constituted a powerful alliance against labor (Kim Hyŏng-gi 1988). Most *chaebŏl* owners and managers were viscerally anti-union. As Samsung's founder stated: "I will have earth cover my eyes before a union is permitted at Samsung" (Ogle 1990: 126). Or, as Hyundai's Chung said: "I will never allow a union in my corporation. There can be a union only over my dead body" (Bello and Rosenfeld 1990: 29). The unionization rate of manufacturing workers was less than 15 percent throughout the 1970s, the lowest rate in the newly industrializing world (Deyo 1989: 69–75).

FKTU, as a para-state agency, exercised corporatist control over workers (Choi Jang Jip 1988: 22–33, 1989a: 169–72). Company-controlled unions and their co-opted union leaders acted at the behest of the state and management (Choi Jang Jip 1989a: 114–15). Some corporations even established a ghost union—a front organization without any substance (Bello and Rosenfeld 1990: 33–34). The police, the KCIA, and corporate thugs terrorized labor (Ogle 1990: 59–62). The ideology of anticommunism discredited labor movements and justified arbitrary interventions to repress nascent organizing efforts (Ogle 1990: 51–53). George Ogle (1977: 88), writing at the time, declared that "Park uses a censored press, the police, and especially the KCIA to stigmatize all opposition as Communists, or 'fellow travelers.'" The pervasive surveillance by the state institutions and employers forced organizing efforts to become clandestine, guerrilla-like activities (Choi Jang Jip 1989a: 92–106).

MILITARIZED MANAGEMENT AND THE CONFUCIAN ETHIC

Low-paid labor is inadequate in and of itself for successful industrialization. An effective office or factory requires adequately trained and motivated workers. This is a pressing problem in developing societies. As Alexander Gerschenkron (1962: 9) argued: "Industrial labor, in the sense of a stable, reliable, and disciplined group that has cut the umbilical cord connecting it with the land and has become suitable for utilization in factories, is not abundant but extremely scarce in a backward country." Furthermore, as E. P. Thompson (1991) emphasized, workers must acquiesce to the mandates of modern industrial production. They must be able to execute commands, deal with the new machinery, and cooperate with other workers.

In South Korea, the military played a crucial role in transforming South Korean men into industrial workers (Janelli 1993: 44–49). Given universal conscription of three years, the military literally disciplined the entire male population. It drilled into them the skills and habits of modern industries and forced every soldier to meet the dictates of modern institutions, such as hierarchical regimentation and punctuality (cf. M. Clark 1954: 172). The quasi-natural rhythm of agrarian life was replaced by the mechanical precision of modern life. By imposing homogeneous training on South Koreans from every status and regional background, the military contributed to national integration and cultural homogeneity. We cannot come to an adequate understanding of contemporary South Korean society without grasping the centrality of the military to the forging of a virtual cultural revolution.

Although some features of the colonial period have survived, much of South Korea's military-cultural revolution can be traced to the management ideas and practices of the U.S. military (Martin 1973; Bark 1984: 274–75). Through conscious imitation and unconscious diffusion, the military became a model for other organizations in South Korea.

The military promoted managerial autocracy. The dominant management style was authoritarian; "one man" rule reverberated down the corporate hierarchy (Lie 1990a). Business corporations imitated the military in institutionalizing hierarchical discipline. The isomorphism of the military and the factory was ensured by the transfer of military officers as corporate managers and the preferential hiring of former military conscripts as factory workers. Hyundai, for example, systematically preferred workers with ROTC training (Kearney 1991: 156). The South Korean sociologist Bae Kyuhan (1987: 37) relayed the following impression of Hyundai's Ulsan factory: "When I visited the factory, many things reminded me of my experiences in the military service." The reminders included the mandatory uniform and the name tag, regulations that pervaded every sphere of life, and the predominance of young males. Given that many manufacturing workers lived in company dormitories, factories resembled disciplined barracks (K. Bae 1987: 37–38).

The South Korean managerial discourse, however, stressed the familial and Confucian nature of the workplace. Companies attempted to instill a sense of loyalty by, for example, giving gifts to employees on holidays, as parents might give presents to their children. The ideal of the family functioned as a means of employee control. As a corporate personnel manager told Robert Kearney (1991: 157), he was looking for "the most normal people. If the office is a family, then those from ordinary families can easily adapt, but those who have had trouble giving up will be likely to encounter trouble in the office." Hence, the corporate personnel office considered parents' marital status when evaluating an employee's adaptability. Four-fifths of the Hyundai factory workers Bae (1987: 44) studied were "recommended by their relatives or friends." Workers were recruited through existing employee networks, which ensured a web of responsibility that prevented subversive activities (K. Bae 1987: 44). Should a worker take part in union activities, for example, not only would the worker's parents be informed of their child's "communist" activities, but the worker's relatives in the same company would be prevented from internal promotion (An 1982: 173–75). Familial ideology was at work in the Factory *Saemaŭl* Movement, which was an offshoot of the rural development program I discuss later. It sought to enhance industrial productivity by propagating the ideology of labor-capital harmony (Choi Jang Jip 1989a: 181–90). A typical slogan urged: "Treat employee like family; Do factory work like your own personal work" (Choi Jang Jip 1989a: 183).

Military-style management does not, however, ensure unquestioned loyalty, obedience, or efficiency. This was particularly true for white-collar workers. South Korean workers have no qualms about leaving a firm (Christie 1972: 221; Lie 1990a). Furthermore, outward conformity with corporate hierarchy belies inward dissent. When I was working at a *chaebŏl* firm in the late 1980s, I was struck by how many workers went around saying "I am busy" in lieu of ordinary greetings. Although they were busily pacing to and fro or conspicuously shuffling papers at their desk, their punctuality and busy-ness masked a variety of efforts to avoid work. Managerial gaze targeted discernible features, such as tardiness, early departure, or a relaxed demeanor. The constant refrain of "I am busy" not only reminded superiors and colleagues of their diligence but protected them from being given additional chores. In the early 1970s, Donald Christie (1972: 142) found that "the men in our section were not working but were reading English novels or a newspaper or just chatting with one another." It was not unusual for my colleagues to take an afternoon off to go to a sauna or to movie theaters.

Why is it, then, that so many observers claim that "Koreans work so hard"? Many scholars regard authoritarian managerial practice as a result of traditional Korean or Confucian culture (Sin Yu-gŭn 1984; B. W. Kim 1992). For most blue-collar workers, militarized management forced them to work long and hard. The situation was, as I have suggested, different for white-collar workers. A particularly memorable experience was symptomatic of the way in which Confucianism was invoked. One day my boss asked me to write a report for the president. Although I had finished a draft soon thereafter, it was ignored for weeks until the night before it was due. Just before I was about to head home, the boss asked me, as well as about a dozen others, to stay behind to work on it. After strenuous hours of rewriting, we finished our task around 3 A.M., at which point the boss insisted that we go out to celebrate. After a few rounds of drinks, he put his arm around me and asked: "Dr. Lie, do you know why we [South Koreans] developed so quickly?" Without waiting for my reply, he triumphantly exclaimed: "Because we work so hard! Because of our Confucian heritage!"

To be sure, as Roger Janelli (1993: 205) notes, South Koreans do take "pride in their long work hours, as when attributing economic growth to hard work" (Janelli 1993: 205). However, the family ideology or Confucianism was especially appealing in times of worker disobedience. As Lucian Pye (1985: 227) argues: "Modernization has thus brought increasing tensions to [South] Korean society, which the government seeks to alleviate by appealing to traditional sentiments." He continues: "The government advanced the doctrine that as a Confucian society [South] Korea did not need the 'wasteful' confrontations of Western labor-management relations" (Pye 1985: 226). In the context of labor militancy in the 1980s, South Korean management theorists and practitioners invoked Confucianism as a normative ideal to attain labor-management harmony.

THE CONDITION OF THE SOUTH KOREAN WORKING CLASS

Even in comparison to other newly industrializing countries, South Korea distinguished itself by extensive and intensive labor exploitation. The situation of South Korean workers in the 1960s and 1970s revealed remarkably little improvement from the colonial period, when Japanese managers relied on female and child labor to ensure a cheap and compliant workforce (Chao 1956: 36).

The working conditions in most factories were poor. South Korea had very high industrial accident rates (Han Hǔi-yǒng 1988: 176–78). Between 1976 to 1988, for example, 60 Poongsan employees died while working. The company, however, was willing to pay only 30 million wǒn ($37,500) to the family of a deceased worker in the late 1980s, when it had donated 3.5 billion wǒn ($4.3 million) to the Ilhae Foundation, President Chun's organization (Clifford 1994: 280). In "A Dwarf Launched a Little Ball," Cho Sehǔi (1990: 344) allows the protagonist, who works for a small firm, to vent his frustration: "We worked until night amidst murky air and deafening noise. Of course we weren't dying right then and there. But the combination of the sordid working conditions, the amount of sweat we shed and the paltriness of pay grated on our nerves." Those workers who complained were fired, while the constant threat of corporate bankruptcy silenced the rest.

Wages were lower than in other developing economies. In 1980, while the average U.S. manufacturing worker earned $10 per hour, the comparable figures were $3 for Mexico and $1 for South Korea (Deyo 1989: 91). Wage increases for manufacturing workers lagged behind productivity increase and wages of other workers; only farmers were worse off (Kim Hyǒng-gi 1988: 379–86). Most telling, the average wage received by manufacturing workers was below the socially necessary minimum wage. The Korea Development Institute (KDI; a government think tank) estimated in 1980 that a minimum monthly income for a family of five was 270,000 wŏn (about US $335). In fact, 31 percent of all workers received less than 70,000 wŏn, 56 percent received less than 100,000 wŏn, and 86 percent received less than 200,000 wŏn. In 1986, FKTU estimated that a family of four required a minimum of 524,000 wŏn a month; the average wage was 339,000 wŏn. Nearly 90 percent of manufacturing workers were earning less than the minimum necessary to support a family of four (Lie 1991a).

Given inadequate social welfare provisions, workers scrambled to meet the needs of the day. Many worked in the informal sector, in casual day labor such as paper and glass recycling, where working conditions were worse and pay lower than in the formal sector (Takizawa 1988: 23–51). The urban informal sector constituted up to a third of the workforce (Chŏng Tong-il 1985: 11–12; Kang Myŏng-sun 1985: pt. 1). The average daily wage for an informal sector job was less than $1 in the early 1970s (Breidenstein 1974: 267). The urban poor, moreover, bore a heavy tax burden (Bahl, Kim, and Park 1986: 211–15). Urban slums proliferated (Sumiya 1976: 63–68; J. Chung 1990: 323).

Cho Chŏngnae's "Land of Exile," first published in 1981, narrates the fate of a downtrodden working-class man. After he entrusts his son to an orphanage, Ch'ŏn Mansŏk, the protagonist, recalls his stint in the People's Army, his years as lowly worker, and his wife who left him. Crying silently as he recalls the time when he was looking for his departed wife, Ch'ŏn ponders on his wretched life:

> Where am I going? What am I doing here in this strange land where I don't know nobody? They call you a human being, but is this how you end up if you never should've been born? You mean to tell me some people are born noble and some people are born low? Where in hell did they get the idea of nobles and commoners, anyway? We're just the same—same faces, same minds. . . . So, what's the difference? Was it my mistake? Just because you're born low class, do you have to live like you are? (C. Cho 1993: 218)

THE SUPER-EXPLOITATION OF FEMALE WORKERS

Development is a gendered process that often adversely affects women (Mies 1986). In South Korea, the super-exploitation of female workers occurred in the context of the exploitation of all workers. Rapid industrialization capitalized on the cultural practice of patriarchal authority, as male power became reified and institutionalized in offices and factories.

The pursuit of extra-cheap labor focused on gender as a central axis of labor differentiation (Lie 1996a). Women have no intrinsic or essential qualities—however they have been socialized—that make their labor less valuable (B. Lee 1994: 74–79). Rather, the relative devaluation of female labor is a cultural phenomenon. The legacy of agrarian patriarchal ideology facilitated the construction of cheap female labor in South Korea, but it was mediated by male workers who struggled for autonomy and patriarchal status in gender-segregated households and workplaces. Whenever male work is defined in terms of family wage, female work is redefined as superfluous. Labor unions often excluded women, while management mobilized male workers to prevent female workers from organizing (Ogle 1990: 20).

In South Korea, female labor participation increased from 25 percent in 1960 to 46 percent in 1990 (Choe, Kong, and Mason 1994: 287). The export-oriented industries in South Korea depended on female workers. In the early 1970s, textile production accounted for 40 percent of all South Korean exports; women workers accounted for 70 to 80 percent of the textile industry workforce (O. Lee 1990: 67, 151).

Women worked longer but were paid less than half what men were (CISJD 1988b: 82, 85). In a 1984 Korea Development Institute report, 40 percent of women workers earned less than 100,000 wŏn a month (Lie 1991a: 506). In 1985, 13 percent of male workers earned less than the minimum cost of living for a single person, while the comparable figure was 64 percent for women (Bello and Rosenfeld 1990: 26). Women in textile factories worked over twelve hours a day in small spaces without ventilation or adequate lighting (Ko Kyŏng-sim 1988; Spencer 1988: chap. 4). Female textile workers made the following appeal in 1977:

Our life in the factory is really miserable. Ours is a confined, stifling existence on the job—prohibited from talking to the workers next to us, poorly fed, not allowed to even go to toilet when
necessary. The company . . . oppresses us by intervening in our
personal lives. . . . We are endlessly plagued by lung tuberculo-
sis, athlete's foot, and various stomach diseases. Women workers have yellow, swollen faces from inadequate sunlight. We are
also tormented by temperatures of 40 [degrees Centigrade] and
by dust. . . . We are struggling to free ourselves from these miserable conditions which are too many to enumerate. (Asian
Women's Liberation Newsletter 1983: 233–34)

Factory dormitories were virtual prisons, characterized by over-
crowding and surveillance (O. Lee 1990: 171–79). Many female
workers were obliged to send their meager earnings back to their
rural homes; in a 1980 study, female textile workers on average
saved nearly 50 percent of their earnings (S. J. Oh 1983: 195). In
addition, many female workers suffered from sexual harassment
and other violence (Ogle 1990: 20).

Alternatives to factory work were worse. From the 1960s to
1980s, many women were employed as domestic workers, often as
live-in help (White and White 1973: chap. 1; Kim Yŏng-mo 1990:
chap. 7). Women also worked in manual and menial jobs, such as
in construction and in peddling cigarettes and candy bars (Son 1983:
13–19; H. Cho 1987: 76–79). In 1989, there were 3 million female
temporary workers, while nearly 2 million women—nearly 20 percent of the labor force—worked in daily contract jobs (A. Park 1992:
16). Sweatshops, often subcontracting from textile manufacturers,
employed minors. According to Ok-Jie Lee (1990: 196): "The working condition for minor workers in the miniature garment work-
shops located in the residential areas . . . appeared close to slavery."

Female super-exploitation was in some cases invisible. Many
South Korean women served as cleaners, cooks, hostesses, enter-
tainers, and prostitutes for GIs stationed in South Korea. In the
colonial period, Korean women served Japanese colonizers; in the
postwar period, they entertained U.S. GIs (Lie 1995). The sex
tour—where *kisaeng* (the Korean equivalent of the Japanese
geisha) entertained Japanese men by acting as escorts and sexual
partners—became popular in the 1970s.

*

As Barrington Moore Jr. (1966: 506) once wrote: "At bottom all forms of industrialization so far have been revolutions from above, the work of a ruthless minority." The ruthlessness exercised by the South Korean minority seems to have had few peers. As exploited as male factory workers were, they could look down on their more exploited female counterparts. Women factory workers, in turn, could feel superior to informal-sector workers. For the vast majority of the labor force, working was a sheer necessity and the effective choice was between bad jobs and horrible ones. What sustained cheap labor beyond the state's antilabor policy was the underdevelopment of the rural sector. With good reason, almost all the urbanites felt superior to their rural counterparts.

The Depression of the Rural Sector

South Korean agriculture made little direct contribution to GNP growth, either in terms of rural savings or rising productivity (Ban, Moon, and Perkins 1980: 12–17). Its role in South Korean development was to supply the cities with both low-paid workers and low-priced grains.

LAND REFORM AND AFTER

As I argued in Chapter 1, land reform (temporarily) obviated peasant discontent. Beyond eradicating extreme poverty and improving productivity, however, land reform was not a panacea. In the post–Korean War era, the condition of farmers steadily worsened. The state's attitude toward the rural sector was indifference and neglect, punctuated by periods of intense attention (Y. Lim 1973: 17). U.S. food aid, especially through P.L. 480, depressed grain prices. The state exploited the countryside by siphoning off agricultural surplus to benefit urban industries (Yi Tae-gŭn 1987).

Industrialization required cheap grains to feed the burgeoning urban working class. The state's dual-price system for the chief staples sold rice and barley at considerably below their market prices (P. Moon 1991a: 377–82). In the 1960s, the government purchase price was 15 percent below the market price (Ban, Moon, and Perkins 1980: 240–41). These staples were sometimes bought under compulsion, but the government mainly used indirect means, such as a rice-fertilizer barter scheme and farm taxes in kind. While the government share of total rice sales was about 10 percent during the 1950s, it rose to about 50 percent by the mid-1970s. The low staple price policy supplied affordable food grains to urban households—food accounted for about 60 percent of the average urban household expenditure in the late 1960s (Pak and Han 1969: 112). In addition, the state also relied on imported rice and barley (Ban, Moon, and Perkins 1980: 24–26). While very little rice was imported in 1964–65, imported rice accounted for 6 percent in 1967–68 and 25 percent in 1970–71 of total consumption. The state was willing to import so much rice in part because it was U.S. surplus shipped to South Korea under the provisions of P.L. 480 and, therefore, did not have to be paid for out of South Korea's jealously guarded foreign exchange reserves (Ban, Moon, and Perkins 1980: 28–31).

Not surprisingly, the condition of the rural population declined relative to their urban counterparts. Between 1963 and 1967, farmers' real income declined by 15 percent (Hasan 1976: 51). Rural per capita income was two-thirds that of urban per capita income by 1970 (M. Moore 1984: 582–84).

By the early 1970s political and economic reasons, however, mandated rural revitalization. Park's support in the countryside had dropped (R. Wade 1982: 18; M. Moore 1988: 144–45), and U.S. food aid was soon to end, which meant that South Korea would soon have to start paying for its grain imports out of its foreign exchange reserves (Burmeister 1988: 69–70). The Third Five-Year Economic Development Plan therefore stressed rural development. It quadrupled the budget for agriculture from the previous Plan and undertook large-scale projects, such as the construction of dams and power plants (Ban, Moon, and Perkins 1980: 188–91). It raised the government price of main staples, particularly rice (Ban, Moon, and Perkins 1980: 250), and pursued protectionist measures. As a result, by the 1980s South Korea had become "one of the most protected agricultural sectors in the world" (Anderson 1989: 110).

Most important, the *Saemaŭl undong* (New Community, or Village, Movement) was started as an attempt to revitalize rural life

(P. Moon 1991b: 4–5). It began by distributing surplus cement to the countryside in the winter of 1970–71 and grew into the first systematic rural development effort—possibly emulating North Korea's Thousand Horses Movement (M. Moore 1984: 584–88). The state sought agricultural mechanization, the spread of high-yielding rice strains, and village beautification. It established inter-village competition to take advantage of village solidarity and to implement various programs in a top-down manner (M. Moore 1984: 588–89). It also encouraged rural industrialization and other forms of off-farm employment (Choe and Kim 1986: 105–9). As Park (1979b: 68) stated: "The *Saemaul* movement being carried out across the nation is a pan-national movement designed to conquer poverty without outside help so as to build a more affluent Korea" (see also Whang 1981: 9). In fact, it was a state-led, not grassroots, effort to insinuate the Yusin regime into the very fabric of rural life.

The *Saemaŭl* movement initially improved rural lives as the urban-rural income gap closed (Wang 1986: 238; cf. Yu and Kim n.d.: 28–32), and it became widely celebrated in the rural development literature (e.g. Whang 1981: 245–54; Watanabe and Fukagawa 1988: 77–79). However, the urban-rural household income differential grew again and the movement became unpopular and ineffectual. Basic needs, such as water sanitation, lagged behind in many villages (Han et al. 1988: 128–36). Authoritarianism reigned in *Saemaŭl* projects. The method of mobilizing rural villages resurrected the specter of colonial-period efforts toward village self-help (R. Wade 1982: 103–4; cf. Helen Kim 1931). It empowered conservative village hierarchies (Steinberg et al. 1984: Appendix D-12), which coerced labor and financial contribution from villagers (Wideman 1974: 295–96). Many decisions were made without any input from the grassroots or organizations knowledgeable about local affairs (R. Wade 1982: 147–49). For example, the autocratic decision-making style of the *Saemaŭl* movement made possible the rapid dispersal of a high-yield strain of rice, which initially increased rice production (Sakurai 1991). However, as far as many South Koreans were concerned, it tasted odd. Even worse, it was not as hardy or as disease resistant as local strains; the harvests were catastrophic in 1979 and 1980 (Burmeister 1988: 60–65).

During the 1970s, the Catholic Farmers Union and others counter-mobilized to empower poor farmers (SSS 1988: 177–93). Government construction of new tile roofs and wide roads in villages lining new national highways only masked the real problems of the countryside that eventually led to farmer mobilization in the 1980s (Abelmann 1996: 213–25).

RAPID RURAL EXODUS

Agrarian underdevelopment had generated massive rural out-migration in many Third World countries: adequate agrarian growth and rural improvement has prevented it (Streeten 1987: 74–75). In South Korea, farmers reacted to the prevailing economic situation by moving to the cities (Y. Cho 1963; H. Koo 1991), depopulating the countryside.

South Korea in the 1960s and 1970s experienced one of the most accelerated rural out-migrations in world history (Mills and Song 1979: 32). Whereas farmers constituted 72 percent of the total South Korean population in 1960, the share declined to 45 percent in 1970, and 28 percent in 1980. From 1967 to 1979, the agricultural population declined at an average annual rate of 3 percent (Kim, Kajiwara, and Watanabe 1984: 113, 119). Migration unleashed chain migration. My paternal grandparents, for example, sent their sons initially to Seoul to be educated. Their five daughters all married men who found employment in Seoul. By the mid-1970s they themselves had moved to Seoul to be near their children. This sort of family chain migration was common. Between 1957 and 1980, 11 million people migrated from the country to the city (South Korean population in the mid-1990s was about 45 million) (H. Koo 1993: 137). The population of Seoul, for example, more than doubled in the 1960s, from 2.4 million to 5.5 million, which accounted for one-third of the total population increase (E. Yu 1982: 89).

More women than men left the countryside. The vast majority of women under the age of 30 who out-migrated went to work as domestic and factory workers (S. Hong 1984: 193). The young men moved to the cities to seek an education (Seok 1982: 110–11). In general, out-migrants tended to be young (Ban, Moon, and Perkins 1980: 374–75) and to come from either the richest or the poorest sectors of rural society; their departure strengthened the egalitarianism of those who remained (Brandt and Lee 1981: 111; Y. Chang 1989: 246–47). The rapid exodus to the cities also generated a large pool of available workers, which consistently depressed wages. The underdevelopment of the countryside contributed to the construction of cheap labor.

The State Against the People

The fundamental contradiction of Park's rule was that economic growth, which he pursued to justify his power, required authoritarian rule. In the name of people's welfare, the state pursued its antilabor and anti-farmer—in short, anti-people—policy. What began as an authoritarian state transmogrified into a massive leviathan during the 1970s.

THE BUREAUCRATIC-AUTHORITARIAN STATE

The Yusin state in some ways exemplified the bureaucratic-authoritarian state (S.-j. Han 1987: 373; H. Im 1987: 239–40). The concept derives from Guillermo O'Donnell's (1979: 91) study of Brazil and Argentina: "The term 'bureaucratic' suggests the crucial features that are specific to authoritarian systems of high modernization . . . [including] the pivotal role played by large (public and private) bureaucracies." There were, however, three differences between the situations O'Donnell described and the South Korea of the 1970s. O'Donnell's explanatory framework stresses the crisis of import-substitution industrialization, but South Korea experienced the problem of export-oriented industrialization. Furthermore, it was not simply the economic but also internal and external political difficulties of the Park regime that gave rise to the South Korean bureaucratic-authoritarian state. Finally, the South Korean state was much more powerful vis-à-vis civil society than either the Brazilian or the Argentinian states (Choi Jang Jip 1993a).

As I have argued, Park ruled in the face of a chronic legitimation crisis. Although economic growth was a means to prop up his rule, it became an end in itself, justifying autocracy. As if to underscore a modernization theorist's postulate regarding the correlation between economic growth and democracy, Prime Minister Kim Jong Pil stated in 1974: "When per capita GNP becomes one thousand dollars, the spectrum of the people's freedom will accordingly be widened" (H. Sohn 1989: 103).

The Yusin state nonetheless claimed to be a democracy, albeit a "Korean-style" democracy. The propaganda had some success: "Our visitor . . . would have found Korea a remarkably open society for one believed by so many non-Koreans to be under a military autocracy" (Keon 1977: 4–5). But the obviously authoritarian regime was incapable of fooling any but a few. The former president Yun Po Sun stated in 1976: "I cannot sit still and see democracy be sacrificed in the name of national cohesiveness. Where democracy is gone there are only three alternatives: Communism, militarism or dictatorship" (*Time*, March 22, 1976: 26).

Under the Yusin state a reign of terror descended on urban life. Dissent led to arrests (H. Sohn 1989: 58–63). Liberal professors were dismissed and jailed. A Seoul National University professor, Ch'oe Chong-gil, was tortured and killed in the early 1970s, although most South Koreans did not know of this fact until fifteen years later (T. K. Sei 1974: 71–72). The most sensational case was the KCIA abduction of Kim Dae Jung from his hotel room in Japan in 1973 (C. S. Kim 1992: chap. 12). The KCIA's tentacles reached abroad, and harassed antigovernment students in Europe and North America (McCormack 1978c: 190–92). Fear of KCIA informants muffled casual conversations (J. A. Kim 1975: 265).

Censorship became heavy-handed; dissenting media organizations were banned (Y. Chang 1994: 253–57). In 1973, two negative articles—the first about pollution in Ulsan and the second about the shoddy quality of South Korean *ramyŏn* [instant noodles]— were suppressed by the KCIA (T. K. Sei 1974: 22). A 1974 free speech movement at two leading newspapers, *Tonga Ilbo* and *Chosŏn Ilbo*, ultimately led to the mass dismissal of editors and journalists in March 1975 (Nam 1989: 78–83). In the mid-1970s, readers of *Time* or *Newsweek* in South Korea could not read articles on South Korea. Japanese publications, such as the left-leaning *Asahi Shimbun*, were also banned in 1974 (H. Sohn 1989: 69). I was frequently told not to bring any Japanese books with the Chinese character for "left" in the title. Names such as "Marx" or words like "socialism" were taboo. In short, freedom of expression was denied.

The accumulation of human tragedies—physical and spiritual anguish—manifested itself in the cultural expression of *han*, which can be loosely translated as *ressentiment*. As Kim Kwan Suk, the general secretary of the Korean National Council of Churches, told Robert Shaplen (1978: 208): "The internalized sense of fear . . . has . . . mesmerized and narcotized so many people." Perhaps the most celebrated literary expression was Kim Chi Ha's narrative poem, "Five Bandits." Kim pillories the five bandits—tycoon, politician, government official, military general, and minister—who lord over the nation. The second bandit, for example, proclaims:

> Revolution, from old evil to new evil!
> Renovation, from illegal profiteering to profiteering illegally!
> Modernization, from unfair elections to elections unfair!
> Physiocracy, from poor farms to abandoned farms!
> Construction, all houses to be built in *Wawoo*[*] style!
> (C. H. Kim 1974: 43; cf. 1978: 68)

Kim's popular poems led to his arrest and death sentence, although he was not executed due to international pressures (C. H. Kim 1978: xlii–xlvi).

ANTICOMMUNISM AND NATIONAL SECURITY

Anticommunism was invoked to justify all aspects of military rule. A mid-1950s government document stated: "Out of a long and tragic experience with Communism, we of [South] Korea believe there is no middle ground, no possibility of coexistence, no road of modus vivendi (OPI 1955: 1). The threat of another war with North Korea provided a powerful rationale for repression in the name of national security.

School lessons and military training disseminated the ideology of anticommunism (Henderson 1976: 139; cf. McGinn et al. 1980: 241). Teachers were responsible for the political activities of their

---

[*] "The collapse of *Wawoo* Apartments in April 1970 was attributed to cheap and faulty construction on the part of Seoul's Bureau of Construction. Seoul's mayor was relieved of his duties as a result of the accident, which claimed some 128 lives" (C. H. Kim 1974: 58–59).

students. The idea that national security was under continual threat was drummed into every South Korean student; it became a central tenet of South Korean anticommunist nationalism. Students were, for example, urged to compose essays imagining the evil North. The absurdity of the fears inculcated during their early school years accounts for the backlash against anticommunism that was common among college students in the 1980s. I narrowly missed a chance to become an anticommunist poster boy in 1974 when I attended a summer school for expatriate Koreans in Seoul. When one of the instructors spotted me reading Alexander Solzhenitsyn's *Gulag Archipelago* (1974), he rejoiced tearfully and embraced what he took to be an embodiment of anticommunist ideology. Only my adolescent shyness prevented me from taking part in the hastily planned national radio interview and a personal audience with President Park.

The ideology of anticommunism (and, in particular, anti–North Korean sentiments) rationalized far-reaching surveillance of the population across time and space. Nightly curfews from midnight to 4 A.M. restricted people's activities. The colonization of night life common in most urbanized societies did not occur in South Korea until the 1980s. Rather, the darkness of the night—the time of danger—came to symbolize the terror of communism. Monthly civilian defense drills alerted the populace to the ever-present possibility of a North Korean attack. Spatial confinement supplemented temporal limitation; South Korean mental cartography became a battle map against North Korea. Many sites were forbidden for citizens to enter or to photograph; the Blue House—the South Korean presidential mansion—was left off all the maps of Seoul until the late 1980s. In the anticommunist imagination, communism was omnipresent and borders were porous. Posters warning of North Korean spies (and huge rewards for locating them) adorned numerous telephone poles and public surfaces. The specter of North Korea necessitated vigilant patrolling of the border between the two Koreas. An extreme manifestation of the siege mentality was the mid-1970s plan to erect a wall 22 feet high and 8 feet thick across the DMZ separating North from South (Shaplen 1978: 192). Anticommunist ideology and policy had turned South Korea into a mirror image of its counterpart to the north (cf. B. C. Koh 1973).

THE DIALECTIC OF REPRESSION AND OPPOSITION

In August 1974, when I was in an auditorium listening to one of Park's soporific speeches, there was an attempt on his life in which his wife was killed. The national mourning that followed generated renewed vigilance and people feared greater repression. In December 1974, a politician who suggested that Park step down was beaten up by his National Assembly colleagues (Shaplen 1976: 74). On the same day, George Ogle, a long-term American missionary and a vocal critic of the Yusin regime, was expelled (Henry 1975: 66). The fall of Saigon also exacerbated tension. Park blamed "lack of unity and the widespread criticism" for "causing the fall of 'democracy' in South Vietnam" (Jack 1975: 302). In May 1975, Park pronounced the Presidential Emergency Decree No. 9, which "effectively blocked all challenges to the Yushin system by banning any form of criticism of the Constitution by whatever means" (H. Sohn 1989: 85; for the text see T.K. 1976: 356–62). The mid-1970s was the height of Yusin repression.

The Yusin state turned into a political system that brooked no criticism whatsoever. Kim Chi Ha's (1974: 90–91) "Cry of the People" makes a mockery of the virtual totalitarian society under Yusin rule:

> The *Yushin* signboard advertisement
> Is merely to deceive the people;
> On democratic constitution's tomb
> Dictatorship has been established;
> Human rights went up in smoke;
> Now sheer survival is at stake.
> The people's leaders thrown in prison
> For espousing democratic rights.
> For their deep belief in freedom
> Students and Christians are labeled "traitors";
> Rule by fear and violence
> Shows total desperation.

The net effect of Yusin repression was the spread of antigovernment sentiments even among the moderate middle class. William J. Parente (1974: 319), visiting South Korea in the mid-1970s, "was impressed by the catholicity of the government's opposition." The

election of Jimmy Carter in 1976 and his intention to withdraw
U.S. troops from South Korea boded ill for Park's beleaguered rule
(McGleish 1977).

Antigovernment forces gathered strength throughout the late
1970s. Students, Christians, politicians, and even farmers expressed their opposition to Yusin rule (CISJD 1985: 94–100). A
Christian group proclaimed in the mid-1970s: "[The] 'Korean style
of democracy' represents no democracy, but a fascist dictatorship.
'Revitalization' [Yusin] is no reform program but maximization of
Park's power" (ECCKP 1975: 10). In addition to political activities,
heightened labor disputes occurred from the late 1970s (K. Nam
1989: 125–26). The best-known dispute occurred on August 11,
1979, when the police arrested the Y.H. textile company's women
workers, who were presenting a list of demands at the New Democratic Party headquarters (CISJD 1985: 107–13).

Park's regime came to a sudden end just over two months later.
When opposition politician Kim Young Sam was expelled from the
National Assembly, students and citizens of Pusan—his home
town—began a demonstration that quickly drew workers from
nearby Masan. The ideological tenor of these demonstrations can
be gleaned in part from a student movement pamphlet:

> The military dictatorship . . . which is based on anti-national
> comprador capitalism, disregarded the desperate national aspi-
> ration to a self-reliant national economy, and blindly pursued a
> foreign-dependent and export-oriented economic growth policy
> which forced workers and farmers to suffer low wages and low
> agricultural prices. The emergency measures were introduced to
> suppress the rightful struggles of working people and the demo-
> cratic forces opposing this policy. . . . The Y.H. incident showed
> clearly that this policy could not but exploit working class peo-
> ple and deprive them of their right to subsistence. (H. Sohn
> 1989: 165)

The Pusan-Masan riot plunged the Park regime into a major crisis
(Tamura 1984: 41–43).

The resolution of the mounting crisis was swift and dramatic.
Apparent disagreements over an appropriate state response to rising protest led the KCIA chief Kim Chae-gyu, Park's protégé, to
shoot Park and his hard-line confidant, Ch'a Chi-ch'ŏl, on Octo-

ber 26, 1979 (for the official reports, see Hinton 1983: 101–16, 120–29).

The ironies of Park's life were manifold. Hoping to champion rural life, his rule made South Korea irremediably urban. Intending to construct a self-sufficient economy, South Korea became enmeshed in the global division of labor. Bringing undreamed of prosperity, he generated widespread resentment against his rule. Repressive state action against young female workers—who had borne the brunt of labor repression—heightened the contradictions of Yusin political economy. And finally, Kim Chae-gyu, the director of KCIA and the very symbol of Park's autocratic rule, resolved these contradictions in a personal feud.

CHAPTER FIVE

Developmental Contradictions and Political Democratization

Development is neither a natural nor a necessary process. A nation-state is not foreordained, whether because of inevitable inner forces or external constraints, to continue on any given trajectory. Take-offs can be aborted; miracles can wither away. From Ernest von Koerber's effort to spur the Austrian economy in the 1900s (Gerschenkron 1977) to a series of post–World War II miracle economies, such as Brazil in the 1960s (Furtado 1976: 174–78), promising beginnings often go awry.

South Korean history is replete with crises and watersheds, but the year 1980 seemed to mark a genuine turning point. Political turmoil followed Park's assassination. The economy was in the doldrums. Sluggish export growth, mounting foreign debt, and rising labor disputes suggested that South Korea was reaching the limits of the single-minded pursuit of economic growth. As *Forbes* reported, the South Korean "economic miracle . . . nearly shattered in 1979" (Minard 1985: 39–40). Yet by 1987, the South Korean economy was booming again, and this time under a democracy.

In this chapter, I address two main questions about the 1980s. First, how did South Korea avoid stagnation, given that its 1970s industrialization effort depended heavily on foreign loans and external trade? Second, why was political democracy possible in 1987 but not in 1980 immediately after Park's death?

The Fifth Republic and Its Discontents

When Park was killed, students, workers, and citizens rose up to demand democracy, but with the Martial Decree No. 10 of March 17, 1980, the military reasserted its power, and General Chun Doo Hwan emerged as the new strong man. The Seoul Spring was over almost before it had begun.

THE 1980 SEOUL SPRING AND THE KWANGJU UPRISING

In accordance with the Yusin Constitution, Choi Kyu Hah became acting president after Park's death. The real power holder, however, was Chung Seung Hwa, who led the Martial Law Command (Cho Kap-je 1989: 86–93). Choi and Chung pursued a moderate course. The interim leadership rescinded Emergency Decree No. 9, the most draconian of the Yusin-era measures, and allowed Kim Dae Jung and other political prisoners to resume political activity (Hinton 1983: 49). Encouraged by U.S. president Jimmy Carter's human rights foreign policy, progressive forces yearned for an end to military rule.

Nonetheless, the moderates in power were soon replaced by hard-liners. Chung was ousted for his alleged collusion with the KCIA Chief Kim Chae-gyu in Park's assassination. The December 12, 1979, military putsch—when the Ninth Division under Roh Tae Woo moved into Seoul—installed Lee Hui Sung as the new Martial Law Commander (Clifford 1994: 143–48). The United States tacitly supported the new government (Baker 1982b: 174). The putsch did not, however, consolidate military rule immediately. In a statement on December 18th, the new military command pledged as a "firm principle that the armed forces should not interfere in politics" (Hinton 1983: 117).

Despite the putsch, students, workers, and citizens continued to mobilize across the nation. Student demonstrations became especially active in anticipation of the twentieth anniversary of *Sa-il-gu*, the April 19th Student Revolution. There were also numerous labor strikes (Shaplen 1980: 192).

The most dramatic expression of dissent, which led to the most brutal response, was the May 1980 Kwangju Uprising (HSSY 1990). Kwangju was not only the home of the leading opposition politician Kim Dae Jung, it was also the capital of the most depressed province in South Korea. In what was tantamount to a military coup, the regime arrested Kim Dae Jung and other politicians on May 17, 1980 (Warnberg 1987: 52). First the students and then the citizens of Kwangju rose to demand not only Kim's freedom but also their fair share of economic growth (L. Lewis 1988: 18–20). As a result, Kwangju became a war zone and remained so for the next ten days. The British poet James Fenton (1988: 241), who was in Kwangju at the time, wrote: "I kept being asked by people: 'Are you going to tell the truth about us?' Government propaganda had branded the insurrectionists as communists. They were not communists, they insisted. They wanted democracy. They wanted an end to the power of General Chun Doo-hwan and the KCIA."

Mobilizing the notorious Black Berets, the military crushed the rebellion, killing some 2,000 people and injuring many more (Cho Kap-je 1989: 196–226). According to one American resident: "Anybody in the soldiers' way was beaten mercilessly. When they saw the injured lying in the street, the soldiers beat them again" (*Time*, June 9, 1980: 41). The poet Ko Un (1993: 65–67) memorialized the event in "When May Is Gone":

> One day in May we all rose up,
> clasping a thousand years' rage in our hands,
> clenching bare fists, we all rose up,
> . . .
> We fought on, proudly bearing the name of
> the Kwangju Struggle Citizens' Army.
> Brought low by foreign interests,
> brought low by compradors,
> brought low by all the dregs of Yushin;
> defending our land from further disgrace,
> our breasts were pierced and so we died.

The military regime stifled or distorted reports on the violence in Kwangju (Warnberg 1987: 46–48). But the truth diffused slowly through the country by hearsay, video copies of foreign TV coverage, and underground publications. The massacre was probably the single most politicizing event for antigovernment activists in the 1980s. Although the state sought to expunge it from memory, it marked the beginning of a new political era and tainted the new regime indelibly (Han Kye-ok 1988: 89–105; Pak Se-gil 1992: chap. 2).

THE RISE OF CHUN DOO HWAN

The consolidation of military rule paralleled the rise of Chun Doo Hwan. Chun assumed the helm of the KCIA in April 1980 and that of the Special Committee for National Security Measures the following month. Yusin sympathizers lined up behind the hard-liner Chun in the face of protests, propelling him to the presidency by August 1980. The September 1980 Constitution inaugurated the Fifth Republic (for the text, see Hinton 1983: 176–203).

Born in 1931, Chun had spent his youth in Manchuria. His childhood, like Park's, was far from affluent. Pursuing the preferred path for ambitious sons from humble backgrounds, he entered the first four-year class of the Korean Military Academy and was classmates with Roh Tae Woo. Park's patronage led to Chun's rise (Shaplen 1980: 174). He cultivated regional and school ties in order to become the head of Hanahoe, an influential group of Korean Military Academy graduates (Han Kye-ok 1988: 42–46; Cho Kap-je 1989: 21–26).

Like most aspiring politicians, Chun assiduously denied his interest in politics or the presidency. He told Robert Shaplen (1980: 178): "Politics is not one of my hobbies. I've always wanted to be a soldier, and I was a happy warrior until October 26, 1979. But events sometimes take over. . . . I was thrust into this position." Like Park, however, he was to prove Lord Acton's adage that power corrupts, and that absolute power corrupts absolutely.

CHUN'S REPRESSIVE RULE

Ronald Reagan's 1980 electoral victory buttressed Chun's rule. Instead of continuing Carter's stress on human rights, Reagan pursued a single-minded anticommunist policy that tolerated repressive but friendly regimes (Sherry 1995: 398–415). The heightened superpower tension in the early 1980s provided a protective umbrella under which Chun could crack down on dissent. Even with U.S. military support, however, Chun's hold on power was far from secure (S. Han 1989a: 283).

Chun was conscious of the problems facing his rule. In order to allay outright opposition, he announced that he would serve only one term. In his September 1, 1980, inaugural address, he called for "a democracy suited to our political climate" and "the attainment of a genuine welfare state" (Hinton 1983: 205). He promised a moderate version of Yusin politics, and sought growth with some redistribution.

In reality, however, Chun and his coterie eliminated political rivals. About 300 senior KCIA agents and nearly 5,000 low-level government bureaucrats were dismissed and replaced by his supporters. Chun weakened the KCIA, which had been Park's ultimate weapon, while he strengthened military intelligence and the riot police (Cumings 1989: 10–11). The military expanded its influence; over half of the 1982 National Assembly members were former military officers, about twice the proportion during the 1970s (Han Kye-ok 1988: 41). The leading dissident politician Kim Dae Jung was sentenced to death in September 1980, although Chun commuted his sentence in response to U.S. pressure (Hinton 1983: 60–61). According to a July 1980 government report, Kim had "engineered the origins of the Kwangju turmoil, an unprecedented national tragedy" (Hinton 1983: 146). As one Westerner in Seoul told the American journalist Tom Mathews (1980: 44) about Kim Dae Jung's crime: "That's called running for President. . . . It doesn't constitute a capital offense in most countries."

Rival politicians were not Chun's only victims. One of Chun's first acts was to fire nearly 400 journalists and shut down 172 periodicals (Cohen and Baker 1991: 201). The press came under stern surveillance (Sin Tu-bŏm 1993: 23–24). Reminiscent of the early phase of Park's rule, Chun engineered a massive purification campaign. The police rounded up "30,578 'hooligans, racketeers and gamblers.' Of these, more than 20,000 were sent to military re-education camps, where they rose at dawn, ran 4 miles, lifted logs and wrote 'confessions' of past misdeeds" (Mathews 1980: 44). A clergyman told the American journalist Donald Kirk (1982: 6): "The police now are stronger than they were under Park. They keep watch on us all the time. They listen to our telephones. We can do nothing without being followed." Chun justified such extensive domestic surveillance by claiming that it was directed against communist infiltrators.

Even though the new regime had implemented extraordinary national security measures, domestic opposition continued. The new president, like his predecessor, staked the regime's survival on economic growth. Quite simply, Chun's hold on power was not firm. His call for a "politics of reconciliation" was not mere rhetoric but an admission of this fact. Even as Chun called for a massive purification campaign, he could not even conceive of challenging big business as Park had done. Rather than ideological purity, technocratic rationale took precedence. He staffed top administrative posts with technocrats, many of whom had obtained Ph.D.'s at U.S. universities.

The middle class—especially the growing number of educated, white-collar workers—was at best lukewarm about military rule even as they benefited from economic growth under its direction. The Chun regime attempted to appeal to them by calling for a "democratic welfare state" and passed a series of social liberalization measures. In January 1982, for example, the midnight curfew that had darkened urban nights for two decades ended. Chun also expanded universities to admit more students to satisfy middle-class demands (S.-B. Kim 1990: 389). In particular, graduate education expanded, which ironically spread opposition to military rule.

Chun's dilemma was that the contradictions of South Korea's rapid industrialization were nearing their limits. He lacked the requisite social support to sustain authoritarian politics. Hence he seesawed between stifling the demands of the masses and meeting them. Consequently, his rule seemed arbitrary. His rule was also tainted by a major loan scandal in 1982. Chang Yŏng-ja, a relative of the president, was found to have made over $300 million by peddling presidential influence (Yun Kyŏng-ch'ŏl 1986: 429–31). The scandal cast skepticism on Chun's claim to purity. The Japanese phrase—"Minna dorobō desu" (We are all thieves)—became a common refrain among the educated Seoulites (Nakagawa 1988: 18–19).

Escaping the Debt Trap

During the period of political turmoil from Park's assassination to the early 1980s, the South Korean economy suffered from serious problems. Exports were down, external debts mounted.

Around 1980, South Korea faced an acute economic crisis. As a government publication noted: "For the [South] Korean economy, 1980 turned out to be an unprecedentedly difficult year" (OAC 1981: 1).

The economic stagnation after the second oil crisis adversely affected South Korean exports and economic growth. The United States and Japan, South Korea's two largest export markets, were hard hit. As Sang-Mok Suh (1992: 24) observed: "Export-led growth became export-led recession." The economy itself was more dependent on industries and industrial exports than it had been six years before and hence suffered more from the higher oil prices. More crucially, South Korea faced financial pressures caused by the amount of debt carried by its industries. Its external debt doubled between 1979 and 1984, accounting for over 53 percent of GNP by 1984 (Dornbusch and Park 1992: 73).

The crisis seemed to corroborate radical critics of the South Korean economy: "The direction of economic growth is such as to lead not to eventual independence, wealth and equality, but to increased subjection to foreign control, mass impoverishment and heightened inequality" (Easey and McCormack 1978: 81). However, the economy began to recover from 1982 and in 1986, South Korea experienced its first positive current account and trade balance. What explains this renewed dynamism?

Many economists seek the source of the post-1982 South Korean economic recovery in the state's liberalization measures (e.g. Kwack 1990: 218). The argument is that loosening state control unleashed economic dynamism. This view merely confirms the neoclassical economic bias of most economists. Internationalization of the economy often requires greater, rather than less, state involvement.

The formula for South Korean economic success had not changed just because it was the 1980s. Low-paid labor was still South Korea's crucial comparative advantage in the global competition for markets. South Korean manufacturers were still closely following Japan and filling the niches left vacant by the Japanese ascent through the product cycle. Transnational diaspora networks and South Koreans educated in the United States and elsewhere still facilitated international trade and transfers.

The state continued to promote exports and industrial production. It also intervened vigorously to enhance South Korea's position in the global economy. Its success in enhancing competition and controlling capital flow encouraged economic recovery and averted IMF-imposed austerity measures. Simultaneously, aggressive antilabor measures controlled wage costs and ensured the competitiveness of South Korean manufacturing exports. The continuation of the previous state strategy and favorable external factors stimulated the recovery of the South Korean economy.

THE CRISIS OF INDEBTED INDUSTRIALIZATION

In the early 1980s, many newly industrializing economies experienced debt crises in their industrial sectors. Beginning with Poland in 1981 and Mexico in 1982, several economies faced problems servicing debt burdens, and some were on the verge of financial collapse (MacEwan 1990: 18–21). In the mid-1980s, Argentina's debt service burden exceeded its total merchandise export, while the ratio for Brazil and Mexico was about 60 percent; interests on debt accounted for 5 to 10 percent of national income in these countries (MacEwan 1990: 20, 106). Many indebted nation-states rescheduled their debts and accepted IMF-imposed austerity measures (Aggarwal 1987: 10).

Third World debt grew throughout the 1970s. The U.S. government encouraged Third World borrowing, and development discourse justified it (Payer 1991: 6). Soon Third World governments were borrowing money to service their debts; debt dependence increased swiftly (Moffitt 1983: 99–103). Given the need for foreign exchange to procure capital goods, raw materials, and consumer commodities, the motivation of Third World governments and corporations to seek foreign loans is clear enough. What motivated the lenders? The international economy experienced rising liquidity and greater financial competition in the 1970s. Financial liberalization and internationalization occurred in tandem with mounting OPEC deposits in the Euromarkets after the 1973 oil crisis (Frieden 1981: 409–10). In this context, international financial firms could reap high interest by aggressively lending money to the Third World (Payer 1991: 68–72). By 1984, U.S. bank loans to Third World and East European countries totaled $550 billion

(Wachtel 1986: 10). Although overlending prompted financiers to speculate about massive collapses, IMF and creditor governments ultimately reached agreements favorable to the banks (Aggarwal 1987: 49). What was agreeable to the banks, however, was not always beneficial for many Third World economies. Although debt rescheduling eased the immediate financial burden, IMF-imposed austerity measures eroded state autonomy and often had deleterious consequences for living standards in the debtor nations (Moffitt 1983: 122–32; Wachtel 1986: 150–52).

The South Korean state, in contrast, disciplined capital and labor in order to encourage export and economic growth. State and business leaders widely agreed on the severity of the crisis, which gave Chun greater room to maneuver. The Chun regime sought better performance from the *chaebŏl* with less state support. The state passed the Fair Trade and Anti-Monopoly Act in April 1981 (Lee, Urata, and Choi 1992: 211–12), which sought to stem the tide toward monopolies and to invigorate competition in order to achieve efficiency and productivity (C. Moon 1988: 73). Instead of colluding among themselves or just making corrupt deals with state officials, large conglomerates were forced to revitalize themselves.

The state also cracked down on labor. Like other major turning points—the 1961 military coup and the 1972 Yusin Constitution— the 1980 military takeover resulted in antilabor measures (Choi Jang Jip 1988: 301–02). The state restrained wage increases during the early 1980s (C. Moon 1988: 71–72) and placed greater restrictions on union activities (Sin Tu-bŏm 1993: 160). The rate of unionization dropped from 17 percent in June 1980 to 12 percent in March 1981 (Nakagawa 1988: 15–16). The state also sought to curtail consumption and to increase domestic savings (Stopford and Strange 1991: 10). Through its antilabor and anti-consumption policies, the state ensured not only the continued competitiveness of South Korean exports but also the continued growth of its foreign exchange reserves.

The state also retained control over the domestic financial market and the interface between it and the international economy (Y. C. Park 1994: 143). Most significant, the state restricted domestic capital flight (Dornbusch and Park 1992: 74–75). Illegal transfer of the jealously guarded foreign exchange was an execrable crime;

transgressors often made newspaper headlines. Thus the state was able to prevent capital flight and to maintain its financial autonomy (cf. Haggard and Maxfield 1993: 312–13). Neither the Brazilian nor the Mexican state had anything like this level of control over domestic capital. The powerful interests of the Brazilian modern industry undermined state policy and ultimately the military regime itself (Frieden 1991: 129–34). Similarly, the Mexican state had little control over domestic capital (Maxfield 1990: 143). According to one estimate, private Mexican assets outside the country were as large as the total foreign debt (MacEwan 1990: 22).

The South Korean state was also able to interface actively with the global economy. Financial autonomy allowed it to maintain low interest rates, which eased the foreign debt financing burden and encouraged economic expansion. To overcome sluggish export growth, the state devalued the wŏn by 20 percent against the U.S. dollar in 1980 (S.-M. Suh 1992: 25). The state also encouraged export diversification. In particular, it targeted the cash-rich Middle East. In 1981 South Korean exports to the Middle East equaled 73 percent of the total South Korean trade deficit and 38 percent of its foreign currency earnings (Chŏng and Mun 1990: 65–66). In addition, trade with other parts of the world grew; in 1981, for example, one-third of export growth was to Latin American and African countries (Michell 1988: 15). South Korea's export orientation facilitated the servicing of the foreign debt burden; in 1982, for example, debt service burden as share of export revenue was 13 percent for South Korea, compared to 34 percent for Mexico and 43 percent for Brazil (Stallings 1990: 83).

External factors also contributed to the economic turnaround. Well aware of South Korea's importance to their economy, the Japanese extended a massive temporary infusion of credit to its neighbor (Wellons 1987: 251). Specifically, Japan lent South Korea $3 billion to facilitate the servicing of its debt (Stopford and Strange 1991: 46). The financial backing of a major economic power was crucial for this debt-ridden developing economy.

Then the condition of the international economy improved dramatically. Low oil prices contributed to world economic recovery after 1982. The consequent revival of the U.S. and Japanese economies after 1982 heightened their demands for South Korean exports (Dornbusch and Park 1992: 82–83). After the 1985 Plaza Accord, the rapid appreciation of the Japanese yen made South Korean exports more economical for the U.S. and Japanese markets. From August 1985 to April 1987, yen appreciated from 240 to the dollar to 140, while the wŏn stayed roughly constant (Hirakawa 1988: 183). South Korean exports—from textiles to automobiles—boomed, doubling from $30 billion in 1985 to $61 billion in 1988 (Clifford 1994: 241).

Thus, the complex confluence of internal and external factors enabled the South Korean economy to regain its earlier dynamism by the mid-1980s.

FOLLOWING THE JAPANESE ASCENT

When we investigate South Korea's industrial successes of the 1980s, we find the same themes that we explored in Chapters 3 and 4: technological transfer from Japan and the United States, the export niche vacated by Japan, favorable credit policy, and the protected domestic market. By the mid-1980s, the center of gravity of South Korean industrial production had shifted to higher value-added production, such as shipbuilding, automobiles, and electronics. Low wages continued to provide a key comparative advantage in the world market. Furthermore, the growth enjoyed by the *chaebŏl* enabled them to pool capital, technology, and business knowledge among their subsidiary firms.

Consider the automobile industry, which is one of South Korea's most important manufacturing industries. South Korea began domestic assembly in 1962, but the first serious call to create a domestic industry was the 1974 Long-Term Plan for the Promotion of the Automobile Industry, which was part of the Heavy and Chemical Industrialization Plan (N.-Y. Lee 1993: 63–69, 78). The state protected the domestic market and facilitated the needed strategic alliances with transnational corporations (Lee and Cason 1994: 232–33). South Korea's infrastructural development and heavy industrialization—especially steel production—also laid the groundwork for automobile production (Kim and Lee 1994: 288).

The first truly South Korean car was the Hyundai Pony, which was put into production in 1976 under technology transfer arrangements with Mitsubishi (Hattori 1989: 56–58). In 1983,

Hyundai first exported subcompacts to Canada and by the following year the Pony had become Canada's most popular import. In 1986, Hyundai successfully entered the U.S. market, when it became the sixth-largest importer of foreign cars in the United States. The Pony's success was due to a number of factors. State patronage—tax breaks, loans, and the protected domestic market— was important. The noncompetitive domestic market not only provided an ideal—and extremely profitable—testing ground but also made possible an economy of scale in production (NSK 1988: 174–77; N.-Y. Lee 1993: 170–72). Technology transfer was facilitated by intense competition among nine major Japanese manufacturers, which eased bargaining (Kim Yŏng-ho 1988: 167–74). Furthermore, there was a niche for low-priced cars in the North American market. Not only was Japan focusing on higher value-added production to generate greater profit, but import restrictions through quotas and voluntary curbs forced Japanese manufacturers to earn more per exported vehicle. Global competition, meanwhile, was weak. U.S., European, and Japanese manufacturers were all focusing on higher value-added models. The newly industrializing economies were concentrating either on their profitable domestic markets or had foundered in the restrictive markets of the advanced economies, which demanded higher quality and low pollution levels (N.-Y. Lee 1993: 148–49). Thus the Yugo was the Pony's only real rival in the mid-1980s (Green 1994: 240–41).

The export success of Hyundai was due above all to low labor costs. Relying on technology transfers and the import of manufactured parts, South Korean manufacturers focused on the final assembly. This strategy worked well as long as South Korea could count on low labor costs. For example, in 1985 the wage cost per small car was $1003 in Japan; the South Korean figure was only about half ($563). This disparity in labor costs was even more pronounced than it seems at first glance: in South Korea each small car required 90 worker hours to produce, in Japan only 34 (Doktor and Lie 1993).

The rise of the medium- and high-tech industries transformed South Korea's economic focus. While textiles accounted for 34 percent of total South Korean exports in 1974, the comparable figure was 23 percent by 1985 (Hong Moon-Shin 1989: 496). Yet it was during this period that the rising wall of protectionism in the United States and growing competition from other developing economies began to endanger South Korean lower-tech exports (Hong Moon-Shin 1989: 499–500). Indonesia, for example, replaced South Korea as the world's leading plywood producer. Although the textile industry was still South Korea's primary export industry in 1987, the next two largest export commodities changed from plywood and wigs in 1970 to communication and transportation equipment by 1987 (J. H. Kim 1989: 15). Wigs and plywood had given way to electronics and heavy industry (NSK 1988: 107–8). Military production also became export-oriented in the course of the 1980s (Brzoska and Ohlson 1987: 116). Many *chaebŏl* moved to higher value-added production, diversified their export markets, and invested overseas (Hong Moon Shin 1989: 509–10). In investing in countries with low-paid labor, South Korean companies often exported their militarized management techniques as well.

Aggressive state policy and the favorable international environment allowed South Korean export expansion through the 1980s. By the mid-1980s, many state officials and big business managers were bullish about their economic prospects; one official told the American journalist Leslie Helm (1985: 52): "This is the first time in our 5,000-year history that we have a chance to become an economically advanced country. We have to do it." By 1988, the year of the Seoul Olympics, few doubted the viability of the economy. Export success in key industrial sectors, including automobiles and some high tech production, seemed to ensure South Korea's imminent status as an advanced—not merely newly—industrialized economy.

Political Democratization

Political democratization usually accompanies industrialization or modernization (Huntington 1991: 59–61; cf. Hirschman 1979). Whether because of their putatively modern values, the decline of their agrarian oligarchies, or the rise of their middle and working classes, wealthy capitalist nation-states are usually democracies. Yet by the time of Park's assassination in 1979, South Korea had a thriving industrial sector and a well-entrenched middle class. The 1980 Seoul Spring amply testified to the widespread support for political democracy, which was corroborated in a national survey (L. Wade 1980: 43–44). But seven more years of military rule followed. To discover why we must look beyond the prerequisites of democracy to consider social changes and contingent processes.

THE MOMENTUM FOR POLITICAL DEMOCRACY

Industrialization expanded the middle-class and working-class populations. These two groups constituted a powerful force from below interested in dismantling three decades of military rule. Active civil society challenged authoritarianism (Cho Hŭi-yŏn 1990).

As I have argued, the educated middle class had never embraced military rule wholeheartedly. Censorship, propaganda, and repression never successfully exterminated democratic yearnings (M. Cho 1989: 95–96). The prevailing democratic temperament was critical of authoritarian rule and the untrammeled pursuit of profit. As Carter Eckert (1993: 116–18) emphasizes, the South Korean elite never managed to make capitalism a hegemonic ideology. The *chaebŏl*, in particular, were associated with corruption and collusion with authoritarian rule. The narrator in Yun Heunggil's 1977 story, "The Man Who Was Left as Nine Pairs of Shoes," expresses this mind-set:

> Like my friends, I believed that we shouldn't despise the poor. But it was all right to look down on the rich. It was only right and natural to do so. . . . My friends and I were frustrated that various social benefits bestowed by the government did not reach the bottom rung of society. Whenever we met people with dead-end lives—on the street, in a coffee shop, or in the newspaper—we tried to compensate for their pitiable circumstances with vicious insults directed toward the mercenary plutocrats who were raking in money any way they could. We considered it our duty and task as educated people not to ignore the difficulties of those who could go no further in life. (H. Yun 1989: 117–18)

As the force behind the 1960 Student Revolution and the subsequent political struggles against the Yusin regime, university students continued to be politically significant. Their numbers grew dramatically in the 1970s. In 1971, for example, only one person in 212 was in college; this fraction had risen to one in 60 by 1982 (Takizawa 1988: 19). Older activists continued to work with student groups, and antigovernment networks among universities expanded. Even as some former activists pursued careers in the state bureaucracy and the *chaebŏl* after graduation, others were expelled from the universities (124,600 between 1980 and 1987) or placed on the black lists that barred them from prestigious jobs (M. Cho 1989: 98). Many imprisoned students became "further radicalized in jail by older political prisoners" (Shaplen 1980: 194). Some activists disguised their educational backgrounds to work in factories in order to organize unions, while others taught workers in night schools. Radical publishers, bookstores, counter-cultural cafés, and other infrastructural bases of the student movement expanded during the 1980s.

The 1980s culture of dissent affected virtually all university students. Student cells showed underground videos of the Kwangju Massacre and promulgated radical social analyses. In this way many students were converted to "antigovernment" thinking. The scorching sensation of being teargassed and the ghastly experience of seeing their peers being beaten by the riot police sealed an entire generation's conversion to an antigovernment position. In Kang Sŏk-kyŏng's 1986 novella, "A Room in the Woods," the narrator expresses a common sentiment as she weeps from the tear gas that shrouded a student demonstration:

> Why did these young people have to shout? Why did they have to wear masks in broad daylight having committed no crime? Why did they have to throw flames toward an indifferent world? Would they knock at the door of this iron-walled government until their fragile fists were shattered? It was the springtime of their life, but instead of being exhilarated by their youth they were shedding their own blood. . . . I had the illusion that blood was spreading through my field of vision, that I was shedding bloody tears. (S. Kang 1989: 111)

What was most remarkable was the extent to which even conservative students came to sympathize with the antigovernment student movement in the 1980s. The effective division was not so much between those who supported the government and those who opposed it but rather between those who were demonstrating on the streets and those who stayed behind. The heroic culture of student activism generated not so much of an opposition as a mass of guilty consciences.

The farmers and the urban poor also began to influence national politics during the 1980s. Their relative economic and social impoverishment propelled them into political action. The declining farming population became more organized in the 1980s. Perhaps the most telling indicator of their plight was their growing debt; while the average debt per rural household was 830,000 wŏn in 1982, that figure had risen to 3.1 million wŏn by 1988. The rate of tenancy rose steadily over the same period. From the low of 8 percent in 1950, it grew to 14 percent in 1960, 18 percent in 1970, 21 percent in 1980, and 31 percent in 1985 (Lie 1991c). Aided by outside organizers, farmers agitated to improve their conditions (Nakagawa 1988: 108–12). In addition, the mobilization of the urban poor occurred in Seoul and other large cities (Kim Yŏng-sŏk 1989: chap. 3). The rural exodus had created a large pool of un- and underemployed workers in urban areas, especially Seoul and Pusan. The Urban Industrial Mission took the lead in organizing them (CCA-URM and ACPO 1987: 7), facilitated by the persistence of rural personal networks in urban areas (Y. Chang 1982: 42, 1991).

The most significant force was the working class. By 1980, manufacturing workers constituted 28 percent of the total labor force and 43 percent of the urban labor force (H. Koo 1987: 177). Labor movements in the 1970s were spearheaded by female textile workers (S.-K. Cho 1985b: 83). Students and church leaders also organized workers to seek higher wages and better working conditions (Song 1985: 181–88; Kim Nak-jung 1985: 407–12; Shimizu 1987: pt. 1, 1774–77). As George Ogle (1990: 84) notes: "Women workers, unlike their male counterparts, often responded to the harshness of the enforcement system by direct resistance. Most of the disputes registered in the [1970s] were registered by women and the few cases of work stoppages were all by women." Sexist labor practices generated gender-based labor movements (S.-K. Cho 1985a: 213). The female workers involved in the Y.H. Incident were not unique.

By the mid-1980s, however, male workers became increasingly active. In 1985, a strike at Daewoo Motors signaled that workers could mobilize autonomously (i.e., independently of FKTU) against a major *chaebŏl* (Ogle 1990: 109–31). By 1987, workers had taken center stage in national politics (CISJD 1987; Nodongbu 1988).

A crucial change in the 1980s was the rise of working-class consciousness. As I have argued, egalitarianism became a widely shared ideal in South Korea after the Korean War. Land reform and the Korean War created a material condition for relative equality; throughout the 1960s and 1970s, South Korea boasted one of the most equal distributions of income in the Third World (Adelman 1974: 284; H. Koo 1984). It stands to reason, therefore, that working-class consciousness should have been stunted in South Korea. Why, then, did it arise?

By the mid-1980s, a new and apparently rigid class structure had appeared. The gulf between the ideology of egalitarianism and the fact of inequality generated conflict. Although the absolute poverty rate declined from 23 percent in 1970 to 10 percent in 1980, the popular perception was that income distribution had worsened over the same period (Leipziger et al. 1992: 16). Even the putatively meritocratic examination system seemed to reproduce a preexisting inequality. High test scores and entrance to prestigious universities depended on urban residence, access to cram schools, and the ability to hire private tutors, all out of reach for the child of the average worker.

In addition, wealth inequality was profound. Its clearest manifestation was the reemergence of land ownership as a crucial marker of social distinction. In the late 1980s, I was often told that single women looked for land (or luxury apartment) ownership, rather than a Seoul National University degree, in selecting a husband. In the late 1980s, over 70 percent of Seoul residents did not own land, and a chronic housing shortage plagued urbanites (Leipziger et al. 1992: 6–7). At the 1987 Berlin Habitat Conference, South Korea was named as "one of the two countries [the other was South Africa] where evictions by force are most brutal and inhuman" (ACHR 1989: 1). The life of the urban poor was described as "a living hell of despair and dehumanization" (CCA-URM and ACPO 1987: 7). The absence of any meaningful social welfare measures further debilitated the urban poor (Kim Yŏng-mo 1990: 104–15; Cho Hŭi-yŏn 1993: chaps. 7–8). By 1988, the modal urban poor household consisted of five people with the men working as day laborers and the women as street vendors. The total monthly household income was $300, from which $70 went for a single-room rental, and $220 for food, leaving only $10 as disposable income (ACHR 1989: 12).

Inequality and class distinctions were stitched into the very fabric of everyday life. The geography of inequality was well-marked (D.-S. Hong 1992). The sights and smells of the poor neighborhoods were visceral class markers. Maids were part and parcel of luxury apartment living in Seoul, while car ownership often implied the service of a chauffeur. These relations of servitude made class distinctions an inescapable reality of urban life. At its most extreme, class prejudices were openly expressed; consider the personal narrative of a factory worker:

> Women working in factories are *kongsuni*; men working in factories are *kongdoli*. *Kongsuni* and *kongdoli* are contemptible guys, nothing worth counting, just loose folks. They call us this way as a whole group. We have to be *kongsuni* even if we hate it, simply because we are working in factories. If someone asks us where we are working, we simply say, "I work at a small company." But *kongsuni* cannot really hide their identity. They show it however hard they try to do makeup and dress up nicely. They pay more attention to clothes, hairdo, and makeup in order to hide it. People fault us for spending money on appearance without making enough money, but our reason is to take off the label of *kongsuni* they put on us. (H. Koo 1993: 152)

In the 1980s labor struggles, the rhetoric of class struggle was plainly evident. At a major demonstration at a *chaebŏl* plant, one pamphlet described white-collar workers as "family members" but blue-collar laborers as "livestock" of the corporation (Watanabe and Fukagawa 1988: 102).

Class—or the divide between the rich and the poor—became a leitmotiv of South Korean protest in the 1980s. Not surprisingly, South Korean sociologists highlight the fact and the perception of class inequality in 1980s South Korea (Sŏ Kwan-mo 1984; Hong and Koo 1993: 196–205; H. Koo 1993: 132).

THE RISE OF THE 'MINJUNG'

The 1980s were characterized by not only the expansion of pro-democratic forces but also the articulation of a powerful antigovernment ideology that bound hitherto separate groups. Authoritarian rule spawned the radical ideology known as *minjung* (literally, "the people")—defined by Tong Hwan Moon (1982: 12) as "oppressed people with a long history of struggle"—and the ubiquitous expression of *han*. This populist ideology became a powerful lens through which to describe and condemn the status quo and served as a shared discourse among agents of social change (Takizawa 1984; Abelmann 1993a; Wells 1995).

The genealogy of *minjung* ideology recapitulates the heroic struggles of the Korean people, including the late-nineteenth-century Tonghak Peasant Rebellion and the 1970 self-immolation of Chŏn T'ae-il. Even more than these historical highlights, the 1980 massacre at Kwangju marked a decisive turning point in the radicalization of students and intellectuals. Im Ch'ŏru's 1984 story, "A Shared Journey," is suggestive of the impact of Kwangju. The protagonist accompanies a friend, who has been in hiding from the authorities, on a night train. The train runs over a woman and as it moves past the corpse, the protagonist has a flashback:

> The moment we saw these things, the blanket with which we had desperately tried to cover our nightmares was mercilessly snatched away. And finally, beneath that blanket we were exposed in our humiliating vulnerability. Beneath that blanket were the chilling memories of the rage of our hometown.

In this epiphany, the Kwangju Massacre, student dissidence, and antigovernment sentiment converge.

The ideology of *minjung* was critical in consolidating opposition to authoritarian rule. In traditional Korea, as I noted, status distance was enormous. The inegalitarian structure was buttressed by Confucian ideology, which justified privilege as well as penury and separated the rulers from the ruled. In spite of rising egalitarian sentiments, the social and ideological gulf between intellectuals and workers (and farmers) persisted in the contemporary era. The April Student Revolution, the anti-Normalization Treaty struggles, and the early anti-Yusin activities were all led by a narrow social base of the educated middle class.

Beginning with the dramatic self-immolation of Chŏn T'ae-il, the political oppression of intellectuals and the economic exploitation of workers and farmers converged. Religious, particularly Protestant, leaders took moral and practical charge of the efforts to ameliorate working-class conditions (Y. Yi 1990). Social interactions with the victims of South Korean development radicalized a significant minority of the expanding Christian community. Similarly, urban intellectuals, particularly students, turned their attention to social issues in the 1970s. Already concerned with the government's disregard for human rights and civil liberties, they found even greater injustice in the afflictions of the poor.

By the 1980s the ideology of *minjung* came to characterize the South Korean culture of dissent. It was at once a mobilizing myth and a philosophy of history. A Christian pamphlet exhorted: "The fundamental structure of history is contradictory relations between the powerful and the powerless, in which the powerless people suffer" (ECCKP 1975: 28). Reverend Cho Wha Soon (1988: 121), who ministered among female factory workers in the 1970s, wrote: "A people's movement . . . cannot be actualized through the unity of a few intellectuals. In a people's movement, the people must become the subject. Only when the people move can a new society be made." *Minjung* history narrated an epic struggle of the Korean people against external and internal oppressors (e.g. HMY 1986). Novels of epic proportions, such as Pak Kyŏng-ni's *T'oji* (Land) (12 vols., 1969–88) and Cho Chŏng-nae's *T'aebaeksanmaek* (T'aebaek Mountain Range) (10 vols., 1986–89), reinscribed people's struggles in the making of Korean history (U. Kim 1993: 185–92).

The discourse of *minjung* pervaded all spheres of South Korean social life. In the realm of literature, the influential literary critic Paik Nak Chung's transformation best captures the changing intellectual terrain. In 1969, Paik promoted *simin munhak* (citizens' literature). Yet in the course of the 1970s, his focus shifted from *minjok munhak* (ethnic literature) to *minjung munhak* (people's literature) (Paik 1993; see also S.-K. Kim 1991: 101). The sociologist Han Wan-sang's 1978 *Minjung kwa chisigin* (People and Intellectuals) identified *minjung* as the subject of history, thereby sundering a long tradition of intellectual leadership, and by the mid-1980s he was advocating a *minjung* sociology as well (Han Wansang 1984).

There was, in effect, a counterculture of South Korean development that challenged state rule and championed *minjung*. In the realm of literature and the arts, *minjung* became a powerful source of inspiration and an object of celebration. The poet Kim Chi Ha, the folksinger Kim Min-gi, and many others were silenced by the state and thrown in jail (S.-K. Kim 1991: 99). But the cultural movement spread far beyond well-known artists and writers (Standish 1994; C. Choi 1995). One significant strand was the effort to recapture native, populist cultural traditions, such as shamanism and farmers' music. On college campuses in the 1980s, the drum beats, the dances, and the songs of "traditional" Korea were inescapable.

The heightened intellectual interest in *minjung* led to serious and radical analyses of the urban poor and the working class. *Minjung*-oriented political economists wrote searing critiques of the South Korean economy (Yi and Chŏng 1984; Pak et al. 1985; Pak Hyŏn-ch'ae 1988). Despite censorship, radical social theory, including Marxism, enjoyed considerable vogue (HTH 1989; Kim and Cho 1990; HSSY 1991).

Minjung political economy in its early phase was exemplified by the work of Pak Hyŏn-ch'ae. Although there had been earlier critics of South Korean political economy, such as Cho Yong-bŏm (1973, 1981) and Yu In-ho (1979, 1982), Pak came to exemplify *minjung* economics (see also Kim et al. 1981). In a series of books, he argued for a self-sufficient economy oriented toward *minjung*, rather than the government's construction of a subservient and anti-*minjung* economy (Pak Hyŏn-ch'ae 1978, 1983). In addition, Latin American dependency theory (Packenham 1992) became widely read in conjunction with the Seoul Spring of 1980. Translated works of Samir Amin and Andre Gunder Frank, along with a spate of English- and Japanese-language surveys, appeared beginning in 1980 (Pyŏn and Kim 1980; Yŏm Hong-ch'ŏl 1980), and distributing them had become a cottage industry by the mid-1980s (Kim Chin-gyun 1983; Yŏm Hong-ch'ŏl 1983; H.-C. Lim 1985).

By the mid-1980s, these two strands of *minjung* political economy had turned on each other. Probably the signal forum was the October 1985 issue of *Ch'angjak kwa pip'yŏng*, featuring Pak Hyŏn-ch'ae and Yi Tae-gŭn. In brief, while Pak characterized South Korea as state monopoly capitalism and stressed the importance of the labor and farmer movement, Yi characterized South Korea as a semiperipheral capitalist economy and emphasized the primacy of democratic movements (see also Pak Hyŏn-ch'ae 1984 and Yi and Chŏng 1984). Although the leading journal of South Korean dissidence, *Ch'angjak kwa pip'yŏng*, would be banned after that issue, the debate on the nature of South Korean society continued in an increasingly divisive fashion (e.g. Pak and Cho 1989; see also HSYH 1990; Takizawa 1992a: chaps. 5–6). Seoul bookstores, especially those near college campuses, were replete with social science books, especially of critical bent. The debate over the nature of South Korean society came to incorporate ever more diverse intellectual influences; I was often shocked to see "respectable" Western Marxist books side by side with "vulgar" Soviet tracts. In effect, the American intellectual hegemony over South Korean social science had been challenged by Marxism and other schools of leftist thought (e.g. Yi Chin-gyŏng 1986). It became difficult to find a non-Marxist among sociology graduate students at the elite universities in Seoul by the late 1980s. Some radical sects went so far as to embrace Kim Il Sung's *chuch'e* ideology. Even as the Soviet empire was collapsing, many students eagerly read about the impending demise of capitalism. In this regard, the American scholar Daniel Chirot's (1994: 259) experience is exemplary:

> On three visits to South Korean universities in 1989 and 1990, I was repeatedly struck by the tenacity with which young South Korean leftist academics could deny the progress going on under their noses, even as they admired a North they believed to be the genuine representation of Korea. The South, in their mind, was only an American colony.

The impact of *minjung* thought was such that, even at elite financial firms, younger employees could be found reading radical analyses of the South Korean economy.

TWO CHRISTIANITIES

The rise of South Korean dissent can be seen in the development of *minjung* Christianity. Christianity entered Korea in the 1880s, first through French Catholic and later through American Protestant missionaries. Its identification with modernity and independence struggles ensured its popularity among educated urbanites. Its phenomenal expansion in post-Liberation South Korea was due to a complex of factors. Many Christians from the Pyongyang area, its pre-Liberation stronghold, moved south. South Korea's first president, Rhee Syngman, was Christian (B.-S. Kim 1990: 52). Christianity became a badge of modernity, especially because of its association with America. Its egalitarian tenor resonated with women and the less privileged. The process of massive rural exodus and the feeling of urban dislocation allowed Seoul's churches to offer communal support, while the persistence of personal ties facilitated chain conversion (Yu Tong-sik 1987: 146–48; B.-S. Kim 1990: 53–56). The total Christian population of South Korea was 2 million by the early 1970s, 10 million by the early 1980s, and reached nearly one-third of the population by the early 1990s (D. K. Suh 1990: 44).

Mainstream Christianity had been nonpolitical and tacitly supported the values of state-led development (D. K. Suh 1990: 29). The Yŏŭido Full Gospel Church in Seoul—the world's largest church with over 800,000 members—features an eclectic blend of traditional shamanism, this-worldly concerns, and Christianity. Harvey Cox (1995: 222–23) describes its "Hallelujah-robics":

> It is a form of dancing to hymns played to an ear-piercing rock beat by an ensemble of electric organ, drums, accordion, and other instruments. The dancing is led by enthusiastic teams from the church's youth division. When the music stops temporarily the congregation takes up what sounds like the religious equivalent of the cheers used at an Ohio State football game. . . . [M]any begin praying in words and phrases of no known language. Then more singing begins, with the songs arranged to the tune of pop melodies. The worshippers rock back and forth and wave their arms. Sometimes the band increases the tempo of the

song . . . and the people move faster and faster until, no longer able to keep it up, they stop in happy exhaustion.

A common theme in the church's sermons is material success. Indeed, as the popular equation of Christianity with modernity suggests, mainstream Christianity benefits from its symbolic association with worldly goods. The zeal of the South Korean Pentecostals has given the world another export; South Korean missionaries—from Moonies to mainline Protestants—are proselytizing around the world, from Japan to Soviet East Asia and the Americas (Mullins 1994).

In contrast to Yŏŭido Full Gospel Church's all-too-worldly celebration, there is another Christianity associated with struggles against oppression (D. Clark 1995). If the Pentecostals celebrate economic growth, then *minjung* Christianity exposes its underside (Kang Ton-gu 1992: 165–201). Although there is a long history of Christian involvement in education, health, and other nonpolitical work, the 1957 formation of Young Catholic Workers and the 1958 Presbyterian Church's industrial evangelism initiated greater Christian involvement in secular affairs (CISJD 1985: 31; Kang In-ch'ŏl 1992). From urban slums to rural areas, Christian groups spearheaded social reform efforts (H. Sohn 1989: 62). Using Saul Alinsky's grassroots organizing methods, the Urban Industrial Mission was active by the late 1960s (CISJD 1981). In addition, Christians, such as Mun Ik-hwan, were central to the anti-Yusin struggles (Yu Tong-sik 1987: 158–73). In particular, the Easter Sunrise Incident of April 22, 1973, marked the first major show of opposition to the Yusin regime (H. Sohn 1989: 58–63). The 1976 Myŏng-dong Incident, when dissidents gathered at the Myŏng-dong Catholic Church on the anniversary of the March First Movement, established Christians as a leading force in the antigovernment struggle (K. Nam 1989: 98–101).

By the 1980s, *minjung* Christianity was a visible force in South Korea. Beginning with the theological efforts to indigenize Christianity in South Korea, *minjung* Christianity developed as a South Korean counterpart to Latin American Liberation Theology (CTC-CCA 1983; Berryman 1987: 164–67). When the African American theologian James Cone visited South Korea in 1975, he was moved

by the struggles of South Korean Christians to write: "For the Koreans who were engaged in the struggle for justice and democracy
reminded me of my own people who have made similar commit-
ments in order to fight against white racism" (Cone 1993: 363).

THE RISE OF ANTI-AMERICANISM

The rise of anti-Americanism was another cultural expression
of the conflicts and contradictions of South Korean development.
Dissidents condemned the United States for sustaining authoritarian rule and for virtually every ill of post-Liberation Korea.

The United States, as I have stressed, played a powerful role in
South Korea. One manifestation of South Korean cultural dependence is the preponderance of South Korean politicians with im-
probable American names, such as Patrick Henry Shinicky (Sin Ik-
hŭi) and John M. Chang (Chang Myŏn). My father, for example, decided on my American name before my Korean name.

The South Korean state ensured that the public held favorable
views of the United States. It was not merely government propaganda, however, that led the Office of Public Information (1955:
2–3) to declare: "We want to say, first of all, that [South] Korea's
gratitude toward the United States is beyond the power of words
to express. Anti-Americanism can never exist in this land. Never
shall our friends hear the cry of 'Yankees, go home.'" Prime Minister Chung Il Kwon told a *New Republic* reporter in the late
1960s: "Where else in Asia are you welcome? Others say, 'Yankee
Go Home.' We alone say, 'Come and establish more bases here'"
(Campbell 1969: 9). Roh Tae Woo (1990: 12) said in a 1989 speech:
"While my country strove endlessly to build a thriving democratic
nation from the poverty and ruin of war, the United States stood
beside us, shoulder to shoulder. For that, the Korean people's gratitude has never wavered."

The pro-American feelings were not, however, often recipro-
cated. Some Americans expressed contempt for, and even racist
sentiments about, Koreans. This was clear as early as the immediate post-Liberation era. The U.S. commander in South Korea, General Hodge, claimed that Koreans "are the same breed of cats as the
Japanese" (Lauterbach 1947: 201). A lieutenant told the Chicago

Sun correspondent Mark Gayn (1948: 349) in 1946 that Koreans were "dirty and treacherous" and that "psychological Warfare [is] the only way to show these gooks we won't stand for any monkey business." According to Alfred Crofts (1960: 544), who served in the United States military government in Korea, his colleagues turned the forebear of Seoul National University into barracks: "I protested that to humiliate scholars is a diplomatic blunder in Confucian society. 'These Gooks,' retorted a Colonel Blimp, 'don't need colleges! Let's close the places up and train them to be coolies.'" The journalist Albert Axelbank (1967: 11), after concluding that he found "little trace of anti-Americanism" in South Korea, offered a caveat that "incidents involving American GIs continue to jar the Koreans" and the following anecdote:

> Some 200 Katusas, or South Korean soldiers attached to US Army units, became enraged and staged a hunger strike. What happened was that a US Army mess sergeant, piqued because he thought the Koreans spread too much jam on their bread, stabbed one Korean in the left eye with a fork, after which he pulled out a pistol and challenged the other Koreans. Memories of such incidents last a lifetime.

Even in the early 1990s, it was still common to hear U.S. soldiers call South Koreans "gooks" and worse.

It should come as no surprise that the respect that South Koreans felt for U.S. cultural and economic might often translated poorly in personal encounters. South Korean literature is full of negative depictions of Americans and American cultural influence (Hahm 1984: 44). A 1976 survey of university students demonstrated the ambivalence in U.S.–South Korean relations (H.-S. Lim 1982: 36–37). This was, in fact, nothing new. In 1946, for example, one survey claimed that one-half of Koreans preferred Japanese colonial rule to U.S. occupation (Lauterbach 1947: 247). Growing South Korean confidence in the 1980s made U.S. military presence problematic (Lee Sookjong 1995: 23). The waning of the North Korean threat made the U.S. military occupation of Yongsan, prime real estate in the middle of Seoul, a visible bone of contention. By the mid-1990s, as Katherine Kim (1996: 28) writes: "Many Koreans believe all GIs are racist young men with little education from rural areas of the U.S." The continuing U.S. support for authoritarian governments, moreover, eroded South Koreans' respect for the United States, especially during the Yusin period. An American writing in the 1970s reported that "my [South Korean] friends see the U.S. forces in Korea and the lack of all but the most benign protests as a symbol of our support for President Park's repression" (McGleish 1977: 101).

Particularly crucial in the rise of anti-Americanism was the U.S. complicity in the 1980 Kwangju Massacre (J. Kim 1989: 761; E. Chang 1992; Shorrock 1996). The U.S. State Department's official response to the Kwangju Uprising, released on May 27, 1980, read as follows: "We recognize that a situation of total disorder and disruption in a major city cannot be allowed to go on indefinitely" (D. Clark 1988: 14). Ronald Reagan's 1983 visit to South Korea generated a great deal of negative sentiments. As Kim Young Sam said at the time: "I had no objection to Mr. Reagan coming here, but his visit should not result in support for the dictatorial regime" (*Time*, November 28, 1983: 44).

Radical students traced South Korean political authoritarianism to U.S. imperialism and military presence. This is the context in which the U.S. Information Service in Pusan was burned in March 1982. Such militant expressions of anti-Americanism became common in the mid-1980s, when students seized U.S. cultural centers and attacked consulates in major cities. As a student movement pamphlet from the mid-1980s charged, the South Korean political system "is a colonial fascist system through which US imperialism and its lackeys have trampled all over the people's democratic rights and national independence, with guns and swords" (CISJD 1986: 46).

In the 1980s, the relationship between the United States and South Korea became a contested topic. Anti-American sentiments carried over into the 1990s, due in large part to trade pressures (D. Clark 1991). There were concerted movements to boycott U.S. commodities, including films (Lent 1990: 122–23). The anti-American movement reflected a xenophobic strand in the culture of dissent. A college student stated: "What we eat is closely related to what we think. We don't want to lose our nationalistic spirit and pride to the taste of Western food. . . . Besides we don't want to pay royalties for what we eat" (*Korea Times,* December 5, 1989: 7). Especially for the student movement, the United States became inextricably linked to military rule and to the failure of reunification (Kang Sŏng-ch'ŏl 1988; Ch'oe Sang-yong 1989).

THE CONTRADICTIONS OF MILITARY MODERNITY

The *minjung* movement and its ideology expressed the contradictions of military modernity. By emphasizing economic growth, the military regime imagined a particular trajectory of South Korea toward national greatness. It valorized materialism and modernity, while preaching anticommunism and nationalism. The very achievement of economic growth and of modernity, as we have seen, generated a social basis for political democracy. By the late 1980s, every ideological prop of military rule had fallen.

Consider nationalism. Cultural nationalism in South Korea originated in the anticolonial independence struggles against the Japanese (C. S. Lee 1963; M. Robinson 1988). As I discussed in Chapter 3, the initial phase of military rule championed populist nationalism. The following passage from Park Chung Hee (1962: 117–18) could have been written by a radical South Korean critic in the 1980s: "The masters of Korean history—the people—had been in long hibernation. . . . We must grasp the subjectivity of the Korean nation, restore the spiritual pillar of Korean history." However, the military rulers of South Korea squandered this source of legitimacy by pursuing nonpopulist policies.

Consider the value of modernity. Military rule came in conflict with the popular perception of modernity. Mass schooling and mass media, even as they regimented the populace, also introduced emancipatory ideas and desires. As Tu Wei-ming (1991: 759) observed: "The irony is that the military junta attempted to revitalize a sense of pride in the Korean past, whereas the cultural elite, the descendants of the *yangban* aristocracy . . . became Westernized and iconoclastically anti-Confucian." In this regard, university students exemplified the contradictions of military modernity. Higher education was necessary in order to train the technocrats and engineers who were to bring about South Korean development. But the university system engendered the most spirited opposition to military rule. A step toward modernity was, in essence, a move away from military rule. By the late 1980s, the vast majority of the middle class regarded military rule as an embarrassing anachronism: in their opinion, modern nation-states are democratic, only backward Third-World countries have military governments. For many South Koreans, the correlation of advanced industrialism and political democracy meant that the military government had to go.

In a related vein, during the 1980s the regime's emphasis on anticommunism gave rise to an anti-anticommunism among the regime's opponents. The cultural delegitimation of anticommunism became part and parcel of South Korean democratization. By the mid-1980s anticommunist ideology had lost its edge, especially among the younger educated population. By the late-1980s many people were nonchalant about civil defense, and the defacing of the posters about North Korean spies had become fairly common (Winchester 1988: 188–89). The fear of the North, in short, dissipated, albeit by no means completely.

The burden of state ideology therefore fell on material achievement. The crucial underpinning of South Korean state nationalism was the celebration of GNP growth. Precisely because of its rapidity, many South Koreans experienced economic growth—however unevenly distributed—as a tangible benefit. Never mind that exploitation and super-exploitation occurred; ordinary South Koreans were given radio and black-and-white and color television in a matter of a few decades. While in 1970 only 2 percent of South Korean households owned refrigerators, 4 percent telephones, and 6 percent televisions, the comparable figures by the late 1980s were 75 percent, 50 percent, and virtually all (Lockwood 1988: 4). By 1983, a popular song, "Oh! South Korea" ("Ah! Taehanmin'guk"), sung by a young female singer, Chŏng Su-ra, openly celebrated South Korean development. The Panglossian lyric described South Korea as a land of urban and rural harmony: "Everyone enjoys happiness here / A place that is always free. . . . We can get what we want / We can achieve what we wish" (Takizawa 1992b: 197–99).

Nonetheless, economic growth in time generated its opposition. As Albert Hirschman (1981: 40) argues, the tolerance for inequality may be high in the initial stages of economic growth, but it withers away over time. He uses the following analogy:

Suppose that I drive through a two-lane tunnel, both lanes going in the same direction, and run into a serious traffic jam. No
car moves in either lane . . . I am in the left lane and feel de-
jected. After a while, the cars in the right lane begin to move.
Naturally, my spirits lift considerably, for I know that the jam
has broken and that my lane's turn to move will surely come
any moment now. . . . But suppose the expectation is disap-
pointed and only the right lane keeps moving: in that case I,
along with my left lane co-sufferers, shall suspect foul play, and
many of us will at some point become quite furious and ready
to correct manifest injustice by taking direct action.

In *grosso modo*, this is what happened in South Korea in the late
1980s. The mass media—especially soap operas on TV—put the
unmistakable wealth of an urban minority on display for all to see.
Conspicuous consumption, exemplified in modern, sprawling department stores, became visible to a large segment of the urban
population. The show of material plenty and the unleashing of
consumer desires combined to turn trickle-down goods into a
Barmecidal feast.

To recapitulate, rapid industrialization created the social basis
of political democracy. The *minjung* movement united hitherto
separate social groups into an entrenched antigovernment political force. But one may still wonder why a permanent democratic
solution was not possible in 1980. Why did the democratic dream
of the Seoul Spring turn into an authoritarian nightmare? Political opposition and cultural changes are insufficient to explain political democratization; the force from below is a necessary but an
insufficient condition.

THE DIFFERENTIATION OF ELITE POWER

Rapid industrialization created alternative sources of gover-
nance and hence contributed to the creation of a polyarchy in
South Korea. As the state expanded and the economy developed,
the sources of elite power became differentiated, which rendered
authoritarian rule tenuous.

Elite power was concentrated under Rhee and Park. Rhee's control over the repressive state apparatus—he used the police to quell

internal dissension and the military to counter both internal and external threat—gave him dictatorial power. The Park regime expanded the police and the military and added the KCIA to forge a troika of naked power. The growth of despotic power coincided with the expansion of infrastructural power. Military officers were placed in powerful nonmilitary organizations. By 1975, 66 percent of the cabinet and 22 percent of the National Assembly were military personnel (Han Kye-ok 1989: 142). Furthermore, as I discussed in the previous chapter, Park exercised considerable power over the *chaebŏl*. Although Park experienced a persistent legitimation crisis, elite power was concentrated and unified.

By the 1980s, however, the military no longer monopolized political and economic power. The expansion of state infrastructures inevitably brought with it the differentiation and diffusion of despotic authority. Because of bureaucratic differentiation, the military itself became less cohesive (Choi Jang Jip 1989b: 222–32). Power differentiation was also evident in the state bureaucracy. By the late 1980s many of the 500,000 local government officials were at best lukewarm to military rule (Clifford 1994: 8). Furthermore, as the *chaebŏl* grew, they relied less and less on state support, which led to their gradual independence from the military in particular and the state in general. Their new independence was evident in their involvement in frenzied real estate speculation in the 1980s against explicit state disapproval. By the late 1980s rapid corporate growth and the development of the stock market had begun to replace the state as a source of financial support (Clifford 1994: 243–44).

Consider the difference between Park and Chun. Park amassed tremendous power and manipulated his closest associates to consolidate and strengthen his position (Lie 1991b: 39–40). Chun, in contrast, could never act as a one-man leader. His constant manipulation of political parties reflected his need to widen his support base. While Park had a very small group of trusted associates, Chun had to rely on a larger, informal network, the Hanahoe (Cho Kap-je 1989: chap. 1; Han Kye-ok 1989: 137–46). Park often acted unilaterally, but Chun's authority was much more circumscribed. In short, by 1987, the power elite was no longer monolithic and hence was vulnerable to a system-wide crisis.

THE FALL OF CHUN

Chun saw his political support plummet in the mid-1980s. Plagued by worker discontent, a disenchanted middle class, and continual domestic corruption scandals (Cho Kap-je 1989: 50–58), Chun turned to brute force to maintain power. But authoritarian terror—even though it may be effective for time—cannot last for long.

Changing international politics further doomed Chun's rule. The waning Cold War—exemplified by Gorbachev's *glasnost*— weakened U.S. support for hardline anticommunist rule (Billet 1990: 301–2). As reports of torture and other forms of state terror began to surface, U.S. support for military rule generated opposition not just within South Korea but in the United States as well (Palais 1986; Oxman, Triffterer, and Cruz 1987). *The New Republic*, for example, noted matter-of-factly: "South Korea is one of the most policed countries in the world" (North 1986: 15). Although the United States remained tepid in opposing military rule—U.S. Secretary of State George Shultz stated that "we are not going around twisting arms in any egregious way" (Lord 1987: 28)—it was far from enthusiastic about Chun or his regime.

Two contingent factors proved important. First, the "People Power" movement in the Philippines and the resulting 1986 democratization left a deep imprint on South Korea (Jin-Hyun Kim 1986: 26; Huntington 1991: 103). As Kim Dae Jung said in 1986: "Next it is Korea's turn" (Desmond 1986: 55). He also declared that "the Philippine situation will have a domino effect on other Asian countries fighting for democracy" (*Time*, March 24, 1986: 51). Second, the 1988 Seoul Olympics made political democracy desirable. The elite and the educated middle class alike worried about the gaze of the world; political democratization was widely seen as a necessary accompaniment to South Korea's economic development. Certainly, the televised images of riot police, tear gas, and rock-throwing students embarrassed South Korean business people. As the *Far Eastern Economic Review* reported the political implications of the Olympics for South Korea: "Indeed, when historians analyse the turbulent events of 1987–88, the desperate desire to keep the Olympics, as much as the political and social dynamics fueled by the nation's surging economy, will figure as one of the most important reasons behind the remarkable transformation from authoritarian to a new and more democratic order" (McBeth and Clifford 1988: 53).

In this context, Chun Doo Hwan's April 13th announcement to annul a democratic transition—to renege on his promise to serve only one term—incited the already mobilized populace to a new level of activism (S. Han 1989a: 286–87). Citing the need to prepare for the upcoming Olympics, Chun claimed that national debates over revisions to the constitution would "split public opinion and waste national energies" (Chua-Eoan 1987: 38). Facing daily demonstrations and constant strikes, Chun stepped up repressive measures. Middle-class opinion swung decisively against him as clashes between the security police and the student movement intensified. In response to state violence, citizens mobilized in a show of defiance. The death of Yonsei University student Yi Han-yŏl during a demonstration inspired a million people to march through central Seoul on June 9, 1987. Even those who had stood solidly behind the economic growth strategy—government bureaucrats, corporate managers, and technicians and engineers—feared Chun's continued rule and his transformation into another Park (Clifford 1994: 264–66). Former bystanders now joined the students to become demonstrators themselves.

The ruling regime faced a protorevolutionary situation (CISJD 1988a). The cost of maintaining authoritarian rule rose precipitously. Rather than risk a civil war, the military opted for democratization (Lie 1991b: 46–49). Chun stepped down, to be replaced by his right-hand man, Roh Tae Woo. In the face of strikes and demonstrations during the hot summer of 1987, Roh enunciated an eight-point democratization program, capitulating to the democratic demands of the opposition. As he announced: "I stand before history and the nation with an extraordinary determination to help build a great homeland in which there is love and harmony among all segments and strata of the population, in which all are proud of being citizens and in which the government can acquire wisdom, courage and genuine strength from the people" (M. Lee 1990: 145). He promised a presidential election and a series of reform measures (Maeda 1988: 10–11; Choi Jang Jip 1989b: 292–310).

The demands of the Seoul Spring had finally been met. As one ruling party official put it: "I thought [Roh] was reading the opposition's platform" (Doerner 1987: 34). The opposition politician Kim Young Sam concurred: "I think [Roh] has given us all that we wanted" (Doerner 1987: 34). Chun himself said on television a few days later: "Our politics must now cast aside its old shabby ways, which are incongruous with our level of economic development, and thus achieve an advanced form of democracy that we can proudly show to the world" (Doerner 1987: 34).

As David Hume (1987: 57) noted more than two centuries ago: "Though men be much governed by interest . . . even interest itself, and all human affairs, are entirely governed by *opinion*." The opinion in South Korea by 1987 had swung decisively for political democracy.

The 1988 Seoul Olympics: The Celebration of South Korean Development

The rivalry between Kim Young Sam and Kim Dae Jung ensured Roh's victory in the December 1987 election (M. Lee 1990: 124–26). In his inaugural address, Roh stated: "The day when freedoms and human rights could be slighted in the name of economic growth and national security has ended. The day when repressive force and torture in secret chambers were tolerated is over" (West and Baker 1988: 137). Chun himself made a public apology: "The seven and a half years when I ruled are now condemned as the age of authoritarianism and irregularities. I am responsible for this. I am very sorry" (M. Lee 1990: 155). Chun's pathetic plea was the revenge of the deferred dream of the 1980 Seoul Spring. Public inquiries into corruption under the Fifth Republic and the Kwangju Uprising dominated South Korean politics in the late 1980s, while the slush-fund scandal led to the arrest of not only Chun but Roh by 1995 (B. Ahn 1995).

The 1988 Seoul Olympics marked a rite of passage for many South Koreans. It was the second time—after the Korean War— that South Korea had taken center stage. An estimated one billion people watched the September 17, 1988, opening ceremony (Larson and Park 1993: 8). It was almost impossible not to be cognizant that the other Asian Olympics, the 1964 Tokyo Olympics, heralded Japan's recovery of its place among the advanced industrial countries. Twenty-four years later, the Seoul Olympics was celebration of similar accomplishment for South Korea.

The triumphant tone of the South Korean establishment is clear from Roh Tae Woo's (1990: 45) speech: "I am convinced that the Seoul Olympics are going to be recorded not only as the biggest Games ever in which the East and West came together for the first time in twelve years, but also as the most splendid Olympiad, outshining any staged in the developed world." Never mind that North Korea boycotted the Seoul Olympics; the participation of the Soviet Union and China was only the beginning of Roh's *Nordpolitik*.

The celebration of the 1988 Olympics was far from a solipsistic act. South Koreans were extremely self-conscious about outsiders' gaze and reaction. Impression management was at work everywhere. The state and corporations spent huge sums to beautify South Korea and South Korean products. As the head of the Seoul Olympic Organizing Committee Park Seh-Jik commented:

> The Games changed the Korean people's view of the world and the world's view of Korea. The world's view of Korea had been mostly formed by the dark days of war-torn Korea. The Seoul Olympic . . . wiped the image away. Television showed a pearl of a city—modern, active, prosperous and peaceful. Since the Seoul Olympics the Korean people have been treated with more respect and so have Korean-made products. (Larson and Park 1993: 190)

Citizens endeavored to be polite to tourists, cleaned the streets, and even cut down on driving to lower the pollution level. The mood of good will and self-congratulation was ubiquitous. After the June 27th, 1987, declaration and the 1988 Olympics, political democracy finally seemed secure in South Korea.

CHAPTER SIX

South Korean Development
in Retrospect

In three decades, South Korea transformed itself from my childhood conception of backwardness to a modern country. Although
hindsight often promotes a sense of inevitability, South Korean development was neither fated nor obvious. The narrator in Yi Munyol's novel *Our Twisted Hero* expresses the sense of surprise at
how things turned out:

> The large conglomerates, which I had felt to be castles built on
> sand, were gradually prospering; my old colleagues who had
> stayed on were being promoted to section chiefs and to depart-
> ment chiefs, their faces shining with success. One of my school
> contemporaries had put his hand on real estate, and already from
> leases alone he was a regular in the golf clubs; a friend of mine
> opened a hole-in-the-wall agency of some sort, made a pile of
> money selling some product—he didn't even know what it was
> for—and now was swaggering around. Another contemporary of
> mine I thought had become a soldier was sitting in a nice un-
> dreamed-of post in the central government. And another fellow,
> who failed even as an entrance exam repeater and finally got
> into a school that was absolutely the pits, now somehow or
> other had got himself a Ph.D. in America and was going around
> with the mien of a professor. (M. Yi 1995: 113–14)

The unexpected advancement of the country as a whole is reflected in the surprising success of individuals.

In this chapter, I present a brief survey of South Korea in the mid-1990s, highlight some changes, and recapitulate the major factors in South Korean development.

South Korea in the Mid-1990s

After a narrow electoral victory in 1987, Roh's ruling Democratic Justice Party suffered a defeat in the 1988 parliamentary election (H. N. Kim 1989: 486). Progressive voices—exemplified by the success of the left newspaper, *Han'gyŏre Sinmun*—seemed dominant (Maeda 1988: 275–78); the ruling party and the government remained objects of derision as reports of corruption and malfeasance dominated the mass media (S. Han 1989b: 31–32).

By 1989, however, the conservatives were once again dominant. The state retracted progressive policies and cracked down on dissent after the 1988 Olympics. The National Security Law was invoked to arrest the opposition (Kihl 1990: 69–70). The progressive Teachers' Movement was banned (Asia Watch 1990: 63–71). The conservatives also seized this opportunity to consolidate their forces. In 1990, all the major opposition political parties, except for Kim Dae Jung's Party for Peace and Democracy, merged to form the Democratic Liberal Party (Dong 1991: 11–12), which was a conscious imitation of the Japanese Liberal Democratic Party, which dominated postwar Japanese politics (Jackson 1990: 6).

In the 1992 presidential election, Kim Young Sam eked out a plurality of votes (42 percent) against Kim Dae Jung (34 percent) and the founder of Hyundai, Chung Ju Yung (16 percent) (Bedeski 1994: 52–55). Kim's cabinet featured many prominent intellectuals and opponents of military rule, including the *minjung* sociologist Han Wan-sang as deputy prime minister and the political scientist Han Sungjoo as foreign minister. The dominance of Seoul National University graduates led the Japanese sociologist Hattori Tamio (1993: 28) to proclaim the return of the *yangban* elite. The civilian element had gained the upper hand over the military. Kim Young Sam himself was a long-term opponent of military rule. The former presidents Chun and Roh were arrested in 1995 and sentenced to death in 1996 for abuse of power. The 1995 local elections, which were widely regarded as clean and fair,

seemed to entrench the principle of representative democracy
(J. Oh 1996).

In terms of foreign policy, South Korea began to make an aggressive adjustment to global geopolitics. The state and corporations promoted *Nordpolitik* to strengthen South Korean relations
with the People's Republic of China and with many former communist countries (Kang Yŏng-ji 1991: 34–50). The large presence
of ethnic Koreans in China and the former Soviet Union facilitated
ties to countries that had once been enemies (Burton 1992: 4). By
the mid-1990s, the dominant political slogan was globalization
(*segyehwa*) (C. Moon 1995).

South Korean economic success resulted in tougher trade and
technology transfer negotiations with the United States and Japan
(Bennett 1991: 49–53). South Korea was pressured to liberalize its
import and financial markets (Yi Yŏng-u 1991: 299–311). Furthermore, escalating wage costs in South Korea and competition from
other newly industrializing economies posed serious challenges to
South Korean manufacturing exports (cf. S.-K. Cho 1985b: 77–84).
In response, South Korea invested more in research and development to undertake higher value-added production (cf. J. Yoon 1989,
1992).

Many *chaebŏl* underwent significant restructuring to become
more competitive in the global market. Facing trade barriers in the
United States and Japan, South Korean enterprises cultivated markets in Europe, Southeast Asia, and the former communist bloc
(B. J. Ahn 1991: 30–38). In addition, foreign direct investment, especially to Southeast Asia, skyrocketed (Fukagawa 1992). Total
South Korean foreign direct investment was just under $32 mil-
lion in 1985, the figure had passed $1 billion by 1991 (S. W. Hong
1993: 14). Import restrictions in the United States and the lure of
low-waged labor led many South Korean textile factories to relo-
cate as far away as the Caribbean Basin (S. W. Hong 1993: 14–16),
where they introduced not only capital and infrastructure but also
draconian labor practices (Pred 1992).

In South Korea itself wages rose steadily and labor unrest diminished. However, major strikes continued into the mid-1990s,
such as the June 1994 railway and subway strike (Dicker 1995:
13–16) and the January 1997 nationwide strike. Signs of newfound

affluence were readily apparent; a veritable consumption explosion began in the late 1980s (Chŏn Kyŏng-su 1992). The luxurious lifestyles of Seoul's middle-class residents generated intense national debate. Meanwhile, the paucity of South Koreans willing to work at low wages increased the number of ethnic Koreans from China and migrant workers from poorer Asian countries (Sŏl 1992; Yi Uk-chŏng 1994). At the same time, lured by the expanding economy, South Koreans educated in the United States returned to their home country.

Although *minjung* rhetoric persisted into the 1990s, the opposition discourse shifted dramatically. The radical debate over the nature of South Korean society peaked in 1989, with the widely discussed eight-part series in *Han'gyŏre Sinmun* in June 1989. Thereafter, intellectual discussions focused on democracy and civil society (HSHC 1992; Yi Ki-ung 1992; Choi Jang Jip 1993c) or on the latest Western intellectual imports, such as postmodernism. Bookstore shelves devoted to radical social criticism rapidly disappeared in the 1990s. Furthermore, new issues superseded *minjung* politics (Nakagawa 1990: 170–88). Citizens focused their concern on issues such as the land speculation scandal known as the Suso Incident (Han To-Hyŏn 1992). The new social movements, including those agitating for women's rights, the environment, and other causes, preoccupied the media and the middle class (HTH 1993; NCY 1993).

The end of the Cold War renewed hopes for the reunification of the two Koreas, but the travails of German unification brought the calculation of costs to the fore (H. S. Lee 1994; Eberstadt 1995a; J. Bae 1996). As the possibility of reunification loomed, the burning passion for it seemed to wane among the affluent middle class (cf. C. S. Kim 1988).

Is South Korea Another Japan?

By the 1990s, books like *Is Korea the Next Japan?* (T. K. Kang 1989) and *Asia's Next Giant* (Amsden 1989) queried South Korea's competitiveness with Japan, while periodical headlines such as "Korea's Challenge to Japan" (Smith 1984) and "Asia's Next Powerhouse" (Neff and Nakarmi 1991) had become common. Many

South Koreans were bullish about their future. One factory manager told a British journalist in the mid-1990s that South Korea
would surpass Japan by the end of the century because "Koreans
are fundamentally superior" (Mallaby 1995: 3; cf. Fallows 1994:
375). Others were skeptical. Noting that South Korean GNP was
less than one-tenth that of Japan, James Abegglen (1994: 58) wrote:
"It is sometimes asked whether [South] Korea will be a 'second
Japan.' The question is as grotesque as the suggestion that Canada
or Brazil will be a 'second United States.'"

Many Japanese remain wary of the South Korean challenge. The
question of whether South Korea will surpass Japan has been a
topic of discussion in Japan since the 1980s (e.g. Adachi 1986). But
in terms of production technology and marketing prowess, South
Korean enterprises remain years behind their Japanese counterparts. Indeed, the very alarm expressed by the Japanese economic
elite about the South Korean threat makes it unlikely that South
Korea will surpass Japan, and the pervasive arrogance in South Korea itself may make it impossible.

Social and Cultural Transformations

Foreign observers often highlight the continuities of South Korean society—images of poverty, war, and authoritarianism lin-
gered for a long time. Simon Winchester (1988: ix) wrote his impressions of South Korea as "frightfully cold, for a start. The Korean people are wretchedly *unfriendly*. Terribly violent place.
Nothing to eat but cabbage." Pico Iyer (1988: 49) noted "the stub-
born spirit of the place," which "is mostly the result of a long history of war, invasion, occupation, resistance, war, destruction, re-
birth, peace—and war."

In a period of massive social and cultural change, however, very
few impressions were likely to withstand the test of time. Michael
Shapiro (1990: 12) noted in the late 1980s: "I have been in South
Korea on and off for much of the year and have begun to feel as if I
were locked in a small room with a manic-depressive, feeling the
alternative pulses of ebullience and melancholy. . . . But in [South]
Korea everything matters." Yet, by the mid-1990s, nothing seemed
to matter. All conviction and intensity had faded, the dull com-

pulsions of organizational life and material desire ruled. Consumerism seemed to thoroughly legitimate South Korean development (cf. Yu Mun-mu 1993).

In considering South Korea from the Korean War to the 1988 Olympics, the crucial transformations are clear enough: from poor to rich, unschooled to overschooled, rural to urban, and farmers to factory and office workers. In the immediate post–Korean War period, most South Koreans were poor. By the 1990s, South Korean per capita GNP was approaching those of poorer OECD countries. While only 6 percent of South Korean households owned TVs in 1970, the figure had risen to 99 percent by 1985. Conspicuous consumption, along with status competition, reigned in urban life. While South Korean newspapers regularly published names and photos of *paksa* (Ph.D. recipients) until the late 1960s, by the early 1990s there were said to be over 100 unemployed American sociology Ph.D.'s in Seoul alone (cf. G. Kim 1989: 238–40). English was the foreign language of choice; the command of classical Chinese—that signifier of literary cultivation—became as rare as the number of Chinese characters in most books. While many university students read a few pages of *Das Kapital*, most are ignorant of the *Analects*. In 1955, more than three-fourths of the population lived in towns and villages with fewer than 50,000 people; by 1990, more than three-fourths lived in cities with over 50,000 people. Seoul alone accounted for one-fourth of the total population. In the mid-1950s, three-fourths of South Koreans were engaged in agriculture; by the mid-1990s, fewer than one-fifth (for these figures, see CISJD 1988c and Lie 1992a).

CHANGING FAMILY AND GENDER RELATIONS

As early as the late 1960s, the South Korean sociologist Lee Hae-yong (1969: 56) wrote: "In the present-day Korea, the patriarchal extended family system, which once was an ideal pattern for the traditional Korean society, is fading away in both the ideological and physical facets." Traditional Confucian practices and ideals, such as ancestor worship and parental authority, steadily declined (E. Yi 1993: 278–80; cf. Kim Dongno 1990). A new conception of the family as a "place to rest," or a haven in a heartless world, had emerged (E. Yi 1993: 365–69). The reproduction of cultural idiom masked the transformation of cultural practice. Consider the example of filial piety. In a 1964 survey, 50 percent of farmers considered the concept to mean "obedience to parents." By 1984, only 6 percent of college students agreed with that definition; 85 percent thought it meant "living a healthy life of my own" (S.-c. Hong 1985: 116). Quite clearly, filial piety meant something different to 1980s university students than it had to farmers two decades before. The respect for the elderly, one of the cardinal social principles of traditional Korea, was clearly on the wane by the 1990s. Until the 1970s, people were quite unlikely to smoke or drink in front of their elders. Yet by the 1990s, the older norm was being superseded by the putatively modern practice. One of my students, who claimed to be a staunch conservative, had no qualms about smoking in my presence. When I inquired about the contradiction between his belief and practice, he merely noted that that was part of the bad tradition. He was, however, quickly angered by the sight of his female peers smoking in his presence.

Notwithstanding the persistence of patriarchal values, gender relations also changed. It is a common refrain that the situation of South Korean women is horrible and that it is due to traditional patriarchy. R. Malcolm Keir (1914: 829), writing in the early twentieth century, pithily noted that Korean "women are treated as slaves." Donald Portway (1953: 110), in the mid-century, wrote: "In general the behaviour of Korean men in their social relations to women is marked by an aloofness possibly unsurpassed by any other nation in the world." In Chosŏn Dynasty Korea, Neo-Confucianism justified the subservience and inferiority of women. *Yangban* women were systematically excluded from political and economic life (Y. Chang 1983; Deuchler 1977). The necessity of female labor in farm households, however, tempered the ideological devaluation of women. Ethnographic accounts of farm life indicate that, despite the ideological profession of male superiority, male-female relations were relatively egalitarian. Although in the *yangban* neighborhoods, "women remain mostly inside their own homes," in the non-*yangban* neighborhoods, "women join in some of the discussions, talking back to men" (Brandt 1971: 46, 48). Farming women created a distinct women's sphere in contradistinction to the male sphere pervaded by Confucianism (Janelli and Janelli 1982: 24–25).

In Korea, the first stirring of women's emancipation occurred primarily among Western-influenced elites. Enlightened *yangban* men propagated progressive ideas on women (S. Choi 1986). My maternal great-grandfather, Yi Hae-jo, wrote a novel, *The Liberty Bell* (*Chayujong*), which didactically discusses the importance of women's liberation. Throughout the colonial period and immediately thereafter, most women active in the public sphere hailed from *yangbąn* background (Y.-c. Kim 1986).

South Korean women's movements became active in the 1970s (Yi Sun-ae 1989; C. Choi 1992: 111–16). Middle-class women began to participate in the public sphere, roughly replicating the Western experience albeit in a compressed time frame. In the 1980s, predominantly middle-class women's groups participated in pro-democratic and other political movements (Palley 1990: 1138). "Alternative Culture" (Tto hana ŭi munhwa) was organized in 1984, the Korea Women's Association (Han'guk yŏsŏng tanch'e yŏnhap) in 1987. Inspired by Western feminism, a wholesale ideological reevaluation of South Korean institutions and discourses occurred (Cho Hae-joang 1988; THM 1988; Louie 1995). Feminist critics assailed marriage and the family system as patriarchal institutions and products of patriarchal ideology (THM 1990; YHSY 1990; Yi et al. 1991; Yun and Cho 1993; cf. Kendall 1996), while others worked for legal changes to redress gender discrimination (S.-K. Cho 1991).

NATIONALISM AND THE MINORITIES

As I discussed in Chapter 5, nationalism became deeply ingrained in South Korea. The military regimes sought legitimation via nationalism from above; the culture of dissent championed *minjung* and promoted nationalism from below. These conflicting nationalisms nonetheless converged in drawing a heroic lineage of colonial-period independence struggles and projecting a triumphant view of a future Korean nation.

In spite of the positive aspects of nationalist sentiments, one deleterious consequence was the denial of heterogeneity. The ritual invocation of South Korea as an ethnically homogeneous coun-

try adversely affected minority groups. Although it would be foolish to deny that South Korea is relatively homogeneous, it would
be equally foolish to deny the existence of minorities altogether.
If nothing else, the denial may perpetuate the difficulties facing
the existing minorities. One sizable, albeit often overlooked, group
is the mixed-race children, estimated to be about 25,000 in the
1980s (S. B. Lee 1987: 83). In a 1965 article, the life of one mixed-
race child, Annie Park, was summarized as follows:

> At six, she followed her Korean mother to a ramshackle bar and
> discovered that her mother was for sale to U.S. servicemen. On
> the way home, alone, the little girl had an even more traumatic
> experience: a man lured her into an alley and assaulted her. At
> eight, she learned why classmates jeered "half-caste!" at her: her
> father had been a white G.I. At 16, she was a full-fledged prosti-
> tute working among American soldiers who liked her slim Oc-
> cidental legs and ample breasts. (*Time*, December 10, 1965: 43)

The Chinese minority, returning ethnic Koreans from China,
Japan, and elsewhere, and descendants of outcast groups face social discrimination as well (Hirai 1993: 92–107). Regional discrimination—most clearly against people from the underdeveloped
Chŏlla provinces—existed in marriage and employment (E. Yu
1990: 37–39). Many *chaebŏl* openly refused to hire people from
certain regions in the 1980s (Janelli 1993: 136–37). Fervent nationalism at times led to xenophobic expressions (Hurst 1985:
442–443).

ECOLOGICAL DESTRUCTION

South Korea's rapid industrialization wreaked havoc on the
countryside. This is ironic given Donald Macdonald's (1990: 6)
claim that "Korean culture lays great emphasis on the country's
natural environment." The fundamental reason for the pollution
of South Korea was the state's single-minded stress on economic
growth (e.g. Eder 1996). In accepting pollution-producing industries from Japan, South Korean corporations and the state ignored
the pollution that ravaged Japan in the 1960s. The World Health
Organization declared in 1978 that Seoul's air had the highest sul-
fur-dioxide content among the major cities of the world (Bello and

Rosenfeld 1990: 98). Onsan, the site of a major industrial center located on the southeastern coast northeast of Pusan, became an ecological nightmare (Han et al. 1988: 132–33), while the Kumi Industrial Complex experienced a major chemical spill in April 1991, threatening Taegu residents (D. Shin 1993: 243). A particularly tragic case was the death of Mun Sŏng-myŏn in 1988. Mun, just fifteen years old when he died, worked in a thermometer factory where, later reporters found, mercury was streaming on the floor like water. Only three months after working in the factory, he fell suddenly ill and died of mercury poisoning (Nishina and Noda 1989: 163–64). In addition, South Korea was one of the highest pesticide users in the world until the 1980s, when measures were finally taken to curb agricultural pollution (Bello and Rosenfeld 1990: 96–97).

Only in the late 1980s did the environmental movement begin to make an impact (Ch'oe Kyŏng-ae 1992; Kim Chin-gyun 1993; Ku 1994). The first survey on environmental awareness in 1982 revealed that over 70 percent of respondents were either "somewhat" or "very" concerned about the environment. One crystallization of this intellectual concern was the 1986 publication of *Han'guk ŭi konghae chido* (The Pollution Map of South Korea) (HKMY 1986), which vividly demonstrated the extent of environmental degradation. In the 1987 wave of the democratization movement, there were three major demonstrations devoted to environmental causes (S.-H. Lee 1993: 361–63). In 1990, for example, the residents of Anmyŏn Island protested against the government plan to store nuclear wastes on the island (D. Shin 1993: 242). As the middle class articulates its grievances, there is likely to be a growing movement for governmental vigilance. Here, again, the example of Japan is at work. Just as pressure from antipollution groups beginning in the late 1960s, along with sheer economic calculus, shifted polluting industries out of Japan to South Korea and elsewhere, South Koreans began to export their most polluting industries to Southeast Asia in the mid-1980s.

Needless to say, I cannot capture all the dimensions of social and cultural change. Nonetheless, the fact of a major social transformation is not deniable. For South Koreans in their thirties and

older, the shift from the old way (*kusik*) to the new (*sinsik*) occurred, as I suggested in the prelude, right before their eyes. From
the material culture and the built environment to interpersonal
relations and intimate thoughts, many South Koreans experienced
phenomenal changes within a few decades.

Explaining South Korean Development

An adequate explanation of South Korean development requires
that we consider the consequences of land reform and the consequent change in class structure; the character of the developmental state; the economic, political, and human dimensions of the production and reproduction of low-paid labor; and the effects of the
international political-economic environment. These factors, moreover, must be understood in terms of concrete historical sequence.
In this book I attempted to explicate South Korean development as
a structured sequence; here, I highlight the major factors.

LAND REFORM

Capitalist development entails not only the rise of the working
class but also the appearance of the industrial bourgeoisie. The
very emergence of these two classes in South Korea depended crit-
ically on land reform. Most agrarian societies are dominated by
landed oligarchs, who are often hostile to industrialization and favor continued peasant exploitation and rentier profiteering. Peasants are trapped on the land because of the lack of opportunities
elsewhere or leave the land only to eke out subsistence in the urban informal sector.

Before the colonization by Japan in the early twentieth century,
the vast majority of the Korean population was engaged in agriculture, while the minority lived off the surplus of peasant labor.
After the end of Japanese colonial rule in August 1945, the external pressure exerted by the United States and the Korean War and
the internal demand generated by peasant struggles led to a sweep-
ing land reform.

Land reform unleashed massive structural changes. The traditional landed class disappeared, which removed a potent obstacle
to industrialization. The *yangban* elite henceforth sought careers

in the state bureaucracy or business enterprises. The post-Liberation land reform also transformed landless tenants into small landholders. But the state preference for industrialization exploited the agricultural sector and contributed to a massive rural exodus. The outflow of farmers into the urban areas created a pool of cheap labor.

THE DEVELOPMENTAL STATE

Land reform was a necessary but insufficient condition for South Korean development. There was limited industrialization in the 1950s due to the triple alliance among the United States with its aid, Rhee and the state, and dependent capitalists. U.S. support and foreign aid sustained elite rule and bureaucratic corruption. By the 1960 Student Revolution, a handful of individuals had amassed spectacular wealth through monopoly profits and rents, while the economy remained less than dynamic.

The developmental state that emerged after the Student Revolution and the 1961 military coup decisively rechanneled the flow of capital into industrial production. Park's chronic legitimation crisis heightened the importance of economic growth. The developmental state prevented the excessive penetration of foreign capital, while soliciting external loans and technology transfers. It provided capital and credit to the *chaebŏl* and protected the domestic market while encouraging exports. The state shaped the *chaebŏl* to execute its economic goals and prevented the capitalist class from backsliding into a stagnant, rentier class.

LABOR EXPLOITATION AND FEMALE SUPER-EXPLOITATION

There is little doubt that export-oriented industrialization fueled dynamic growth in South Korea. Buoyed above all in the late 1960s by the demands generated by the U.S. intervention in Vietnam and the integration in the Japanese economic sphere, South Korean exports expanded. Low-cost labor enabled South Korean enterprises to undercut their global competitors in such industries as textiles, electronic goods, and footwear.

State policy sought to disorganize workers and to forestall their demands for higher wages. Capitalist domination and exploitation went unimpeded. The KCIA and the police, reinforced by corporate goon squads, squelched labor activism. The Yusin regime overrode extant labor regulations to support management and silence worker grievances.

The untrammeled pursuit of cheap labor led to an extreme dehumanization of the industrialization process. Wages were lower than in developing economies and often fell below the socially necessary minimum. Female workers' conditions were especially dire, characterized by long working hours, low pay, and harsh managerial discipline.

Labor exploitation inside and outside factories was crucial in promoting export through cheap labor. The exploitation of women was instrumental in accumulating crucial foreign exchange earnings to promote heavy industrialization, infrastructural development, and export-oriented light industrialization.

INTERNATIONAL POLITICAL ECONOMY

Land reform, the developmental state, and low-paid labor— three inextricably intertwined factors—were crucial in propelling South Korean development. These internal factors, however, are necessary but insufficient to explain economic growth. It is impossible to ignore the international environment.

The geopolitical significance of the United States to South Korea cannot be overemphasized. The threat of North Korea—and behind it the specter of international communism—provided ample motivation for the United States to offer vital military and economic support to South Korea. The U.S. military presence generated revenues for South Korea and contributed to the development of the repressive apparatuses. In particular, the Vietnam War proved South Korea's value as a strategic ally of the United States. South Korea not only supplied combat soldiers but also products to fill the demands generated by the U.S. intervention in Vietnam. The Vietnam War provided a major spur to South Korean industrialization.

Regional division of labor also played a critical role. South Korea followed the ascent of Japan toward higher value-added production. The production and export niches vacated by the Japanese were filled by South Korea. Japan was also important in transferring much-needed capital and technology to South Korea, without which South Korean development might never have occurred.

The relatively open international trade regime of the 1960s and 1970s favored South Korea's export-oriented industrialization strategy. While exports moved relatively freely, the South Korean state tightly controlled imports.

IS THE SOUTH KOREAN MODEL REPLICABLE?

The indisputable economic development of South Korea inevitably beckons imitators. As Manmohan Singh, the finance minister of India in the early 1990s, asked: "What does South Korea have that India doesn't?" (*Economist*, May 23, 1992: 21). Most accounts of South Korean development offer guidelines for other developing countries (Amsden 1989: 320–24; P. Kuznets 1994: 133–35). But the South Korean model is unsuitable for the aspiring economies of the 1990s.

To put it simply, the conditions that fueled South Korean development do not exist in most developing countries. Land reform remains an urgent agenda in many Third World countries. Powerful landed oligarchs prevent redistribution of land and often oppose all efforts to industrialize. The state's capacity to promote development remains circumscribed in countries with a powerful agrarian elite. Dependence on transnational corporations and IMF-imposed austerity measures also limit governmental decision-making authority in many developing economies. Powerful labor unions in some countries prevent the possibility of cheap labor.

The international political economic environment has also changed. The advanced industrial economies are less open to free trade in the 1990s, in part because they are wary of the emergence of new South Koreas. The penetration of transnational capital is ever more extensive and intensive in many parts of the world. Although industrialization will undoubtedly spread to other peripheral economies, this should not be mistaken as the Koreanization of the Third World.

However, even if it were plausible to dismantle state welfare functions and to intensify capital accumulation and labor repression, one must ask: at what cost? Industrialization occurred on the backs of factory workers and farmers, whose long work days and below-subsistence wages propelled the miracle. Indeed, suffering continues: stories of sweat shops with sub-minimal working conditions and below-subsistence wages, of sexual slavery and the attendant violence against women, of the farmers' growing debts, and of many more social problems fill the pages of the newspapers. Muffled cries of the invisible majority still clamor for justice in the pages of history books.

South Korean development also entailed a quarter-century of military rule. The KCIA was at one point the largest organization in the country. Protests against authoritarian rule resulted in the imprisonment and torture of countless people. Broken lives abounded in a country that was politically and intellectually stifled in the name of economic growth.

South Korea today is the envy of many developing countries; the prosperity and freedom which it enjoys have proven unattainable for many others. Yet that prosperity was made possible by a complex set of external conditions that no longer exist and was purchased at a cost so high that beneath the surface of material abundance South Korea remains a nation fraught with social problems and deep social divisions.

Postlude

One mark of affluence is a nostalgic yearning for the purity of poverty. Among impoverished and struggling people, the repose necessary for such reflection is in short supply. This was the case for South Korea in the post-Liberation period. Gregory Henderson (1980: 95) remarked: "Koreans are not specially prone to backward glances. . . . Korean culture seems now to lack the freight of nostalgia which Yi Dynasty *sijo* (classic Korean poetry) bring with them." As material desire became sated, nostalgia was unleashed.

The fulfillment of basic needs and the longing for the past is clear in Sonu Hwi's story, "Thoughts of Home." The protagonist says: "And, the more comfortable I have become, the more intense have grown thoughts of my old home" (Sonu 1980: 24). The story focuses on the father of the narrator's friend, who had fled North Korea in 1946, nearly two decades prior to the opening of the story, but who now desires only to re-create his childhood home in North Korea—down to the rats gnawing in the ceiling. The old man comes to resemble his own father and drowns while reaching out for what he thinks is his father's image but which is actually his own reflection in the water.

The desire for the past ironically, if predictably, increased with capitalist industrialization that literally pulverized tradition and the physical environment. In the 1970s, an American-educated South Korean told Robert Shaplen (1972: 142):

> When I came back [from the United States], I felt lost. I went to
> the country, to where my grandfather had lived, and there found
> all sorts of beautiful things—furniture, pottery, paintings—rot-
> ting away in a barn. I brought these back to Seoul, and now I
> have them in my house. They're part of the Korean heritage I
> have to rediscover if I'm going to be able to come to terms with
> modernization.

Such sentiments are common among South Koreans who have
lived abroad or among diasporic Koreans with strong ties to South
Korea.

By the late 1980s—along with the ubiquitous celebration of the
miracle on the Han—nostalgia became a palpable theme in many
popular novels and television dramas. In one TV show, the president of a company, who lives in an affluent home, disappears. As
family members and friends wonder about his whereabouts, a
close friend guesses correctly that he has gone back to his ancestral village. His wife finds him, perched on a rock by a stream,
staring blankly at nature. When she asks him why he left, he says
that he wanted to eat *ramyŏn* (instant noodles; shorthand for
cheap food) and enjoy nature. In effect, he wanted to return to the
simplicity of his upbringings, rather than live in the congested city
and eat Western food. Such a sentiment—an uneasy and ironic
mixture of nostalgia and resentment—is the stuff out of which ordinary lives come to be reckoned. My father spent much of his life
running away from the backwardness of his native village. Eventually he emigrated to the United States and thereby fulfilled one
of his life-long yearnings. Yet by the time of his retirement, he was
pondering whether he should live out his last years in his ancestral village. "Life would be cheap and simple," he said.

During the 1988 Olympics, people expressed their pride and de-
lightedly pointed to high-rises, highways, and high-class shops and
restaurants. Meanwhile, the government forcefully destroyed the
legacy of the bad old days: outdoor cafés and street vendors. The
cultural fabric of the nation unraveled: the spirit of the gift was replaced by the spirit of the deal, the investment, and the purchase.
The first generation was ambitious, but the second generation may
have been only greedy. People scurried back and forth, and the
daily greeting became "I am busy, you must be busy, too." On

buses in the 1960s, strangers rushed to offer my grandfather their seat. In the late 1980s, people scrambled their way into buses and subway trains, even if it meant shoving aside frail grandmothers. Stars have disappeared along with cows and fields; children spend nights in libraries attempting to get into good schools in order to get good jobs. And behind the surface glitz and material plenty, a significant minority toils and lives in shacks.

When I lived in Seoul in the late 1980s, I spent an inordinate amount of time at Insa-dong—the residential area of Chosŏn state officials and of Japanese colonial-period bureaucrats—which was one of the few places in Seoul with remnants of traditional Korea. Its used bookshops, craft stores, and traditional tea houses were a respite from the Japanese-style department stores and the American fast food franchises. Yet every time I returned I could see the encroachment of modern construction. As I pondered the past and the present, I came to lament the future. Sipping traditional Korean tea and watching the well-heeled businessmen in Western suits pass by, I could not help but recall a passage in Tacitus's *Agricola* (1970: 67), where he describes the Roman colonization of Britain: "The wearing of our dress became a distinction . . . and little by little the Britons went astray into alluring vices: to the promenade, the bath, the well-appointed dinner table. The simple natives gave the name of 'culture' to this factor of their slavery." Such a reflection is, of course, the privilege of an outsider and a product of the post-affluent West. Others view the same phenomenon as, willy nilly, development.

APPENDIX

Appendix: Salting the Past

Although it would have been tempting to narrate this book from the very beginning of Korea, such an account would have obscured, not illuminated, the dynamics of contemporary development.[*] It is not necessarily better, after all, to search farther into the past. Only the mythologically minded would start from Tan'gun, the first Korean according to the thirteenth-century *Samguk yusa* (*Memorabilia of the Three Kingdoms*). Furthermore, I disagree with explanations of South Korean development that stress the legacies of traditional Korea or even that of Japanese colonialism.

Tradition and Its Legacy

It seems sensible to appeal to traditional Korean culture, values, or national character to explain development (e.g. K. Chung 1956: 30–31). In this vein, Edward Mason (1982: 134) writes: "It is too much to say that South Korea has grown because it is occupied by Koreans but the individual and social discipline, work habits, passion for education, and desire for personal and family advancement that characterise that population have had a lot to do with it." Such blanket praise, however, is a generic characterization of most successful countries. The celebration of Korean character, culture, and values fails to explain

[*]Readers wishing an overview of Korean history should consult Eckert et al. (1990). I regret that Bruce Cuming's *Korea's Place in the Sun* (1997), along with the promised volumes of the *Cambridge History of Korea*, appeared too late for this book.

present success because the same set of factors has been used to explain past failures (e.g. Weems 1960: 14).

The temptation to try to capture the essence of a culture—the original sin of Orientalism—steers analyses away from history and heterogeneity. Cultural generalizations are notoriously fraught with pitfalls. Consider Louise Yim's (1951: 276) remark that "[Koreans] were and are volatile. We are called 'The Irish of Asia.'" Robert Shaplen (1972: 136) similarly observed that Koreans "have a sort of boisterous, Irish emotional range that shows in their spontaneity, their laughing and weeping and singing." Although such a characterization may have made sense in the agrarian 1950s, it rings hollow in the industrial 1990s. Peasant cultures, not surprisingly, exhibit numerous points of convergence. Russians, according to Lauterbach (1947: 244), thought Koreans to be much like the Poles. The Japanese anthropologist Nakane Chie (1973: 186) found South Koreans to be like Russians and Italians. One might ask: Shouldn't they have compared Koreans to the industrious Prussians, the ingenious Yankees, or perhaps even the diligent Japanese?

Indeed, the very assertion of Koreanness is problematic before the twentieth century. The absence of mass media and mass schooling hindered the integration and homogenization of the Korean population. Chosŏn Dynasty Korea was also a rigidly stratified society with limited geographical and status mobility. Regional differences and status inequality prevented, or at least hindered, the emergence of proto-national feelings among most Koreans (cf. Sin Yong-ha 1987: chap. 1). The *yangban*, like most elites from culturally backward areas, emulated the metropolis: which in Korea's case, meant China. Although the *yangban* were undoubtedly aware of their distinctive cultural, even proto-national, identity, a national culture as such hardly existed before the twentieth century.

Tradition is, moreover, not something that flows majestically and uninterruptedly through time. What passes as a venerable national tradition is often a recent invention to legitimate a particular lineage of state rule. Consider "Arirang," by now the undisputed national folk song of South Korea. According to David McCann (1979: 55–56), "Arirang" in its contemporary guise can be traced to the 1926 movie of the same title: "The various attempts to demonstrate a venerable pedigree for this national song have obscured its importance as a document in the social history of the transition period from traditional to modern Korea."

The contemporary construction of tradition aside, even "authentic" traditional Korea was far from static. Five hundred years of dynastic rule testify to the state's robustness but robustness should not be mistaken for stasis. The Confucianization of Korea was, for example, a long and protracted process (Haboush 1991; Deuchler 1992). The number and status of different groups of slaves shifted markedly during this period (Chŏn Tong-t'aek 1989). Agrarian technology changed (Yi T'ae-jin 1986: chap. 13), while commercialization proceeded with the rise and fall of different types of merchants (O Sŏng 1989). These examples can be multiplied to make the simple point that tradition is ever in flux.

The question is how to make sense of continuities and discontinuities. Rather than project a reified contemporary understanding of traditional Korea onto the past, we should trace contemporary ideas, practices, and institutions to a concrete time period. There are obviously continuities in family lineages, linguistic usages, and cultural practices. However, nominal continuities often mask qualitative ruptures. No one doubts that Seoul, albeit under different names, has existed for centuries. But the Seoul of 1900 would be a small regional city in contemporary South Korea and cannot be compared to the current city of over 10 million people. Or compare the state in the Chosŏn period and in the 1980s. The Chosŏn state lacked a national police force; indeed, in the mid-nineteenth century there were only 330 magistrates for a country of perhaps 10 million people (Palais 1975: 12). In contrast, by the late 1980s, there were nearly a million people in the military and the police, as well as 500,000 local government officials (Clifford 1994: 8).

Tradition in and of itself does not explain South Korean development.

Some scholars nonetheless seek the origins of later development in traditional, or Chosŏn Dynasty, Korea. There are two principal explanatory efforts.

The "sprouts" (*maenga*) of capitalism, in one argument, were nipped by Japanese colonial rule (Kim Yong-sŏp 1970; Kajimura 1977). This argument is a healthy antidote to the Japanese colonial-period historiography that portrayed Korea as a backward and stationary society (Yi T'ae-jin 1989: 115–26; Kang Sang-jung 1993).

Chosŏn Dynasty Korea was, however, far from achieving conditions for an autonomous capitalist development (cf. Palais 1996: 1018–19). Late-nineteenth-century Korea lacked adequate inland transportation and communication, a unified national system of finance, and an extensive interregional division of labor (cf. Kang Mangil 1984a). More important, there were no agents on the horizon who would have been capable of transforming the limited commerce in agricultural produce into modern trade and industries. The state lacked infrastructural capacity, while the *yangban* had little incentive to become merchants or industrialists. Urban dwellers were limited in number while peasants eked out subsistence. Capitalist enterprises and modern industries originated during the Japanese colonial period (Kobayashi 1975; Eckert 1991). Although the counterfactual possibility of autonomous development cannot be denied altogether, the search for the origins of capitalism in Chosŏn Korea seems quixotic.

A more popular explanation is the Confucian ethic thesis. Confucianism is said to stress learning and encourage hard work; the well-educated and disciplined labor force in turn spurs development (Harrison 1992: 106–9; K.-D. Kim 1994: 102–3; cf. Lie 1996b).

The impact of Confucianism on education and diligence is, however, ambiguous. Although Confucianism existed for centuries in Korea, it was only in the post-Liberation period that the U.S. military government and the Rhee regime institutionalized mass education. Furthermore, as late as 1960, the Filipino and Thai literacy rates were equal to that of South Korea. Thailand had instituted compulsory schooling as early as 1935 and its literacy rate was higher than that of South Korea in 1960 (Pak Kŭn-ho 1993: 5–6). Yet the Philippines and Thailand were neither influenced by Confucianism nor went on to experience the kind of development South Korea did. Education by itself is clearly inadequate to explain South Korean development (McGinn et al. 1980: 240–41). Furthermore, working hours have been long in other Asian countries without Confucianism or development. Although hard work is necessary, it hardly constitutes a sufficient condition for development. Slaves and peasants may toil to the point of physical exhaustion, but their blood and sweat do not necessarily lead to development (Tax 1953: 17–19).

The Confucian ethic thesis is a *post hoc* explanation. As Ernest Gellner (1981: 7) wryly remarks, Muslim economic growth would undoubtedly have prodded Ibn Weber to write *The Kharejite Ethic and the Spirit of Capitalism*. The Korean work ethic was certainly not evident to observers of traditional Korea. Isabella Bird, traveling through Korea in the 1890s, wrote:

> The energies of [Korean] people lie dormant. The upper classes, paralysed by the most absurd of social obligations, spend their lives in inactivity. . . . The lower classes work no harder than is necessary to keep the wolf from the door. . . . The author of the Korean Dictionary states that the word for *work* in Korean is synonymous with "loss," "evil," "misfortune," and the man who leads an idle life proves his right to a place among the gentry. (Bird 1986, 2: 278, 280; see also Gale 1898: 177)

In point of fact, Confucianism was widely regarded as a major obstacle to South Korean development. As Hong Yi-Sup (1973: 111) wrote:

"Confucianism was . . . a soil cultivating an authoritative [*sic*] and bu-reaucratic spirit and containing elements hindering modernization" (see also M. G. Lee 1982: 5). This is not surprising given that Confucianism was widely regarded as a philosophy that devalues pecuniary pursuits (Hahm 1967: 27–28; Palais 1975: 174).

There are qualitative differences between Chosŏn Dynasty Korea and contemporary South Korea. Twentieth-century Korea was no longer the land of "morning calm" but rather the land of "broken calm," as in Shannon McCune's (1966) apt subtitle. I am not dismissing Chosŏn Dynasty legacy *tout court*; it simply needs to be documented and argued. Tradition as such is an ideological construct; we need to trace concrete connections, whether in the realm of ideas, values, practices, or institutions, in order to make a case for the contemporary relevance of the past. In their absence, we should stress more recent and intervening influences and events to explain contemporary political economy.

Colonial Rule and Its Legacy

The Japanese intervention in Korea intensified gradually (Duus 1995). After defeating the Chinese bid to maintain its traditional dominance over Korea in the Sino-Japanese War (1894–95), Japan ensured its supremacy over Korea by winning the Russo-Japanese War (1904–5). What had already been part of the Japanese sphere of influence became a Japanese Protectorate in 1905. Five years later, Korea was annexed, thereby inaugurating thirty-five years of colonial rule (Beasley 1987; Unno 1995).

The Japanese colonial period, like all of modern Korean history, is rife with controversies and polemics. The popular South Korean view portrays the "thirty-six years of Japanese colonial rule" as a period of unmitigated disaster and social evil (Kang Man-gil 1984b: pt. 1). Japanese colonialism remains for many South Koreans a master metaphor for injustice and misfortune. In Sŏ Kiwŏn's 1963 story, "The Heir," the young protagonist asks his grandfather whether he had taken a civil service examination to enter the state bureaucracy. The grandfather replies: "By the time I was old enough for the examination, the Japanese were here, and the examination was banned" (K. Sŏ 1990: 172). In fact, the protagonist learns later that his grandfather, having been a dissolute youth, had no one to blame but himself for his failure. In a similar fashion, the rhetoric of Japan-bashing often masks the complexities of twentieth-century Korea.

Very few deny that Japanese colonialism entailed brutal police rule, racial discrimination, thought control, and the exploitation of peasants and workers. But colonialism also implicated Korea in the Japanese quest for power, wealth, and modernity and thereby lodged Korea inescapably on the stage of modern world history. The Korea of 1945 was indisputably not the Korea of the Chosŏn Dynasty period. Hence, some scholars stress the benefits, while acknowledging the costs, of colonial rule for South Korean development (Henderson 1973: 266–67; McNamara 1990: 3). In this line of argument, Japanese colonialism provided a powerful springboard for later development.

The search for the positive effects of Japanese colonialism neglects a crucial context. The fundamental truth of Japanese colonial rule is that Japan relentlessly pursued its own interests. The Korean economy was a classic case of an underdeveloped colonial economy. However, what is more crucial than the argument over costs and benefits of Japanese colonialism is that the colonial period provided a crucial background to post-Liberation political economy. The seeds of the modern economy and modern politics were sown during this period, including the explosive struggles of the immediate post-Liberation years.

THE IMPACT OF JAPANESE COLONIALISM

An export-oriented monocultural economy is a paradigmatic colonial economy. Surplus is seized by and repatriated to the colonizer. The encroachment of capitalist agriculture, furthermore, leads to the polarization of the peasantry. The indigenous ruling group retains its power by collaborating with the colonial power (Frank 1969: chap. 4).

The Japanese agricultural policy in Korea met many of the conditions of a classic export-oriented monocultural economy. Although the total agricultural output doubled between 1910 and 1941, much of the growth was siphoned off to Japan and the condition of peasants deteriorated in real terms (S.-C. Suh 1978: 167). Between 1915 and 1938, Korean peasants' consumption of all cereals declined; the per capita rice consumption dropped roughly 40 percent (Grajdanzev 1944: 118–19). According to Sang-Chul Suh (1978: 83): "Over 62 percent of total tenant-farm households were short of even the minimum amount of food required for an adequate diet."

Furthermore, commercialization, rigorously enforced taxation, and usurious interest rates increased the number of landless tenants. Tenant rents averaged over 50 percent and were as high as 90 percent (Grajdanzev 1944: 114). Between 1918 and 1938, the percentage of households with no land increased from 38 percent to 58 percent (H. K. Lee 1936: 148–61). As tenancy increased, a rapid rural exodus occurred. Although only 60,000 Koreans on average left agriculture from

1930 to 1935, the number rose to 220,000 per year between 1935 and 1940. By 1944, at least 10 percent of Koreans were living outside of Korea (Grajdanzev 1944: 81).

Agrarian commercialization, peasant impoverishment, and rural exodus nonetheless left the structure of local rule and land ownership largely intact (Cumings 1981: 41–48; G. Shin 1990: 6; Duus 1995: 395). The Korean agrarian elite—despite noteworthy exceptions—collaborated with Japanese colonial rule and thereby retained their local power.

If Japanese rule contributed to agrarian misery, then what about its industrialization efforts? As Andrew Grajdanzev (1944: 4) observed: "The very exercise of a domination over a colony demands railways, roads, some schools, and some hospitals." Furthermore: "The Korean economy was Japanese-owned and Japanese-directed" (G. McCune 1950: 37). The benefits of Japanese-imposed rapid industrialization did not trickle down to either the traditional Korean economy or to Korean workers (S.-C. Suh 1978: 155). The Japanese-created modern economic sector remained integrated into the Japanese, not the colonial Korean, economy (S.-C. Suh 1978: 111). Most bureaucrats, managers, technicians, and engineers were Japanese. Modern factories and electricity generators were largely located in northern Korea. What was left in South Korea was destroyed during the Korean War (Yi Tae-gŭn 1990). Rapid industrialization left little direct legacy for the post–Korean War South Korean economy.

The benefits of Japanese colonialism seem plausible because Japan delivered the modern to Korea. Modernity—whether Western architecture and industries, European ideas and arts, or cosmopolitan food and manners—were disseminated to Korea through colonial rule. What was true for the Japanese rule in Korea was true for the French rule in Morocco or the British rule in Egypt (Rabinow 1989: chap. 9; T. Mitchell 1991: chap. 3). The indelible affects and effects of colonial modernity—the universal feature of postcolonial societies—do not, however, lead to development in most postcolonial societies. The postmodern architecture of a Third World capital coexists with the premodern shacks for the majority of the population.

Neither does the existence of a Western-educated, modernizing elite guarantee national development. Long-term colonial rule requires the co-optation of ever larger numbers of the colonized population who benefit from it. South Korean officials, business people, and even intellectuals became part and parcel of colonial rule (Im Chung-guk 1966, 1982; M. Robinson 1988). Ch'ae Mansik's *Peace Under Heaven* (1993), originally published in 1938, is a fictional indictment of the material enrichment and the spiritual impoverishment of the

Korean elite under Japanese rule. Learning that his grandson had been arrested for being a socialist, Master Yun blurts out: "Don't ever forget to thank your lucky stars we live in this wonderful world, where the Japanese have mobilized a huge army . . . to protect us Koreans! It's a world of peace where we can keep what is ours and live in comfort! Peace under heaven, that's what it is!" The colonial elite—armed with modern administrative and repressive institutions—often perpetuate corrupt rule. Westernized Moroccans or elite Egyptians have been unable to achieve successful national development. As we saw in Chapter 2, even in post–land reform South Korea, elite rule impeded national development.

JAPANESE LEGACY FOR SOUTH KOREAN DEVELOPMENT

Although I have minimized the direct impact of Japanese rule for South Korean development, the colonial period profoundly shaped the trajectory of South Korean political economy.

Japanese colonial rule brought state centralization and national integration; Japan effectively created modern Korea. As Carter Eckert and his colleagues (1990: 254) argue: "By the end of Japanese rule in 1945, there was not one aspect of Korean life that lay unaffected by the pervasiveness and will of Japanese rule." Centralizing rule consolidated local governments and intensified institutional and police control over the country. The successive rulers of South Korea built on the Japanese repressive apparatuses.

Japanese colonialism also transformed Korean politics. The anticolonial, independence struggles—exemplified by the March First Movement of 1919—gave a powerful boost to both nationalist and communist movements (Kang Chae-ŏn 1986: chap. 8). Indeed, both Kim Il Sung and Rhee Syngman based their legitimacy on their participation in independence struggles against the Japanese. Furthermore, commercialized agriculture and rising tenancy had contributed to widespread local dissidence against Japanese rule (G. Shin 1990). Although there were only 15 tenancy disputes involving 4,000 peasants in 1920, at its peak in 1937, there were 31,799 disputes involving 77,515 people (Pak Kyŏng-sik 1973: 1: 281–82). Three decades of peasant dissent formed a crucial background for the immediate post-Liberation peasant mobilization.

The colonial period also sowed the seeds of modern industries. Capitalists, administrators, engineers, and workers, as well as managerial knowledge and the habits of industry, all had their start in the first half of the twentieth century (Eckert 1991). Throughout the later phase of the colonial period, the number of Korean-owned enterprises increased. Almost all of them were, to be sure, small-scale enterprises working in the interstices of the Japanese-controlled economy (Grajdanzev 1944: 175). Industrialization also accelerated urbanization and proletarianization.

Finally, Japanese influence proved to be pervasive throughout the post-Liberation period. The colonial government had mandated the Japanization (*kōminka*; literally, to become Emperor's people) of Korea, ranging from mass schooling to the enforced adoption of Japanese names and language (Miyata 1985: chap. 4). Although the Koreans resisted Japanization efforts, the Japanese legacy would persist especially among the educated elite. For example, Park Chung Hee, despite his professed anti-Japanese sentiments, was profoundly shaped by and remained an adherent of the Japanese military ethos (Han Kye-ok 1989: 35–38). The sheer geographical proximity and the lure of Japan's booming economy, not to mention a common language and at times shared school ties, influenced the architects and engineers of South Korean development. In the late 1980s, I was constantly struck by conspicuously Japanese mannerisms and phrases used by corporate executives, even by those for whom the colonial period was a distant childhood memory. It is impossible to make sense of South Korean development without acknowledging the pervasive, albeit often denied, influence of Japan.

REFERENCE MATTER

References

Abegglen, James C. 1994. *Sea Change: Pacific Asia as the New World Industrial Center.* New York: Free Press.

Abelmann, Nancy. 1993a. "*Minjung* Theory and Practice." In Harumi Befu, ed., *Cultural Nationalism in East Asia: Representation and Identity,* pp. 139–65. Berkeley: Institute of East Asian Studies, University of California.

———. 1993b. "Siblings, Soaps, and Social Mobility: South Korean Women's Mobility Narratives." Paper presented at the annual meeting of the American Anthropological Association, Washington, D.C.

———. 1996. *Echoes of the Past, Epics of Dissent: A South Korean Social Movement.* Berkeley: University of California Press.

Abelmann, Nancy, and John Lie. 1995. *Blue Dreams: Korean Americans and the Los Angeles Riots.* Cambridge, Mass.: Harvard University Press.

Adachi Tetsuo. 1986. *Kankoku keizai wa Nihon o nukuka: sono katsuryoku no gensen o saguru.* Tokyo: Kyōikusha.

Adelman, Irma. 1974. "South Korea." In Hollis Chenery, Montek S. Ahluwalia, C.L.G. Bell, John H. Duloy, and Richard Jolly, eds., *Redistribution with Growth,* pp. 280–85. New York: Oxford University Press.

———. 1980. "Economic Development and Political Change in Developing Countries." *Social Research* 47: 213–34.

———, ed. 1969. *Practical Approaches to Development Planning: Korea's Second Five-Year Plan.* Baltimore, Md.: Johns Hopkins University Press.

Agarwal, Bina. 1994. *A Field of One's Own: Gender and Land Rights in South Asia.* Cambridge: Cambridge University Press.

Aggarwal, Vinod K. 1985. *Liberal Protectionism: The International Politics of Organized Textile Trade.* Berkeley: University of California Press.

———. 1987. *International Debt Threat: Bargaining Among Creditors and Debtors in the 1980s.* Berkeley: Institute of International Studies, University of California.

Ahluwalia, Montek S. 1974. "Income Inequality: Some Dimensions of the Problem." In Hollis Chenery, Montek S. Ahluwalia, C.L.G. Bell, John H. Duloy, and Richard Jolly, *Redistribution with Growth*, pp. 3–37. New York: Oxford University Press.

Ahn, Byung-Joon. 1991. "Foreign Relations: An Expanded Diplomatic Agenda." In Chong Sik Lee, ed., *Korea Briefing, 1990*, pp. 23–38. Boulder, Colo.: Westview Press.

Ahn, Byung-young. 1995. "Korean Politics After Slush Fund Scandal." *Korea Focus* 3(6): 5–16.

Ahn, Junghyo. 1989. *White Badge.* New York: SoHo.

Allen, Richard C. 1960. *Korea's Syngman Rhee: An Unauthorized Portrait.* Rutland, Vt.: Charles E. Tuttle.

Amsden, Alice H. 1989. *Asia's Next Giant: South Korea and Late Industrialization.* New York: Oxford University Press.

———. 1992. "The South Korean Economy: Is Business-Led Growth Working?" In Donald N. Clark, ed., *Korea Briefing 1992*, pp. 71–96. Boulder, Colo.: Westview Press.

An Ch'un-sik. 1982. *Shūshin kōyōsei no Nikkan hikaku.* Tokyo: Ronsōsha.

Anderson, Kym. 1989. "Korea: A Case of Agricultural Protection." In Terry Sicular, ed., *Food Price Policy in Asia: A Comparative Study*, pp. 109–53. Ithaca, N.Y.: Cornell University Press.

Anderson, Perry. 1996. "Diary." *London Review of Books*, October 17, pp. 28–29.

Apel, Karl-Otto. [1979] 1984. *Understanding and Explanation: A Transcendental-Pragmatic Perspective.* Trans. Georgia Warnke. Cambridge, Mass.: MIT Press.

Asia Watch. 1990. *Retreat from Reform: Labor Rights and Freedom of Expression in South Korea.* Washington, D.C.: Asia Watch.

Asian Coalition for Housing Rights. 1989. *Battle for Housing Rights in Korea: Report of the South Korean Project of the Asian Coalition for Housing Rights.* Bangkok: Asian Coalition for Housing Rights, Third World Network.

Asian Women's Liberation Newsletter. 1983. "Outcries of the Poor Workers: An Appeal from South Korea." In Miranda Davies, ed., *Third World Second Sex: Women's Struggles and National Liberation*, pp. 233–39. London: Zed.

Axelbank, Albert. 1967. "Why the Reelection of Park Is Practically Certain." *New Republic*, April 29, pp. 9–11.

Bae, Jin-Young. 1996. "The Fiscal Burden of Korean Reunification and Its Impact on South Korea's Macroeconomic Stability." *Joint U.S.-Korean Academic Studies* 6: 185–202.

Bae, Kyuhan. 1987. *Automobile Workers in Korea*. Seoul: Seoul National University Press.

Bahl, Roy, Chuk Kyo Kim, and Chong Kee Park. 1986. *Public Finances During the Korean Modernization Process*. Cambridge, Mass.: Council on East Asian Studies, Harvard University.

Bairoch, Paul. 1988. *Cities and Economic Development: From the Dawn of History to the Present*. Trans. Christopher Braider. Chicago: University of Chicago Press.

———. 1993. *Economics and World History: Myths and Paradoxes*. Chicago: University of Chicago Press.

Baker, Edward J. 1982a. "The New South Korean Constitution." In Wonmo Dong, ed., *Korean-American Relations at Crossroads*, pp. 71–84. Princeton Junction, N.J.: Association of Korean Christian Scholars in North America.

———. 1982b. "Politics in South Korea." *Current History*, April, pp. 173–78.

Ban, Sung Hwan, Pal Yong Moon, and Dwight H. Perkins. 1980. *Rural Development*. Cambridge, Mass.: Council on East Asian Studies, Harvard University.

Baran, Paul A. 1957. *The Political Economy of Growth*. New York: Monthly Review Press.

Bark, Dong Suh. 1967. "Policy Making in the Korean Executive Branch." In Byung Chul Koh, ed., *Aspects of Administrative Development in South Korea*, pp. 30–64. Kalamazoo, Mich.: Korea Research and Publication.

———. 1984. "The American-Educated Elite in Korean Society." In Youngnok Koo and Dae-Sook Suh, eds., *Korea and the United States: A Century of Cooperation*, pp. 263–80. Honolulu: University of Hawaii Press.

Barnet, Richard J., and John Cavanagh. 1994. *Global Dreams: Imperial Corporations and the New World Order*. New York: Simon & Schuster.

Barnet, Richard J., and Ronald E. Müller. 1974. *Global Reach: The Power of the Multinational Corporations*. New York: Simon & Schuster.

Bartz, Patricia M. 1972. *South Korea*. Oxford: Clarendon Press.

Bauer, P. T. [1971] 1976. *Dissent on Development*. Rev. ed. Cambridge, Mass.: Harvard University Press.

Beasley, W. G. 1987. *Japanese Imperialism, 1894–1945*. Oxford: Clarendon Press.

Becker, David G. 1983. *The New Bourgeoisie and the Limits of Dependency: Mining, Class, and Power in "Revolutionary" Peru*. Princeton, N.J.: Princeton University Press.

Bedeski, Robert E. 1994. *The Transformation of South Korea: Reform and Reconstruction in the Sixth Republic Under Roh Tae Woo, 1987–1992*. London: Routledge.

Bell, C.L.G., and John H. Duloy. 1974. "Rural Target Groups." In Hollis Chenery, Montek S. Ahluwalia, C.L.G. Bell, John H. Duloy, and Richard Jolly, eds., *Redistribution with Growth*, pp. 113–35. New York: Oxford University Press.

Bello, Walden, and Stephanie Rosenfeld. 1990. *Dragons in Distress: Asia's Miracle Economies in Crisis*. San Francisco: Institute for Food and Development Policy.

Bennett, John T. 1991. "The South Korean Economy: Recovery Amidst Uncertainty and Anguish." In Donald N. Clark, ed., *Korea Briefing, 1991*, pp. 27–56. Boulder, Colo.: Westview Press.

Berger, John. 1979. *Pig Earth*. New York: Pantheon.

Berry, Sara. 1993. *No Condition Is Permanent: The Social Dynamics of Agrarian Change in Sub-Saharan Africa*. Madison: University of Wisconsin Press.

Berryman, Phillip. 1987. *Liberation Theology*. New York: Pantheon.

Bhagwati, Jagdish N. 1988. *Protectionism*. Cambridge, Mass.: MIT Press.

Biersteker, Thomas J. 1987. *Multinationals, the State, and Control of the Nigerian Economy*. Princeton, N.J.: Princeton University Press.

Billet, Bret L. 1990. "South Korea at the Crossroads: An Evolving Democracy or Authoritarianism Revisited?" *Asian Survey* 30: 300–311.

Bird, Isabella L. [1898] 1986. *Korea and Her Neighbours: A Narrative of Travel, with an Account of the Recent Vicissitudes and Present Position of the Country*. 2 vols. in 1. Rutland, Vt.: Charles E. Tuttle.

Bix, Herbert P. 1974. "Regional Integration: Japan and South Korea in America's Asian Policy." In Frank Baldwin, ed., *Without Parallel: The American-Korean Relationship Since 1945*, pp. 179–232. New York: Pantheon.

Block, Fred L. 1977. *The Origins of International Economic Disorder: A Study of United States International Monetary Policy from World War II to the Present*. Berkeley: University of California Press.

Bloom, Martin. 1992. *Technological Change in the Korean Electronics Industry*. Paris: Development Centre of the Organisation for Economic Co-operation and Development.

Boettcher, Robert. 1980. *Gifts of Deceit: Sun Myung Moon, Tongsun Park, and the Korean Scandal.* New York: Holt, Rinehart & Winston.

Bognanno, Mario F. 1987. "Collective Bargaining in Korea: Laws, Practices, and Recommendations for Reform." In Il Sakong, ed., *Human Resources and Social Development Issues*, pp. 108–80. Seoul: Korea Development Institute.

———. 1988. *Korea's Industrial Relations at the Turning Point.* Seoul: Korea Development Institute.

Bonner, Raymond. 1987. *Waltzing with a Dictator: The Marcoses and the Making of American Policy.* New York: Times Books.

Boone, Catherine. 1992. *Merchant Capital and the Roots of State Power in Senegal, 1930–1985.* Cambridge: Cambridge University Press.

Borden, William S. 1984. *The Pacific Alliance: United States Foreign Economic Policy and Japanese Trade Recovery, 1947–1955.* Madison: University of Wisconsin Press.

Bornschier, Volker, Christopher Chase-Dunn, and Richard Rubinson. 1978. "Cross-National Evidence of the Effects of Foreign Investment and Aid on Economic Growth and Inequality: A Survey of Findings and a Reanalysis." *American Journal of Sociology* 84: 651–83.

Brandt, Vincent S.R. 1971. *A Korean Village: Between Farm and Sea.* Cambridge, Mass.: Harvard University Press.

———. 1991. "South Korean Society." In Chong Sik Lee, ed., *Korea Briefing 1990*, pp. 75–95. Boulder, Colo.: Westview Press.

Brandt, Vincent S.R., and Man-gap Lee. 1981. "Community Development in the Republic of Korea." In Ronald Dore and Zoë Mars, eds., *Community Development: Comparative Case Studies in India, the Republic of Korea, Mexico, and Tanzania*, pp. 49–136. London: Croom Helm.

Braudel, Fernand. 1977. *Afterthoughts on Material Civilization and Capitalism.* Trans. Patricia M. Ranum. Baltimore, Md.: Johns Hopkins University Press.

Bray, Francesca. [1986] 1994. *The Rice Economies: Technology and Development in Asian Societies.* Berkeley: University of California Press.

Breidenstein, Gerhard. 1974. "Capitalism in South Korea." In Frank Baldwin, ed., *Without Parallel: The American-Korean Relationship Since 1945*, pp. 233–70. New York: Pantheon.

Brown, Gilbert T. 1973. *Korean Pricing Policies and Economic Development in the 1960s.* Baltimore, Md.: Johns Hopkins University Press.

Brun, Ellen, and Jacques Hersh. 1976. *Socialist Korea: A Case Study in the Strategy of Economic Development.* New York: Monthly Review Press.

Brzoska, Michael, and Thomas Ohlson. 1987. *Arms Transfers to the Third World, 1971–85.* Oxford: Oxford University Press.

Bulmer-Thomas, Victor. 1994. *The Economic History of Latin America Since Independence.* Cambridge: Cambridge University Press.

Burchett, Wilfred G. 1968. *Again Korea.* New York: International Publishers.

Burmeister, Larry L. 1988. *Research, Realpolitik, and Development in Korea: The State and the Green Revolution.* Boulder, Colo.: Westview Press.

Burton, John. 1992. "Korean Investors Unfurl Red Flags with Eye to China." *Financial Times,* September 30, p. 4.

Caldwell, John. 1952. *The Korea Story.* Chicago: Henry Regnery.

Campbell, Alexander. 1960. "Seoul: The Angry Students and the Clatter of Carbines." *Life,* May 2, pp. 31–32.

———[Alex Campbell]. 1969. "Come and Establish More Bases Here." *New Republic,* June 7, pp. 9–11.

Cathie, John 1989. *Food Aid and Industrialisation: The Development of the South Korean Economy.* Aldershot, U.K.: Avebury.

CCA-URM and ACPO. 1987. *People's Power, People's Church: A Short History of Urban Poor Mission in South Korea.* Hong Kong: CCA-URM and ACPO.

Central Intelligence Agency. 1978. *Korea: The Economic Race Between the North and the South.* Washington, D.C.: Central Intelligence Agency.

Ch'ae, Man-Sik. 1993. *Peace Under Heaven.* Trans. Kyung-Ja Chun. Armonk, N.Y.: M. E. Sharpe.

Chai, Jae Hyung. 1972. "The Military and Modernization in Korea." Ph.D. diss., Case Western Reserve University.

Chambers, Robert. 1983. *Rural Development: Putting the Last First.* London: Longman.

Chang, Dal-Joong. 1985. *Economic Control and Political Authoritarianism: The Role of Japanese Corporations in Korean Politics, 1965–1979.* Seoul: Sogang University Press.

Chang, Edward Taehan. 1992. "Anti-Americanism and Student Movements in South Korea." In Eui-Young Yu and Terry R. Kandal, eds., *The Korean Peninsula in the Changing World Order,* pp. 147–72. Los Angeles: Center for Korean-American and Korean Studies, California State University, Los Angeles.

Chang Myŏng-guk. 1985. "Haebanghu Han'guk nodong undong ŭi paljach'wi." In Kim Kŭm-su et al., *Han'guk nodong undongnon,* pp. 113–45. Seoul: Miraesa.

Chang, Yunshik. 1967. "Population in Early Modernization: Korea." Ph.D. diss., Princeton University.

———. 1982. "Personalism and Social Change in South Korea." In Yunshik Chang, Tai-Hwan Kwon, and Peter J. Donaldson, eds., *Society in Transition with Special Reference to Korea*, pp. 29–43. Seoul: Seoul National University Press.

———. 1983. "Women in a Confucian Society: The Case of Chosun Dynasty Korea." In Eui-Young Yu and Earl H. Phillips, eds., *Traditional Thoughts and Practices in Korea*, pp. 67–96. Los Angeles: Center for Korean-American and Korean Studies, California State University, Los Angeles.

———. 1989. "Peasants Go to Town: The Rise of Commercial Farming in Korea." *Human Organization* 48: 236–51.

———. 1990. "Education, Equality and Society: A Comparison of North and South Korea." *California Sociologist* 13: 87–121.

———. 1991. "The Personalist Ethic and the Market in Korea." *Comparative Studies in Society and History* 33: 106–29.

———. 1994. "From Ideology to Interest: Government and Press in South Korea, 1945–1979." In Dae-Sook Suh, ed., *Korean Studies: New Pacific Currents*, pp. 249–62. Honolulu: Center for Korean Studies, University of Hawaii.

Chao, Lien. 1956. "Distinctive Patterns of Industrial Relations in Korea." Ph.D. diss., University of Minnesota.

Chapin, Emerson. 1969. "Success Story in South Korea." *Foreign Affairs* 47: 560–74.

Cheong, Sung-Hwa. 1991. *The Politics of Anti-Japanese Sentiment in Korea: Japan-South Korean Relations Under American Occupation, 1945–1952*. New York: Greenwood.

Chesnais, Jean-Claude. 1992. *The Demographic Transition: Stages, Patterns, and Economic Implications*. Trans. Elizabeth Kreager and Philip Kreager. Oxford: Clarendon Press.

Chirot, Daniel. 1994. *Modern Tyrants: The Power and Prevalence of Evil in Our Age*. New York: Free Press.

Cho, Chang-Hyun. 1972. "Bureaucracy and Local Government in South Korea." In Se Jin Kim and Chang-Hyun Cho, eds., *Government and Politics of Korea*, pp. 91–126. Silver Springs, Md.: Research Institute on Korean Affairs.

Cho, Chŏngnae. [1981] 1993. "Land of Exile." Trans. Marshall R. Pihl. In Marshall R. Pihl, Bruce Fulton, and Ju-Chan Fulton, eds., *Land of Exile: Contemporary Korean Fiction*, pp. 200–243. Armonk, N.Y.: M. E. Sharpe.

Cho Hae-joang [Cho Hye-jŏng]. 1988. *Han'guk ŭi yŏsŏng kwa namsŏng*. Seoul: Munhak kwa Chisŏngsa.

Cho Hŭi-yŏn. 1993. *Kyegŭp kwa pin'gon*. Seoul: Hanul.

———, ed. 1990. *Han'guk sahoe undongsa*. Seoul: Chuksan.

Cho, Hyoung. 1987. "The Position of Women in the Korean Work Force." In Eui-Young Yu and Earl H. Phillips, eds., *Traditional Thoughts and Practices in Korea*, pp. 85–102. Los Angeles: Center for Korean-American and Korean Studies, California State University, Los Angeles.

Cho, Jae Hong. 1964. "Post-1945 Land Reforms and Their Consequences in South Korea." Ph.D. diss., Indiana University.

Cho Kap-je. 1989. *Gunbu*. Trans. Hwang Min-gi. Tokyo: JICC.

Cho Mi-hye. 1988. "Tosi pinmin yŏsŏng ŭi silt'ae wa ŭisik." *Yŏsŏng* 3: 171–84.

Cho, Myung Hyun. 1989. "The New Student Movement in Korea: Emerging Patterns of Ideological Orientation in the 1980's." *Korea Observer* 20: 93–110.

Cho, Sehŭi. 1990. "A Dwarf Launched a Little Ball." In Peter Lee, ed., *Modern Korean Literature: An Anthology*, pp. 328–67. Honolulu: University of Hawaii Press.

Cho, Soon. 1994. *The Dynamics of Korean Economic Development*. Washington, D.C.: Institute for International Economics.

Cho, Soon-Kyoung. 1985a. "The Labor Process and Capital Mobility: The Limits of the New International Division of Labor." *Politics and Society* 14: 185–222.

———[S. K. Cho]. 1985b. "The Dilemmas of Export-Led Industrialization: South Korea and the World Economy." *Berkeley Journal of Sociology* 30: 65–94.

———. 1987. "How Cheap Is 'Cheap Labor'? The Dilemmas of Export-led Industrialization." Ph.D. diss., University of California, Berkeley.

———[Cho Sun-gyŏng]. 1991. "Namnyŏ koyong p'yŏngdŭngpŏp ŭi han'gye wa kwaje." In *Kyoyuk kwa pŏp e taehan yŏsŏnghakchŏk chŏpkŭn*, pp. 73–94. Seoul: Ch'ŏngha.

Cho, Wha Soon. 1988. *Let the Weak Be Strong: A Woman's Struggle for Justice*. Ed. Sun Ai Lee and Sang Nim Ahn. Bloomington, Ind.: Meyer Stone.

Cho Yong-bŏm. 1973. *Hujin'guk kyŏngjeron*. Seoul: Pagyŏngsa.

———. 1981. *Han'guk kyŏngje ŭi nolli*. Seoul: Chŏnyewŏn.

Cho Yong-bŏm and Chŏng Yun-hyŏng, eds. 1984. *Han'guk tokchŏm chabon kwa chaebŏl*. Seoul: P'ulbit.

Cho, Yong Sam. 1963. *"Disguised Unemployment" in Underdeveloped Areas with Special Reference to South Korean Agriculture*. Berkeley: University of California Press.

Ch'oe Chae-suk. 1983. *Han'guk kajok chedosa yŏn'gu*. Seoul: Iljisa.

Choe, Chong-hui. [1946] 1983. "The Ritual at the Well." Trans. Genell Y. Poitras. In Genell Y. Poitras, ed., *The Cruel City and Other Korean Short Stories*, pp. 61–94. Seoul: Si-sa-yong-o-sa.

Ch'oe Kyŏng-ae. 1992. "Han'guk hwan'gyŏng undong ŭi sŏngjang kwa kach'i chihyang." In Han'guk Sahoesa Yŏn'guhoe, ed., *Han'guk sanŏp sahoe ŭi hyŏnsil kwa chŏnmang*, pp. 192–242. Seoul: Munhak kwa Chisŏngsa.

Choe, Minja Kim, Sae-Kwon Kong, and Karen Oppenheim Mason. 1994. "Korean Women's Labor Force Participation: Attitudes and Behavior." In Dae-Sook Suh, ed., *Korean Studies: New Pacific Currents*, pp. 283–98. Honolulu: Center for Korean Studies, University of Hawaii.

Choe, Sang-Chul, and Jong-Gie Kim. 1986. "Rural Industrial Policy in Korea: Past Experiences and New Approach." In Yang-Boo Choe and Fu-Chen Lo, eds., *Rural Industrialization and Non-Farm Activities of Asian Farmers*, pp. 99–119. Seoul: Korea Rural Economics Institute.

Ch'oe Sang-yong. 1989. *Migunjŏng kwa Han'guk minjokjuŭi*. Rev. ed. Seoul: Nanam.

Choi, Chungmoo. 1992. "Korean Women in a Culture of Inequality." In Donald N. Clark, ed., *Korea Briefing, 1992*, pp. 97–106. Boulder, Colo.: Westview Press.

———. 1995. "The Minjung Culture Movement and the Construction of Popular Culture in Korea." In Kenneth M. Wells, ed., *South Korea's Minjung Movement: The Culture and Politics of Dissidence*, pp. 105–18. Honolulu: University of Hawaii Press.

Choi, Jang Jip [Ch'oe Chang-jip]. 1988. *Han'guk ŭi nodong undong kwa kukka*. Seoul: Yŏrŭmsa.

———. 1989a. *Labor and the Authoritarian State: Labor Unions in South Korean Manufacturing Industries, 1961–1980*. Seoul: Korea University Press.

———[Ch'oe Chang-jip]. 1989b. *Han'guk hyŏndae chŏngch'i ŭi kujo wa pyŏnhwa*. Seoul: Kkach'i.

———. 1993a. "Political Cleavages in South Korea." In Hagen Koo, ed., *State and Society in Contemporary Korea*, pp. 13–50. Ithaca, N.Y.: Cornell University Press.

———. 1993b. "Building a Strong State and Development in South Korea." In Ken'ichiro Hirano, ed., *The State and Cultural Transformation: Perspectives from East Asia*, pp. 256–78. Tokyo: United Nations University Press.

———[Ch'oe Chang-jip]. 1993c. *Han'guk minjujuŭi ŭi iron*. Seoul: Han'gilsa.

Choi, Sook-kyung. 1986. "Formation of Women's Movements in Korea: From the Enlightenment Period to 1910." In Sei-wha Chung, ed., *Challenges for Women: Women's Studies in Korea*, trans. Chang-hyun Shin et al., pp. 103–26. Seoul: Ewha Womans University Press.

Chomsky, Noam. 1993. *Year 501: The Conquest Continues*. Boston: South End Press.

Chŏn Kwang-hŭi. 1992. "Han'guk chŏnjaeng kwa Nam-Pukhan in'gu ŭi pyŏnhwa." In Han'guk Sahoehakhoe, ed., *Han'guk chŏnjaeng kwa Han'guk sahoe pyŏndong*, pp. 60–92. Seoul: P'ulbit.

Chŏn, Kwangyong. [1962] 1993. "Kapitan Ri." Trans. Marshall R. Pihl. In Marshall R. Pihl, Bruce Fulton, and Ju-Chan Fulton, eds., *Land of Exile: Contemporary Korean Fiction*, pp. 58–83. Armonk, N.Y.: M. E. Sharpe.

Chŏn Kyŏng-su. 1992. "Tosi chungsanch'ŭng ap'at'ŭch'on ŭi sobija kyŏngje saenghwal." In Mun Ok-p'yo, Kim Kwang-ŏk, Kim Pu-sŏng, Im Pong-gil, and Chŏn Kyŏng-su, *Tosi chungsanch'ŭng ŭi saenghwal munhwa*, pp. 143–74. Seoul: Han'guk Chŏngsin Munhwa Yŏn'guwŏn.

Chon, Soohyun. 1992. "Political Economy of Regional Development in Korea." In Richard P. Appelbaum and Jeffrey Henderson, eds., *States and Development in the Asian Pacific Rim*, pp. 150–75. Newbury Park, Calif.: Sage.

Chŏn Tong-t'aek. 1989. *Chosŏn hugi noye sinbun yŏn'gu*. Seoul: Iljogak.

Chŏng Chang-yŏn and Mun Kyŏng-su. 1990. *Gendai Kankoku e no shiten*. Tokyo: Ōtsuki Shoten.

Chŏng Ku-hyŏn. 1989. "Han'guk esŏ ŭi chŏngbu wa kiŏp kan ŭi kwan'gye." In Lee Hak-Chong, Chŏng Ku-hyŏn, and Kae H. Chung, eds., *Han'guk kiŏp ŭi kujo wa chŏllyak*, pp. 71–94. Seoul: Pŏmmunsa.

Chŏng Tong-il. 1985. *Tosi pinmin yŏn'gu*. Seoul: Ach'im.

Chŏng Yo-sop. 1971. *Hanguk yŏsŏng undongsa*. Seoul: Iljogak.

Chŏng Yun-hyŏng. 1988. "Pak Chong-hŭi chŏnggwŏn ŭi kyŏngje kaebal inyŏm." In Cho Yong-bŏm et al., *Han'guk chabonjuŭi sŏnggyŏk nonjaeng*, pp. 396–414. Seoul: Taewangsa.

Christian Institute for the Study of Justice and Development. 1981. *Presence of Christ Among Minjung*. Seoul: Christian Institute for the Study of Justice and Development.

———. 1984. *Bechtel Case: An Alleged Korean Bribery Scandal*. Seoul: Christian Institute for the Study of Justice and Development.

———. 1985. *Democratization Movement and the Christian Church in Korea During the 1970s*. Seoul: Christian Institute for the Study of Justice and Development.

———. 1986. *Korean Situationer*. Vol. 2. Seoul: Christian Institute for the Study of Justice and Development.

———. 1987. *Korean Situationer*. Vol. 9. Seoul: Christian Institute for the Study of Justice and Development.

———. 1988a. *Lost Victory*. Seoul: Minjungsa.

————. 1988b. *Korean Situation and Women*. Seoul: Christian Institute for the Study of Justice and Development.

————. 1988c. *Social Justice Indicators in Korea*. 2d ed. Seoul: Christian Institute for the Study of Justice and Development.

Christie, Donald Earle. 1972. "Seoul's Organization Men: The Ethnography of a Businessmen's Association in Industrializing Korea." Ph.D. diss., University of Illinois at Urbana-Champaign.

Chua-Eoan, Howard G. 1987. "Reforms on Hold." *Time*, April 27, pp. 38–39.

Chung, Joseph Hee-Soo. 1990. "Housing Policies in Korea: Search for New Orientation." In Gill-Chin Lim and Wook Chang, eds., *Dynamic Transformation: Korea, NICs, and Beyond*, pp. 309–25. Urbana, Ill.: Consortium on Development Studies.

Chung, Kyung Cho. 1956. *Korea Tomorrow: Land of the Morning Calm*. New York: Macmillan.

Chung, Un-chang. 1982. "The Development of the Korean Economy and the Role of the United States." In Sungjoo Han, ed., *After One Hundred Years: Continuity and Change in Korean-American Relations*, pp. 167–92. Seoul: Asiatic Research Center, Korea University.

Clark, Donald N. 1986. *Christianity in Modern Korea*. Lanham, Md.: University Press of America.

————. 1991. "Bitter Friendship: Understanding Anti-Americanism in South Korea." In Donald N. Clark, ed., *Korea Briefing 1991*, pp. 147–62. Boulder, Colo.: Westview Press.

————. 1995. "Growth and Limitations of Minjung Christianity in South Korea." In Kenneth M. Wells, ed., *South Korea's Minjung Movement: The Culture and Politics of Dissidence*, pp. 87–103. Honolulu: University of Hawaii Press.

————, ed. 1988. *The Kwangju Uprising: Shadows over the Regime in South Korea*. Boulder, Colo.: Westview Press.

Clark, Mark W. 1954. *From the Danube to the Yalu*. New York: Harper & Brothers.

Clifford, Mark. 1991. "Land of the Bribe." *Far Eastern Economic Review*, February 28, pp. 8–9.

————. 1994. *Troubled Tiger: Businessmen, Bureaucrats, and Generals in South Korea*. Armonk, N.Y.: M. E. Sharpe.

Clough, Ralph N. 1987. *Embattled Korea: The Rivalry for International Support*. Boulder, Colo.: Westview Press.

Cohen, Jerome Alan, and Edward J. Baker. 1991. "U.S. Foreign Policy and Human Rights in South Korea." In William Shaw, ed., *Human Rights in Korea: Historical and Policy Perspectives*, pp. 171–219. Cambridge, Mass.: Council on East Asian Studies, Harvard University.

Cole, David C., and Princeton N. Lyman. 1971. *Korean Development: The Interplay of Politics and Economics.* Cambridge, Mass.: Harvard University Press.

Cole, David C., and Young Woo Nam. 1969. "The Pattern and Significance of Economic Planning in Korea." In Irma Adelman, ed., *Practical Approaches to Development Planning: Korea's Second Five-Year Plan*, pp. 11–37. Baltimore, Md.: Johns Hopkins University Press.

Cole, David C., and Yung Chul Park. 1983. *Financial Development in Korea, 1945–1978.* Cambridge, Mass.: Council on East Asian Studies, Harvard University.

Colson, Elizabeth. 1982. *Planned Change: The Creation of a New Community.* Berkeley: Institute of International Studies, University of California.

Colson, Elizabeth, and Thayer Scudder. 1988. *For Prayer and Profit: The Ritual, Economic, and Social Importance of Beer in Gwembe District, Zambia, 1950–1982.* Stanford, Calif.: Stanford University Press.

Commission on Theological Concerns of the Christian Conference of Asia, ed. [1981] 1983. *Minjung Theology: People as the Subjects of History.* London: Zed.

Conde, David W. 1967. *Kaihō Chōsen no rekishi.* 2 vols. Trans. Okakura Koshirō et al. Tokyo: Taihei Shuppan.

Cone, James H. [1980] 1993. "A Black American Perspective on the Asian Search for Full Humanity." In James H. Cone and Gayraud S. Wilmore, eds., *Black Theology: A Documentary History*, vol. 2, *1980–1992*, pp. 358–70. Maryknoll, N.Y.: Orbis Books.

Constantino, Renato. 1975. *A History of the Philippines: From the Spanish Colonization to the Second World War.* New York: Monthly Review Press.

Cornford, F. M. [1900] 1994. "Microcosmographia Academica." In Gordon Johnson, ed., *University Politics: F. M. Cornford's Cambridge and His Advice to the Young Academic Politicians*, pp. 85–110. Cambridge: Cambridge University Press.

Cotler, Julio. 1978. *Clases, estado y nación en el Perú.* Lima: Instituto de Estudios Peruanos.

Cox, Harvey. 1995. *Fire from Heaven: The Rise of Pentecostal Spirituality and the Reshaping of Religion in the Twenty-first Century.* Reading, Mass.: Addison-Wesley.

Crofts, Alfred. 1960. "Our Falling Ramparts." *Nation*, June 25, pp. 544–48.

Cumings, Bruce. 1981. *The Origins of the Korean War.* Vol. 1, *Liberation and the Emergence of Separate Regimes.* Princeton, N.J.: Princeton University Press.

————. 1984. "The Origins and Development of the Northeast Asian Political Economy: Industrial Sector, Product Cycles, and Political Consequences." *International Organization* 38: 1–40.

————. 1989. "The Abortive Abertura: South Korea in the Light of Latin American Experience." *New Left Review* 173: 5–32.

————. 1990a. *The Origins of the Korean War.* Vol. 2, *The Roaring of the Cataract, 1947–1950.* Princeton, N.J.: Princeton University Press.

————. 1990b. *The Two Koreas: On the Road to Reunification.* Washington, D.C.: Foreign Policy Association.

————. 1997. *Korea's Place in the Sun: A Modern History.* New York: Norton.

David, Steven R. 1987. *Third World Coups d'État and International Security.* Baltimore, Md.: Johns Hopkins University Press.

Davidson, Basil. 1992. *The Black Man's Burden: Africa and the Curse of the Nation-State.* New York: Times Books.

de Janvry, Alain. 1981. *The Agrarian Question and Reformism in Latin America.* Baltimore, Md.: Johns Hopkins University Press.

De Waal, Alexander. 1989. *Famine That Kills: Darfur, Sudan, 1984–1985.* Oxford: Clarendon Press.

Desmond, Edward W. 1986. "Lunch at the Blue House." *Time,* March 10, p. 55.

Deuchler, Martina. 1977. "The Tradition: Women During the Yi Dynasty." In Sandra Mattielli, ed., *Virtues in Conflict: Tradition and the Korean Women Today,* pp. 1–47. Seoul: Royal Asiatic Society, Korea Branch.

————. 1992. *The Confucian Transformation of Korea: A Study of Society and Ideology.* Cambridge, Mass.: Council on East Asian Studies, Harvard University.

Deyo, Frederic C. 1989. *Beneath the Miracle: Labor Subordination in the New Asian Industrialism.* Berkeley: University of California Press.

Di Lampedusa, Giuseppe. [1958] 1960. *The Leopard.* Trans. Archibald Colquhoun. New York: Pantheon.

Dicker, Richard. 1995. "South Korea: Labor Rights Violations Under Democratic Rule." *Human Rights Watch / Asia* 7(14): 1–31.

Disney, Nigel. 1978. "Korea and the Middle East." In Gavan McCormack and Mark Selden, eds., *Korea, North and South: The Deepening Crisis,* pp. 199–206. New York: Monthly Review Press.

Doerner, William R. 1987. "Suddenly, A New Day." *Time,* July 13, pp. 34–37.

Doktor, Robert, and John Lie. 1993. "The Impact of Information Technology on Organizational Democracy: The Case of South Korea." In

William M. Lafferty and Eliezer Rosenstein, eds., *International Handbook of Participation in Organization,* vol. 3, *The Challenge of New Technology and Macro-Political Change,* pp. 173–89. Oxford: Oxford University Press.

Donaldson, Peter J. 1990. *Nature Against Us: The United States and the World Population Crisis, 1965–1980.* Chapel Hill: University of North Carolina Press.

Dong, Wonmo. 1991. "Domestic Politics in 1990: A Year of Crisis." In Donald N. Clark, ed., *Korea Briefing, 1991,* pp. 5–25. Boulder, Colo.: Westview Press.

Dore, Ronald. 1990. "Reflections on Culture and Social Change." In Gary Gereffi and Donald L. Wyman, eds., *Manufacturing Miracles: Paths of Industrialization in Latin America and East Asia,* pp. 353–67. Princeton, N.J.: Princeton University Press.

Dornbusch, Rudiger, and Yung-Chul Park. 1992. "The External Balance." In Vittorio Corbo and Sang-Mok Suh, eds., *Structural Adjustment in a Newly Industrialized Country: The Korean Experience,* pp. 68–94. Baltimore, Md.: Johns Hopkins University Press.

Dumont, René. 1965. *Lands Alive.* Trans. Suzanne Sale and Gilbert Sale. New York: Monthly Review Press.

Dumont, René, with Marcel Mazoyer. [1969] 1973. *Socialisms and Development.* Trans. Rupert Cunningham. London: Andre Deutsch.

Duus, Peter. 1995. *The Abacus and the Sword: The Japanese Penetration of Korea, 1895–1910.* Berkeley: University of California Press.

Easey, Walter, and Gavan McCormack. 1978. "South Korean Society: The Deepening Nightmare." In Gavan McCormack and Mark Selden, eds., *Korea, North and South: The Deepening Crisis,* pp. 77–90. New York: Monthly Review Press.

Eberstadt, Nicholas. 1995a. *Korea Approaches Reunification.* Armonk, N.Y.: M. E. Sharpe.

———. 1995b. "Policy and Economic Performance in Divided Korea, 1945–1995." Ph.D. diss., Harvard University.

Eckert, Carter J. 1991. *Offspring of Empire: The Koch'ang Kims and the Colonial Origins of Korean Capitalism, 1876–1945.* Seattle: University of Washington Press.

———. 1993. "The South Korean Bourgeoisie: A Class in Search of Hegemony." In Hagen Koo, ed., *State and Society in Contemporary Korea,* pp. 95–130. Ithaca, N.Y.: Cornell University Press.

Eckert, Carter J., Ki-baik Lee, Young Ick Lew, Michael Robinson, and Edward W. Wagner. 1990. *Korea Old and New: A History.* Seoul: Ilchokak.

Eder, Norman. 1996. *Poisoned Prosperity: Development, Moderniza-*

tion, and the Environment in South Korea. Armonk, N.Y.: M. E. Sharpe.

Emergency Christian Conference on Korean Problems. 1975. *Documents on the Struggle for Democracy in Korea.* Tokyo: Shinkyō Shuppansha.

Emmanuel, Arghiri. [1969] 1972. *Unequal Exchange: A Study of the Imperialism of Trade.* Trans. Brian Pearce. New York: Monthly Review Press.

Evans, Peter. 1979. *Dependent Development: The Alliance of Multinational, State, and Local Capital in Brazil.* Princeton, N.J.: Princeton University Press.

Fallows, James. 1994. *Looking at the Sun: The Rise of the New East Asian Economic and Political System.* New York: Pantheon.

Fehrenbach, T. R. 1963. *This Kind of War: Korea: A Study in Unpreparedness.* New York: Macmillan.

Fenton, James. 1988. *All the Wrong Places: Adrift in the Politics of the Pacific Rim.* New York: Atlantic Monthly Press.

Ferguson, James. 1990. *The Anti-Politics Machine: "Development," Depoliticization, and Bureaucratic Power in Lesotho.* Cambridge: Cambridge University Press.

Fields, Karl J. 1995. *Enterprise and the State in Korea and Taiwan.* Ithaca, N.Y.: Cornell University Press.

Food and Agriculture Organization of the United Nations. 1954. *Rehabilitation and Development of Agriculture, Forestry, and Fisheries in South Korea.* New York: Columbia University Press.

Frank, Andre Gunder. [1967] 1969. *Capitalism and Underdevelopment in Latin America: Historical Studies of Chile and Brazil.* Rev. and enl. ed. New York: Monthly Review Press.

Frank, Charles R., Jr., Kwang Suk Kim, and Larry E. Westphal. 1975. *Foreign Trade Regimes and Economic Development: South Korea.* New York: National Bureau of Economic Research.

Frieden, Jeffry A. 1981. "Third World Indebted Industrialization: International Finance and State Capitalism in Mexico, Brazil, Algeria, and South Korea." *International Organization* 35: 407–31.

———. 1991. *Debt, Development, and Democracy: Modern Political Economy and Latin America, 1965–1985.* Princeton, N.J.: Princeton University Press.

Fröbel, Folker, Jürgen Heinrichs, and Otto Kreyre. [1977] 1980. *The New International Division of Labour: Structural Unemployment in Industrialised Countries and Industrialisation in Developing Countries.* Cambridge: Cambridge University Press.

Fukagawa Yukiko. 1992. "Kankoku no tai ASEAN tōshi: genjō to tenbō." In Kohama Hirohisa, ed., *Chokusetsu tōshi to kōgyōka: Nihon, NIES, ASEAN*, pp. 103–27. Tokyo: Nihon Bōeki Shinkōkai.

Furtado, Celso. [1970] 1976. *Economic Development of Latin America: Historical Background and Contemporary Problems*. 2d ed. Trans. Suzette Macedo. Cambridge: Cambridge University Press.

Fussell, Paul, ed. 1991. *The Norton Book of Modern War*. New York: W. W. Norton.

Gale, James S. 1898. *Korean Sketches*. New York: Fleming H. Revell.

Gallie, W. B. 1964. *Philosophy and the Historical Understanding*. London: Chatto & Windus.

Gayn, Mark. 1948. *Japan Diary*. New York: William Sloane Associates.

———. 1954. "What Price Rhee? Profile of a Despot." *Nation*, March 13, pp. 214–17.

Gellner, Ernest. 1981. *Muslim Society*. Cambridge: Cambridge University Press.

Gereffi, Gary, and Miguel Korzeniewicz. 1990. "Commodity Chains and Footwear Exports in the Semiperiphery." In William G. Martin, ed., *Semiperipheral States in the World-Economy*, pp. 45–68. New York: Greenwood.

Gerschenkron, Alexander. 1943. *Bread and Democracy in Germany*. Berkeley: University of California Press.

———. 1962. *Economic Backwardness in Historical Perspective and Other Essays*. Cambridge, Mass.: Harvard University Press.

———. 1977. *An Economic Spurt That Failed: Four Lectures in Austrian History*. Princeton, N.J.: Princeton University Press.

Gibbs, David N. 1991. *The Political Economy of Third World Intervention: Mines, Money, and U.S. Policy in the Congo Crisis*. Chicago: University of Chicago Press.

Gibney, Frank. 1954. "Syngman Rhee: The Free Man's Burden." *Harper's Magazine*, February, pp. 27–34.

Goldberg, Charles N. 1979. "Spirits in Place: The Concept of Kohyang and the Korean Social Order." In David R. McCann, John Middleton, and Edward J. Schultz, eds., *Studies on Korea in Transitition*, pp. 89–101. Honolulu: Center for Korean Studies, University of Hawaii.

Goncahrov, Sergei N., John W. Lewis, and Xue Litai. 1993. *Uncertain Partners: Stalin, Mao, and the Korean War*. Stanford, Calif.: Stanford University Press.

Gopnik, Adam. 1995. "Status Quo Forever." *New Yorker*, December 18, pp. 67–69.

Gragert, Edwin H. 1994. *Landownership Under Colonial Rule: Korea's Japanese Experience, 1900–1935*. Honolulu: University of Hawaii Press.

Grajdanzev, Andrew J. 1944. *Modern Korea: A Study of Social and*

Economic Changes Under Japanese Rule. New York: Institute of Pacific Relations.

Green, Andrew E. 1994. "Moving Beyond the State: The International Context of South Korea's Comparative Advantage." In Dae-Sook Suh, ed., *Korean Studies: New Pacific Currents*, pp. 227–45. Honolulu: Center for Korean Studies, University of Hawaii.

Griffin, Keith. 1974. *The Political Economy of Agrarian Change: An Essay on the Green Revolution.* Cambridge, Mass.: Harvard University Press.

Ha, Joseph Man-Kyung. 1971. "Politics of Korean Peasantry: A Study of Land Reforms and Collectivization with Reference to Sino-Soviet Experiences." Ph.D. diss., Columbia University.

Ha, Young-Sun. 1984. "American-Korean Military Relations: Continuity and Change." In Youngnok Koo and Dae-Sook Suh, eds., *Korea and the United States: A Century of Cooperation*, pp. 111–30. Honolulu: University of Hawaii Press.

Habakkuk, John. 1994. *Marriage, Debt, and the Estates System: English Landownership, 1650–1950.* Oxford: Clarendon Press.

Haboush, JaHyun Kim. 1988. *A Heritage of Kings: One Man's Monarchy in the Confucian World.* New York: Columbia University Press.

———. 1991. "The Confucianization of Korean Society." In Gilbert Rozman, ed., *The East Asian Region: Confucian Heritage and Its Modern Adaptation*, pp. 84–110. Princeton, N.J.: Princeton University Press.

Haggard, Stephan, and Sylvia Maxfield. 1993. "Political Explanations of Financial Policy in Developing Countries." In Stephan Haggard, Chung H. Lee, and Sylvia Maxfield, eds., *The Politics of Finance in Developing Countries*, pp. 293–325. Ithaca, N.Y.: Cornell University Press.

Haggard, Stephan, and Chung-In Moon. 1993. "The State, Politics, and Economic Development in Postwar South Korea." In Hagen Koo, ed., *State and Society in Contemporary Korea*, pp. 51–93. Ithaca, N.Y.: Cornell University Press.

Hahm, Pyong-Choon. 1967. *The Korean Political Tradition and Law: Essays in Korean Law and History.* Seoul: Royal Asiatic Society, Korea Branch.

———. 1984. "The Korean Perception of the United States." In Youngnok Koo and Dae-Sook Suh, eds., *Korea and the United States: A Century of Cooperation*, pp. 23–52. Honolulu: University of Hawaii Press.

Hahn, Bae-ho. 1975. "The Authority Structure of Korean Politics." In Edward Reynolds Wright, ed., *Korean Politics in Transition*, pp. 289–301. Seattle: University of Washington Press.

Haksul Tanch'e Hyŏbŭihoe, ed. 1989. *1980-nyŏndae Han'guk sahoe wa chibae kujo.* Seoul: P'ulbit.

———, ed. 1993. *Han'guk minjujuŭi ŭi hyŏnjaejŏk kwaje.* Seoul: Ch'angjak kwa Pip'yŏngsa.

Hall, John A. [1985] 1986. *Powers and Liberties: The Causes and Consequences of the Rise of the West.* Berkeley: University of California Press.

Halliday, Jon, and Bruce Cumings. 1988. *Korea: The Unknown War.* New York: Pantheon.

Han Hŭi-yŏng. 1988. *Kankoku kigyō keiei no jittai.* Tokyo: Tōyō Keizai Shinpōsha.

Han Kye-ok. 1988. *Kankoku hankyōgunsei to minshuka.* Tokyo: Dōjidaisha.

———. 1989. *Kankokugun chūkan beigun.* Tokyo: Kaya Shobō.

Han, Sang-bok. 1993. "Cultural Transformation in Rural and Urban Korea." In Ken'ichiro Hirano, ed., *The State and Cultural Transformation: Perspectives from East Asia,* pp. 279–96. Tokyo: United Nations University Press.

Han, Sang-bok, Tai-Hwan Kwon, Kyung-Soo Chun, and Chang-Kyu Moon. 1988. *Water Supply and Sanitation in Korean Communities.* Seoul: Population and Development Studies Center, Seoul National University.

Han, Sang-jin. 1987. "Bureaucratic-Authoritarianism and Economic Development in Korea During the Yushin Period: A Reexamination of O'Donnell's Theory." In Kyong-Dong Kim, ed., *Dependency Issues in Korean Development: Comparative Perspectives,* pp. 362–74. Seoul: Seoul National University Press.

Han, Sungjoo. 1972. "Political Dissent in South Korea, 1948–61." In Se Jin Kim and Chang-Hyun Cho, eds., *Government and Politics of Korea,* pp. 43–69. Silver Springs, Md.: Research Institute on Korean Affairs.

———. 1974. *The Failure of Democracy in South Korea.* Berkeley: University of California Press.

———. 1978. "South Korea's Participation in the Vietnam Conflict: An Analysis of the U.S.-Korean Alliance." *Orbis* 21: 893–912.

———. 1985. "Policy Towards the United States." In Youngnok Koo and Sungjoo Han, eds., *The Foreign Policy of the Republic of Korea,* pp. 139–66. New York: Columbia University Press.

———. 1989a. "South Korea: Politics in Transition." In Larry Diamond, Juan J. Linz, and Seymour Martin Lipset, eds., *Democracy in Developing Countries,* vol. 3, *Asia,* pp. 267–303. Boulder, Colo.: Lynne Rienner.

————. 1989b. "South Korea in 1988: A Revolution in the Making." *Asian Survey* 29: 29–38.

Han To-hyŏn. 1992. "Hyŏndae Han'guk esŏ ŭi chaebŏl ŭi t'oji chibae silt'ae." In Han'guk Sahoesa Yŏn'guhoe, ed., *Han'guk sanŏp sahoe ŭi hyŏnsil kwa chŏnmang*, pp. 99–147. Seoul: Munhak kwa Chisŏngsa.

Han Wan-sang. 1978. *Minjung kwa chisigin*. Seoul: Chŏngusa.

————. 1984. *Minjung sahoehak*. Seoul: Chongno Sŏjŏk.

Han, Woo-keun. [1970] 1974. *The History of Korea*. Trans. Kyung-shik Lee. Ed. Grafton K. Mintz. Honolulu: University Press of Hawaii.

Hancock, Graham. 1989. *Lords of Poverty: The Power, Prestige, and Corruption of the International Aid Business*. New York: Atlantic Monthly Press.

Han'guk Konghae Munje Yŏn'guso. 1986. *Han'guk ŭi konghae chido*. Seoul: Ilwŏl Sŏgak.

Han'guk Minjungsa Yŏn'guhoe. 1986. *Han'guk minjungsa*. Vol. 2. Seoul: P'ulbit.

Han'guk Sahoehakhoe and Han'guk Chŏngch'ihakhoe, eds. 1992. *Han'guk ŭi kukka wa simin sahoe*. Seoul: Hanul.

Han'guk Sahoekwahak Yŏn'gu Hyobŭihoe, ed. 1990. *Han'guk sahoe ŭi insik nonjaeng*. Seoul: Pŏmmunsa.

Han'guk Sanŏp Sahoe Yŏn'guhoe, ed. 1991. *Han'guk sahoe wa chibae ideollogi*. Seoul: Noktu.

Harding, Colin. 1975. "Land Reform and Social Conflict in Peru." In Abraham F. Lowenthal, ed., *The Peruvian Experiment: Continuity and Change Under Military Rule*, pp. 220–53. Princeton, N.J.: Princeton University Press.

Harrison, Lawrence E. 1992. *Who Prospers? How Cultural Values Shape Economic and Political Success*. New York: Basic Books.

Hart, Keith. 1982. *The Political Economy of West African Agriculture*. Cambridge: Cambridge University Press.

Hart-Landsberg, Martin. 1993. *The Rush to Development: Economic Change and Political Struggle in South Korea*. New York: Monthly Review Press.

Hasan, Parvez. 1976. *Korea: Problems and Issues in a Rapidly Growing Economy*. Baltimore, Md.: Johns Hopkins University Press.

Hattori Tamio. 1984. "Kōdo seichōki ni okeru sangyō erīto no keisei." In Itō Teiichi, ed., *Hatten tojōkoku no bijinesu rīdāshippu*, pp. 157–86. Tokyo: Ajia Keizai Kenkyūsho.

————. 1988. *Kankoku no keiei hatten*. Tokyo: Bunshindō.

————. 1989. "Hyundai Motor Company: The New Standard-Bearer of Korean Industrialization." *East Asian Cultural Studies* 28: 45–61.

———. 1992. *Kankoku: nettowāku to seiji bunka*. Tokyo: Tokyo Daigaku Shuppankai.

———. 1993. "Kim Yŏng-sam seiken no jinji seisaku." *UP* 250: 23–28.

Hawes, Gary. 1987. *The Philippine State and the Marcos Regime: The Politics of Export*. Ithaca, N.Y.: Cornell University Press.

Hayami, Yujiro, and Saburo Yamada. 1991. *The Agricultural Development of Japan: A Century's Perspective*. Tokyo: University of Tokyo Press.

Hayter, Teresa. 1971. *Aid as Imperialism*. Harmondsworth, U.K.: Penguin.

Hayter, Teresa, and Catharine Watson. 1985. *Aid: Rhetoric and Reality*. London: Pluto Press.

Helm, Leslie. 1985. "The Koreans Are Coming." *Business Week*, December 23, pp. 46–52.

Henderson, Gregory. 1968. *Korea: The Politics of the Vortex*. Cambridge, Mass.: Harvard University Press.

———. 1973. "Japan's Chōsen: Immigrants, Ruthlessness and Developmental Shock." In Andrew C. Nahm, ed., *Korea Under Japanese Colonial Rule: Studies of the Policy and Techniques of Japanese Colonialism*, pp. 261–69. Kalamazoo: Center for Korean Studies, Western Michigan University.

———. 1976. "Korea: Militarist or Unification Policies?" In William J. Barnds, ed., *The Two Koreas in East Asian Affairs*, pp. 123–66. New York: New York University Press.

———. 1980. "Lee In-Soo's Cloud Cuckoo Land." In David R. McCann, ed., *Black Crane 2: An Anthology of Korean Literature*, pp. 95–97. Ithaca, N.Y.: China-Japan Program, Cornell University.

———. 1989. "Korea, 1950." In James Cotton and Ian Neary, eds., *The Korean War in History*, pp. 175–82. Atlantic Highlands, N.J.: Humanities Press International.

———. 1991. "Human Rights in South Korea 1945–1953." In William Shaw, ed., *Human Rights in Korea: Historical and Policy Perspectives*, pp. 125–69. Cambridge, Mass.: Council on East Asian Studies, Harvard University.

Henning, Charles N. 1952. "The Economic Basis of an Independent Korea." Ph.D. diss., University of California, Los Angeles.

Henry, Carl F.H. 1975. "South Korea in the Balances." *Christianity Today*, July 4, pp. 65–66.

Hill, Polly. 1986. *Development Economics on Trial: The Anthropological Case for a Prosecution*. Cambridge: Cambridge University Press.

Hinton, Harold C. 1983. *Korea Under New Leadership: The Fifth Republic*. New York: Praeger.

Hirai Hisashi. 1993. *Souru taryon*. Tokyo: Tokuma Shoten.

Hirakawa Hitoshi. 1988. "Kankoku no yushutsu shikōgata seichō to bōeki." In Ogawa Yūhei, ed., *Kankoku keizai no bunseki*, pp. 167–89. Tokyo: Nihon Hyōronsha.

Hirschman, Albert O. 1958. *The Strategy of Economic Development*. New Haven, Conn.: Yale University Press.

———. 1979. "The Turn to Authoritarianism in Latin America and the Search for Its Economic Determinants." In David Collier, ed., *The New Authoritarianism in Latin America*, pp. 61–98. Princeton, N.J.: Princeton University Press.

———. [1945] 1980. *National Power and the Structure of Foreign Trade*. Exp. ed. Berkeley: University of California Press.

———. [1973] 1981. "The Changing Tolerance for Income Inequality in the Course of Economic Development." In Hirschman, *Essays in Trespassing: Economics to Politics and Beyond*, pp. 39–58. Cambridge: Cambridge University Press.

Hobsbawm, Eric. 1994. *The Age of Extremes: A History of the World, 1914–1991*. New York: Pantheon.

Hofstadter, Richard. 1955. *The Age of Reform: From Bryan to F.D.R.* New York: Knopf.

Hong, Doo-Seung. 1992. "Spatial Distribution of the Middle Classes in Seoul, 1975–1985." *Korea Journal of Population and Development* 21: 73–83.

Hong Doo-Seung [Hong Tu-sŭng] and Koo Hagen [Ku Hae-gŭn]. 1993. *Sahoe kyech'ŭng, kyegŭmnon*. Seoul: Tasan.

Hong, Moon-Shin. 1989. "The Restructuring Experience of the Korean Textile Industry." In Wolfgang Klenner, ed., *Trends of Economic Development in East Asia: Essays in Honour of Willy Kraus*, pp. 493–511. Berlin: Springer Verlag.

Hong, Sawon. 1984. "Urban Migrant Women in the Republic of Korea." In James T. Fawcett, Seiw-Ean Khoo, and Peter C. Smith, eds., *Women in the Cities of Asia: Migration and Urban Adaptation*, pp. 191–210. Boulder, Colo.: Westview Press.

Hong, Sung-chick. 1969. "Values of the Farmers, Businessmen, and Professors." In C. I. Eugene Kim and Ch'angboh Chee, eds., *Aspects of Social Change in Korea*, pp. 165–86. Kalamazoo, Mich.: Korea Research and Publication.

———. 1985. "Korean Social Values in the Year 2000." In Sungjoo Han, ed., *Korea in the Year 2000: Prospects for Development and Change*, pp. 111–21. Seoul: Asiatic Research Center, Korea University.

Hong, Sung Woong. 1993. *Multinationals in Asia: The Case of the Republic of Korea*. Geneva: International Labour Office.

Hong, Wontack. 1976. *Factor Supply and Factor Intensity of Trade in Korea*. Seoul: Korea Development Institute.

Hong, Yi-Sup. 1973. *Korea's Self-Identity*. Seoul: Yonsei University Press.

Hume, David. [1777] 1987. "Whether the British Government Inclines More to Absolute Monarchy, or to a Republic." In Hume, *Essays, Moral, Political, and Literary*, ed. Eugene F. Miller, pp. 47–53. Indianapolis: Liberty Classics.

Huntington, Samuel P. 1957. *The Soldier and the State: The Theory and Politics of Civil-Military Relations*. Cambridge, Mass.: Harvard University Press.

———. 1968. *Political Order in Changing Societies*. New Haven, Conn.: Yale University Press.

———. 1991. *The Third Wave: Democratization in the Late Twentieth Century*. Norman: University of Oklahoma Press.

Hurst, G. Cameron. 1985. "'Uri Nara-ism': Cultural Nationalism in Contemporary Korea." *UFSI Reports* 33: 435–44.

Hwang, Eui-Gak. 1993. *The Korean Economies: A Comparison of North and South*. Oxford: Clarendon Press.

Hwang, Suk-Young. [1985–88] 1994. *The Shadow of Arms*. Trans. Kyung-Ja Chun. Ithaca, N.Y.: East Asia Program, Cornell University.

Hymer, Stephen Herbert. 1979. *The Multinational Corporation: A Radical Approach*. Ed. Robert B. Cohen, Nadine Felton, Morley Nkosi, and Jaap van Liere. Cambridge: Cambridge University Press.

Hyun, Peter. 1974. "A Talk with President Park." *National Review*, May 24, pp. 590–91.

Im Chong-nyŏl. 1985. "Nodong pŏp ŭi chemunje." In Pak Hyŏn-ch'ae et al., *Han'guk chabonjuŭi wa nodong munje*, pp. 179–203. Seoul: Tolbegae.

Im, Ch'ŏru. [1984] 1993. "A Shared Journey." Trans. Bruce Fulton and Ju-Chan Fulton. In Marshall R. Pihl, Bruce Fulton, and Ju-Chan Fulton, eds., *Land of Exile: Contemporary Korean Fiction*, pp. 264–84. Armonk, N.Y.: M. E. Sharpe.

Im Chung-guk. 1966. *Ch'inil munhaknon*. Seoul: P'yŏnghwa Ch'ulp'ansa.

———. 1982. *Ilje ch'imnyak kwa ch'inilp'a*. Seoul: Ch'ŏngsa.

Im, Hyug Baeg. 1987. "The Rise of Bureaucratic Authoritarianism in South Korea." *World Politics* 34: 231–57.

Ishizaka Kōichi. 1993. *Kindai Nihon no shakaishugi to Chōsen*. Tokyo: Shakai Hyōronsha.

Iyer, Pico. 1988. "The Yin and Yang of Paradoxical, Prosperous Korea." *Smithsonian*, August, pp. 47–58.

J.D. 1957. "Korea: We Can't Go Home." *Fortune*, June, p. 159.

Jack, Homer A. 1975. "South Korea: Another South Vietnam?" *America*, November 8, pp. 302–3.

Jackson, Tim. 1990. "South Korea: An Impromptu Performance." In *Economist*, August 18.

Jalée, Pierre. 1968. *The Pillage of the Third World.* Trans. Mary Klopper. New York: Monthly Review Press.

James, William E., Seiji Naya, and Gerald M. Meier. 1989. *Asian Development: Economic Success and Policy Lessons.* Madison: University of Wisconsin Press.

Janelli, Roger L., and Dawnhee Yim Janelli. 1982. *Ancestor Worship and Korean Society.* Stanford, Calif.: Stanford University Press.

Janelli, Roger L., with Dawnhee Yim. 1993. *Making Capitalism: The Social and Cultural Construction of a South Korean Conglomerate.* Stanford, Calif.: Stanford University Press.

Janowitz, Morris. 1964. *The Military in Political Development of New Nations: An Essay in Comparative Analysis.* Chicago: University of Chicago Press.

Johansen, Frida. 1993. *Poverty Reduction in East Asia: The Silent Revolution.* Washington, D.C.: World Bank.

Johnson, Harry G. 1967. "The Ideology of Economic Policy in the New States." In Johnson, ed., *Economic Nationalism in Old and New States*, pp. 124–41. Chicago: University of Chicago Press.

Johnson, R. H. 1972. "Social Development Aspects of the Third Five-Year Plan." In Sung-Hwan Jo and Seong-Ywang Park, eds., *Basic Documents and Selected Papers of Korea's Third Five-Year Economic Development Plan (1972–1976)*, pp. 184–93. Seoul: n.p.

Johnston, Bruce F., and Peter Kilby. 1975. *Agriculture and Structural Transformation: Economic Strategies in Late-Developing Countries.* New York: Oxford University Press.

Jones, Leroy P. 1975. *Public Enterprise and Economic Development: The Korean Case.* Seoul: Korea Development Institute.

Jones, Leroy P., and Il SaKong. 1980. *Government, Business, and Entrepreneurship in Economic Development: The Korean Case.* Cambridge, Mass.: Council on East Asian Studies, Harvard University.

Jones, Leroy P., and Edward S. Mason. 1982. "Role of Economic Factors in Determining the Size and Structure of the Public-Enterprise Sector in Less-Developed Countries with Mixed Economies." In Leroy P. Jones, ed., *Public Enterprise in Less-Developed Countries*, pp. 17–47. Cambridge: Cambridge University Press.

Kahin, George McT. 1986. *Intervention: How America Became Involved in Vietnam.* New York: Knopf.

Kahn, E. J. 1961. "Our Far-Flung Correspondent: Spring in Korea." *New Yorker*, May 27, pp. 43–71.

Kajimura Hideki. 1977. *Chōsenshi: sono hatten.* Tokyo: Kōdansha.

Kang Chae-ŏn. 1986. *Chōsen kindaishi.* Tokyo: Heibonsha.

Kang Haeng-u. 1986. *Minamichōsen keizairon.* Tokyo: Aoki Shoten.
Kang In-ch'ŏl. 1992. "Haebanghu Han'guk kaesin'gyohoe wa kukka, simin sahoe (1945–1960)." In Han'guk Sahoesa Yŏn'guhoe, ed., *Hyŏndae Han'guk ŭi chonggyo wa sahoe,* pp. 98–141. Seoul: Munhak kwa Chisŏngsa.
Kang Man-gil. 1984a. *Chosŏnsidae sanggongŏpsa yŏn'gu.* Seoul: Han'gilsa.
————. 1984b. *Han'guk hyŏndaesa.* Seoul: Ch'angjak kwa Pip'yŏngsa.
Kang Myŏng-sun. 1985. *Pinmin yŏsŏng, pinmin adong.* Seoul: Ach'im.
Kang, Myung Hun. *The Korean Business Conglomerate: Chaebol Then and Now.* Berkeley: Institute of East Asian Studies, University of California.
Kang Sang-jung. 1993. "Shakai kagakusha no shokuminchi ninshiki: shokuminchi seisakugaku to orientarizumu." In Yamanouchi Yasushi et al., eds., *Iwanami kōza shakaikagaku no hōhō,* vol. 3, *Nihon shakaikagaku no shisō,* pp. 101–30. Tokyo: Iwanami Shoten.
Kang, Sŏk-kyŏng. [1986] 1989. "A Room in the Woods." Trans. Bruce Fulton and Ju-Chan Fulton. In Sŏk-kyŏng Kang, Chi-wŏn Kim, and Chŏng-hŭi O, *Words of Farewell: Stories by Korean Women Writers,* pp. 28–147. Seattle: Seal Press.
Kang Sŏng-ch'ŏl. 1988. *Chuhan Migun.* Seoul: Ilsongjŏng.
Kang, T. W. 1989. *Is Korea the Next Japan?: Understanding the Structure, Strategy, and Tactics of America's Next Competitor.* New York: Free Press.
Kang Ton-gu. 1992. *Han'guk kŭndae chonggyo wa minjokjuŭi.* Seoul: Chipmundang.
Kang Yŏng-ji. 1991. *Higashi Ajia no saihen to Kankoku keizai.* Tokyo: Shakai Hyōronsha.
Kawai Kazuo. 1988. "Kōgyōka seisaku no henbō." In Ogawa Yūhei, ed., *Kankoku keizai no bunseki,* pp. 71–89. Tokyo: Nihon Hyōronsha.
Kearney, Robert P. 1991. *The Warrior Worker: The Challenge of the Korean Way of Working.* New York: Henry Holt.
Keidel, Albert, III. 1981. *Korean Regional Farm Product and Income: 1910–1975.* Seoul: Korea Development Institute.
Keim, Willard D. 1979. *The Korean Peasant at the Crossroads: A Study in Attitudes.* Bellingham: Center for East Asian Studies, Western Washington University.
Keir, R. Malcolm. 1914. "Modern Korea." *Bulletin of the American Geographical Society* 46: 756–69, 817–30.
Kendall, Laurel. 1996. *Getting Married in Korea: Of Gender, Morality, and Modernity.* Berkeley: University of California Press.
Keon, Michael. 1977. *Korean Phoenix: A Nation from the Ashes.* Englewood Cliffs, N.J.: Prentice-Hall International.

Kerkvliet, Benedict J. 1977. *The Huk Rebellion: A Study of Peasant Revolt in the Philippines*. Berkeley: University of California Press.

———. 1990. *Everyday Politics in the Philippines: Class and Status Relations in a Central Luzon Village*. Berkeley: University of California Press.

Khong, Yuen Foong. 1992. *Analogies at War: Korea, Munich, Dien Bien Phu, and the Vietnam Decisions of 1965*. Princeton, N.J.: Princeton University Press.

Kihl, Young Whan. 1984. *Politics and Policies in Divided Korea: Regimes in Contest*. Boulder, Colo.: Westview.

———. 1990. "South Korea in 1989: Slow Progress Toward Democracy." *Asian Survey* 30: 67–73.

Kim, Byong Kuk. 1965. *Central Banking Experiment in a Developing Economy*. Seoul: Korea Research Center.

Kim, Byong-Soh. 1990. "The Explosive Growth of the Korean Church Today: A Social Analysis." In Christian Institute for the Study of Justice and Development, ed., *Korean Church*, pp. 47–60. Seoul: Christian Institute for the Study of Justice and Development.

Kim, Byung-Kook. 1987. "Bringing and Managing Socioeconomic Change: The State in Korea and Mexico." Ph.D. diss., Harvard University.

Kim, Byung Whan. 1992. *Seniority Wage System in the Far East: Confucian Influence over Japan and South Korea*. Aldershot, U.K.: Avebury.

Kim, C.I. Eugene. 1971. "The Military in the Politics of South Korea: Creating Political Order." In Morris Janowitz and Jacques van Doorn, eds., *On Military Intervention*, pp. 361–86. Rotterdam: Rotterdam University Press.

Kim, Chang Nam, Hirokazu Kajiwara, and Toshio Watanabe. 1984. "A Consideration of the Compressed Process of Agricultural Development in the Republic of Korea." *Developing Economies* 22: 113–36.

Kim, Chi Ha. 1974. *Cry of the People and Other Poems*. Hayama, Japan: Autumn Press.

———. 1978. *The Gold-Crowned Jesus and Other Writings*. Ed. Sun Kim Chong and Shelly Killen. Maryknoll, N.Y.: Orbis.

Kim Chin-gyun, ed. 1983. *Che-3 segye wa sahoeiron*. Seoul: Hanul.

Kim Chin-gyun and Cho Hŭi-yŏn, eds. 1990. *Han'guk sahoeron*. Seoul: Hanul.

Kim Chong-gil. 1993. "Hwan'gyŏng munje wa hwan'gyŏng undong." In Im Hŭi-sŏp and Pak Kil-sŏng, eds., *Onŭl ŭi Han'guk sahoe*, pp. 319–44. Seoul: Nanam.

Kim, Choong Soon. 1988. *Faithful Endurance: An Ethnography of Korean Family Dispersal*. Tucson: University of Arizona Press.

————. 1992. *The Culture of Korean Industry: An Ethnography of Poongsan Corporation.* Tucson: University of Arizona Press.

Kim Ch'ung-sik. 1992. *Namsan ŭi pujangdŭl.* 2 vols. Seoul: Tonga Ilbosa.

Kim, Chung-yum. 1994. *Policymaking on the Front Lines: Memoirs of a Korean Practitioner, 1945–79.* Washington, D.C.: World Bank.

Kim, Dae Jung. 1987. *Prison Writings.* Trans. Sung-il Choi and David R. McCann. Berkeley: University of California Press.

Kim, Dongno. 1990. "The Transformation of Familism in Modern Korean Society: From Cooperation to Competition." *International Sociology* 5: 409–25.

Kim, Eun Mee. 1988. "From Dominance to Symbiosis: State and Chaebol in Korea." *Pacific Focus* 3(2): 105–21.

————. 1989–90. "Foreign Capital in Korea's Economic Development, 1960–1985." *Studies in Comparative International Development* 24(4): 24–45.

Kim, Eun-Shil. 1993. "The Making of the Modern Female Gender: The Politics of Gender in Reproductive Practices in Korea." Ph.D. diss., University of California, San Francisco.

Kim, Gyu-Won. 1989. "Unemployment Among the Educated in South Korea: A Consequence of Export-led Growth Policy." Ph.D. diss., University of Wisconsin, Madison.

Kim, Han K., ed. 1972. *Reunification of Korea: 50 Basic Documents.* Washington, D.C.: Institute for Asian Studies.

Kim, Helen Kiteuk. 1931. *Rural Education for the Regeneration of Korea.* New York: n.p.

Kim, Hong Nack. 1989. "The 1988 Parliamentary Election in South Korea." *Asian Survey* 29: 480–95.

Kim Hyŏng-gi. 1988. *Han'guk ŭi tokchom chabon kwa imnodong.* Seoul: Kkach'i.

Kim, Hyung Kook, and Su-Hoon Lee. 1994. "Commodity Chains and the Korean Automobile Industry." In Gary Gereffi and Miguel Korzeniewicz, eds., *Commodity Chains and Global Capitalism,* pp. 281–96. Westport, Conn.: Praeger.

Kim, Illsoo. 1981. *New Urban Immigrants: The Korean Community in New York.* Princeton, N.J.: Princeton University Press.

Kim, Jae-On, and B. C. Koh. 1980. "The Dynamics of Electoral Politics: Social Development, Political Participation, and Manipulation on Electoral Laws." In Chong Lim Kim, ed., *Political Participation in Korea: Democracy, Mobilization and Stability,* pp. 59–84. Santa Barbara, Calif.: CLIO.

Kim, Jai-Hyup. 1970. "The Economic Effects of the Vietnam War in Southeast and East Asia." Master's thesis, Indiana University.

————. 1978. *The Garrison State in Pre-War Japan and Post-War Korea: A Comparative Analysis of Military Politics.* Lanham, Md.: University Press of America.

Kim, Ji Hong. 1989. "Korea's Industrial Policies for Declining Industries." Seoul: Korea Development Institute.

Kim, Jin-Hyun. 1986. "South Korea on Edge." *World Press Review,* October 26–28.

Kim, Jinwung. 1989. "Recent Anti-Americanism in South Korea: The Causes." *Asian Survey* 29: 749–63.

Kim, Joon-Kyung, Sang Dal Shim, and Jun-Il Kim. 1995. "The Role of the Government in Promoting Industrialization and Human Capital Accumulation in Korea." In Takatoshi Ito and Anne O. Krueger, eds., *Growth Theories in the Light of the East Asian Experience,* pp. 181–200. Chicago: University of Chicago Press.

Kim, Joungwon Alexander. 1975. *Divided Korea: The Politics of Development, 1945–1972.* Cambridge, Mass.: East Asian Research Center, Harvard University.

Kim, Jung Sae. 1975. "Recent Trends in the Government's Management of the Economy." In Edward Reynolds Wright, ed., *Korean Politics in Transition,* pp. 255–81. Seattle: University of Washington Press.

Kim, Katherine Y. 1996. "A Few Bad Apples." *Far Eastern Economic Review,* February 22, pp. 27–28.

Kim, Kihwan, and Danny M. Leipziger. 1993. *The Lessons of East Asia: Korea—A Case of Government-Led Development.* Washington, D.C.: World Bank.

Kim, Kwang Bong. 1971. *The Korea-Japan Treaty Crisis and the Instability of the Korean Political System.* New York: Praeger.

Kim, Kwang Chung, and Shin Kim. 1989. "Kinship Group and Patrimonial Executives in a Developing Nation: A Case Study of Korea." *Journal of Developing Areas* 24: 27–46.

Kim, Kwang Suk, and Michael Roemer. 1981. *Growth and Structural Transformation.* Cambridge, Mass.: Council on East Asian Studies, Harvard University.

Kim, Kyong-Dong. 1979. *Man and Society in Korea's Economic Growth: Sociological Studies.* Seoul: Seoul National University Press.

————[Kim Kyong-dŏng]. 1992. *Han'gugin ŭi kach'igwan kwa sahoeŭisik.* Seoul: Pagyŏngsa.

————. 1994. "Confucianism and Capitalist Development in East Asia." In Leslie Sklair, ed., *Capitalism and Development,* pp. 87–106. London: Routledge.

Kim, Mahn Kee. 1991. "The Administrative Culture of Korea: A Comparison with China and Japan." In Gerald E. Caiden and Bun Woong Kim, *A Dragon's Progress: Development Administration in Korea*, pp. 26–39. West Hartford, Conn.: Kumarian Press.

Kim Nak-jung. 1982. *Han'guk nodong undongsa: haebanghu p'yŏn.* Seoul: Ch'ŏngsa.

—————. 1985. "Chisigin kwa nodong undong." In Pak Hyŏn-ch'ae et al., *Han'guk chabonjuŭi wa nodong munje*, pp. 391–418. Seoul: Tolbegae.

Kim Paek-san. 1985. "Han'guk nodong chohap undong ŭi t'ŭksŏng." In Pak Hyŏn-ch'ae et al., *Han'guk chabonjuŭi wa nodong munje*, pp. 205–26. Seoul: Tolbegae.

Kim, Quee-Young. 1983. *The Fall of Syngman Rhee.* Berkeley: Institute of East Asian Studies, University of California.

Kim, Se Jin. 1971. *The Politics of Military Revolution in Korea.* Chapel Hill: University of North Carolina Press.

Kim, Seok Ki. 1987. "Business Concentration and Government Policy: A Study of the Phenomenon of Business Groups in Korea, 1945–1985." D.B.A. diss., Harvard University.

Kim, Seong-Kon. 1991. "On Native Grounds: Revolution and Renaissance in Art and Culture." In Chong Sik Lee, *Korea Briefing, 1990*, pp. 97–117. Boulder, Colo.: Westview Press.

Kim, Seung Hee. 1970. *Foreign Capital for Economic Development: A Korean Case Study.* New York: Praeger.

Kim, Shin-Bok. 1990. "Educational Policy Changes in Korea: Ideology and Praxis." In Gill-Chin Lim and Wook Chang, eds., *Dynamic Transformation: Korea, NICs, and Beyond*, pp. 383–403. Urbana, Ill.: Consortium on Development Studies.

Kim Sŏk-jun. 1992. *Han'guk sanŏphwa kukkanon.* Seoul: Nanam.

Kim Sun-il. 1973. "Betonamu sensō to Kankoku." *Sekai*, March, pp. 135–43.

Kim, Sŭngok. [1965] 1993. "Seoul: 1964, Winter." Trans. Marshall R. Pihl. In Marshall R. Pihl, Bruce Fulton, and Ju-Chan Fulton, eds., *Land of Exile: Contemporary Korean Fiction*, pp. 84–101. Armonk, N.Y.: M. E. Sharpe.

Kim, Taek Il, John A. Ross, and George C. Worth. 1972. *The Korean National Family Planning Program: Population Control and Fertility Behavior.* New York: Population Council.

Kim, Uchang. 1993. "The Agony of Cultural Construction: Politics and Culture in Modern Korea." In Hagen Koo, ed., *State and Society in Contemporary Korea*, pp. 163–95. Ithaca, N.Y.: Cornell University Press.

Kim, W. S. 1991. "The President's Emergency Decree for Economic Stability and Growth (1972)." In Lee-Jay Cho and Yoon Hyung Kim, eds., *Economic Development in the Republic of Korea: A Policy Perspective*, pp. 163–81. Honolulu: East-West Center

Kim Yŏng-ho. 1988. *Higashi Ajia kōgyōka to sekai shihonshugi: dai 4-sedai kōgyōkaron*. Tokyo: Tōyō Keizai Shinpōsha.

Kim Yŏng-mo. 1990. *Han'guk pin'gon yŏn'gu*. Seoul: Han'guk Pokchi Chŏngch'aek Yŏn'guso.

Kim, Yŏng-nok. [1964] 1973. "On Korean Entrepreneurship." Trans. T'ae-yŏng Pak. In Marshall R. Pihl, ed., *Listening to Korea: A Korean Anthology*, pp. 227–37. New York: Praeger.

Kim Yŏng-sŏk. 1989. *Han'guk sahoe sŏnggyŏk kwa tosi pimmin undong*. Seoul: Ach'im.

Kim Yong-sŏp. 1970. *Chosŏn hugi nongŏpsa yŏn'gu: nongch'on kyŏngje sahoe pyŏndong*. Seoul: Iljogak.

Kim, Yoon Hyung. 1991. "Policy Response to the Oil Crisis and the Presidential Emergency Decree (1974)." In Lee-Jay Cho and Yoon Hyung Kim, eds., *Economic Development in the Republic of Korea: A Policy Perspective*, pp. 183–206. Honolulu: East-West Center.

Kim Yun-hwan et al. 1981. *Han'guk kyŏngje ŭi chŏn'gae kwajŏng*. Seoul: Tolbegae.

Kim, Yung-chung. 1986. "Women's Movement in Modern Korea." In Sei-wha Chung, ed., *Challenges for Women: Women's Studies in Korea*, trans. Chang-hyun Shin et al., pp. 75–102. Seoul: Ewha Womans University Press.

King, Russell. 1977. *Land Reform: A World Survey*. Boulder, Colo.: Westview Press.

Kirk, Donald. 1982. "Democracy without Dissent in Korea." *New Leader*, March 8, pp. 5–7.

———. 1994. *Korean Dynasty: Hyundai and Chung Ju Yung*. Armonk, N.Y.: M. E. Sharpe.

Klein, Sidney. 1958. *The Pattern of Land Tenure Reform in East Asia After World War II*. New York: Bookman Associates.

Ko Kyŏng-sim. 1988. "Han'guk yŏsŏng nodongja ŭi kŏn'gang munje." *Yŏsŏng* 3: 50–68.

Ko, Un. 1993. *The Sound of My Waves: Selected Poems by Ko Un*. Trans. Brother Anthony of Taizé and Young-Moo Kim. Ithaca, N.Y.: East Asia Program, Cornell University.

Kobayashi Hideo. 1975. *"Dai Tōa kyōeiken" no keisei to hōkai*. Tokyo: Ochanomizu Shobō.

———. 1983. *Sengo Nihon shihonshugi to "Higashi Ajia keizaiken."* Tokyo: Ochanomizu Shobō.

Koh, B. C. 1973. "Convergence and Conflict in the Two Koreas." *Current History*, November, pp. 205–27.

Koh, Byung-ik. 1973. "The Attitude of Koreans Toward Japan." Trans.

Jame B. Palais. In Marshall R. Pihl, ed., *Listening to Korea: A Korean Anthology*, pp. 43–51. New York: Praeger.

Koh, Kwang Il. 1963. "In Quest of National Unity and Power: Political Ideas and Practices of Syngman Rhee." Ph.D. diss., Rutgers University.

Koh, Soo Kohn. 1973. "Commodity Composition of Exports of Manufactures from a Developing Country: The Case of Republic of Korea." Ph.D. diss., New York University.

Koh, Yeong-kyeong. 1962. "Land Reform and Agricultural Structure in Korea." *Korean Affairs* 1: 428–39.

Kolko, Gabriel. 1988. *Confronting the Third World: United States Foreign Policy, 1945–1980.* New York: Pantheon.

———. 1994. *Century of War: Politics, Conflict, and Society Since 1914.* New York: New Press.

Kong Che-uk. 1992. "1950-nyŏndae kukka ŭi chaejŏng-kŭmyung chŏngch'aek kwa taegiŏp ŭi sŏngjang." In Han'guk Sahoesa Yŏn'guhoe, ed., *Han'guk chabonjuŭi wa chaebŏl.* Seoul: Munhak kwa Chisŏngsa.

Koo, Bohn Young. 1985. "The Role of Direct Foreign Investment in Korea's Recent Economic Growth." In Walter Galenson, ed., *Foreign Trade and Investment: Economic Development in the Newly Industrializing Asian Countries*, pp. 176–216. Madison: University of Wisconsin Press.

Koo, Hagen. 1984. "The Political Economy of Income Distribution in South Korea: The Impact of the State's Industrialization Policies." *World Development* 12: 1029–1037.

———. 1987. "The Interplay of State, Social Class, and World System in East Asian Development: The Cases of South Korea and Taiwan." In Frederic C. Deyo, ed., *The Political Economy of the New Asian Industrialism*, pp. 165–81. Ithaca, N.Y.: Cornell University Press.

———. 1991. "From Farm to Factory: Proletarianization in Korea." *American Sociological Review* 55: 669–81.

———. 1993. "The State, *Minjung*, and the Working Class in South Korea." In Hagen Koo, ed., *State and Society in Contemporary Korea*, pp. 131–62. Ithaca, N.Y.: Cornell University Press.

Koo, Hagen, and Eun Mee Kim. 1992. "The Developmental State and Capital Accumulation in South Korea." In Richard P. Appelbaum and Jeffrey Henderson, eds., *States and Development in the Asian Pacific Rim*, pp. 121–49. Newbury Park, Calif.: Sage.

Koo, Suk Mo. 1994. "Korea's Big Business Groups and International Competitiveness." In Seung Yeung Kwack, ed., *The Korean Economy at a Crossroad: Development Prospects, Liberalization, and South-North Economic Integration*, pp. 151–66. Westport, Conn.: Praeger.

Koo, Youngnok. 1975. "The Conduct of Foreign Affairs." In Edward Reynolds Wright, ed., *Korean Politics in Transition*, pp. 207–42. Seattle: University of Washington Press.

Korea Development Institute. 1975. *Korea's Economy: Past and Present*. Seoul: Korea Development Institute.

Korzeniewicz, Miguel. 1994. "Commodity Chains and Marketing Strategies: Nike and the Global Athletic Footwear Industry." In Gary Gereffi and Miguel Korzeniewicz, eds., *Commodity Chains and Global Capitalism*, pp. 247–65. Westport, Conn.: Praeger.

Krasner, Stephen D. 1978. *Defending the National Interest: Raw Materials Investments and U.S. Foreign Policy*. Stanford, Calif.: Stanford University Press.

————. 1985. *Structural Conflict: The Third World Against Global Liberalism*. Berkeley: University of California Press.

Ku To-wan. 1994. "Han'guk hwan'gyŏng undong ŭi yŏksa wa t'ŭksŏng." Ph.D. diss., Seoul National University.

Kuk, Minho. 1988. "The Governmental Role in the Making of *Chaebol* in the Industrial Development of South Korea." *Asian Perspective* 12: 107–33.

Kuramochi Kazuo. 1985. "Kankoku ni okeru nōchi kaikaku to sonogo no kosaku no tenkai." *Ajia kenkyū* 32(2): 1–33.

Kuznets, Paul W. 1977. *Economic Growth and Structure in the Republic of Korea*. New Haven, Conn.: Yale University Press.

————. 1994. *Korean Economic Development: An Interpretive Model*. Westport, Conn.: Praeger.

Kuznets, Simon. 1973. *Population, Capital, and Growth: Selected Essays*. New York: Norton.

Kwack, Seung Yeung. 1990. "The Economy of South Korea, 1980–1987." In Lawrence J. Lau, ed., *Models of Development: A Comparative Study of Economic Growth in South Korea and Taiwan*, rev. and exp. ed., pp. 217–36. San Francisco: ICS Press.

Kwon, Tai Hwan. 1977. *Demography of Korea: Population Change and Its Components, 1925–66*. Seoul: Seoul National University Press.

Ladurie, Emmanuel Le Roy. 1979. "Peasants." In Peter Burke, ed., *The New Cambridge Modern History XIII: Companion Volume*, pp. 115–63. Cambridge: Cambridge University Press.

LaFeber, Walter. [1983] 1993. *Inevitable Revolutions: The United States in Central America*. 2d ed., rev. and exp. New York: Norton.

Larson, James F., and Heung-Soo Park. 1993. *Global Television and the Politics of the Seoul Olympics*. Boulder, Colo.: Westview Press.

Lary, Hal B. 1968. *Imports of Manufactures from Less Developed Countries*. New York: National Bureau of Economic Research.

Lautensach, Hermann. 1950. *Korea: Land, Volk, Schicksal.* Stuttgart, Germany: K. F. Koehler Verlag.

Lauterbach, Richard E. 1947. *Danger from the East.* New York: Harper & Brothers.

League of Nations [Folke Hilgerdt]. 1945. *Industrialization and Foreign Trade.* Geneva: League of Nations.

Lee, Bun Song. 1994. "Sex Discrimination in Korea's Job Market." In Seung Yeung Kwack, ed., *The Korean Economy at a Crossroad: Development Prospects, Liberalization, and South-North Economic Integration,* pp. 73–105. Westport, Conn.: Praeger.

Lee, Chong Sik. 1963. *The Politics of Korean Nationalism.* Berkeley: University of California Press.

———. 1985. *Japan and Korea: The Political Dimension.* Stanford, Calif.: Hoover Institution Press.

Lee, Chung Hoon. 1991. "Promotion Measures for Construction Service Exports to the Middle East (1975)." In Lee-Jay Cho and Yoon Hyung Kim, eds., *Economic Development in the Republic of Korea: A Policy Perspective,* pp. 527–49. Honolulu: East-West Center.

Lee, Eun Ho, and Yong Soon Yim. 1980. *Politics of Military Civic Action: The Case of South Korean and South Vietnamese Forces in the Vietnamese War.* Hong Kong: Asian Research Service.

Lee, Gin-Fu Larry. 1973. "The Structure of the Hardwood Plywood Industry in the Far East Exporting Countries: Japan, Republic of China, Republic of Korea, and the Philippines." Ph.D. diss., Oregon State University.

Lee, Hae-yong. 1969. "Modernization of the Family Structure in an Urban Setting—with Special Reference to Marriage Relation." In C. I. Eugene Kim and Ch'angboh Chee, eds., *Aspects of Social Change in Korea,* pp. 44–69. Kalamazoo, Mich.: Korea Research and Publication.

Lee, Hahn-Been. 1968. *Korea: Time, Change, and Administration.* Honolulu: East-West Center Press.

———. 1982. *Future, Innovation and Development.* Seoul: Panmun Book.

Lee, Hoon K. 1936. *Land Utilization and Rural Economy in Korea.* Chicago: University of Chicago Press.

Lee, Hy Sang. 1994. "Economic Factors in Korean Reunification." In Young Whan Kihl, ed., *Korea and the World: Beyond the Cold War,* pp. 189–215. Boulder, Colo.: Westview Press.

Lee, Jeong Taik. 1988. "Dynamics of Labor Control and Labor Protest in the Process of Export-oriented Industrialization in South Korea." *Asian Perspective* 12: 134–58.

Lee, Joe Won. 1966. "Planning Efforts for Economic Development." In

Joseph S. Chung, ed., *Korea: Patterns of Economic Development*, pp. 1–24. Kalamazoo, Mich.: Korea Research and Publication.

Lee, Ki-baik. 1984. *A New History of Korea*. Trans. Edward W. Wagner with Edward J. Shultz. Cambridge, Mass.: Harvard University Press.

Lee, Kyu-Uck, Shujiro Urata, and Inbom Choi. 1992. "Industrial Organization: Issues and Recent Developments." In Vittorio Corbo and Sang-Mok Suh, eds., *Structural Adjustment in a Newly Industrialized Country: The Korean Experience*, pp. 204–27. Baltimore, Md.: Johns Hopkins University Press.

Lee, Man Gap. 1982. *Sociology and Social Change in Korea*. Seoul: Seoul National University Press.

Lee, Manwoo. 1990. *The Odyssey of Korean Democracy: Korean Politics, 1987–1990*. New York: Praeger.

Lee, Nae-Young. 1993. "The Politics of Industrial Restructuring: A Comparison of the Auto Industry in South Korea and Mexico." Ph.D. diss., University of Wisconsin, Madison.

Lee, Naeyoung, and Jeffrey Cason. 1994. "Automobile Commodity Chains in the NICs: A Comparison of South Korea, Mexico, and Brazil." In Gary Gereffi and Miguel Korzeniewicz, eds., *Commodity Chains and Global Capitalism*, pp. 223–43. Westport, Conn.: Praeger.

Lee, Nak-ho. 1989. "Korea Suffers Ill Name as Baby Exporter." *Korea Times*, November 1, p. 14.

Lee, Ok-jie. 1990. "Labor Control and Labor Protest in the South Korean Textile Industry, 1945–1985." Ph.D. diss., University of Wisconsin, Madison.

Lee Sookjong [Yi Suk-chong]. 1992. "Han'guk chŏnjaeng kwa ilbon ŭi kyŏngjejŏk sŏngjang." In Han'guk Sahoehakhoe, ed., *Han'guk chŏnjaeng kwa Han'guk sahoe pyŏndong*, pp. 360–83. Seoul: P'ulbit.

———. 1995. "Korean Perceptions on National Security." *Korea Focus* 3(4): 13–23.

Lee, Steven Hugh. 1995. *Outposts of Empire: Korea, Vietnam, and the Origins of the Cold War in Asia, 1949–1959*. Montreal: McGill-Queen's University Press.

Lee, Su-Hoon. 1993. "Transitional Politics of Korea, 1987–1992: Activation of Civil Society." *Pacific Affairs* 66: 351–67.

Lee, Suk Bok. 1987. *The Impact of U.S. Forces in Korea*. Washington, D.C.: National Defense University Press.

Lee, Suk-Chae. 1991. "The Heavy and Chemical Industries Promotion Plan (1973–79). In Lee-Jay Cho and Yoon Hyung Kim, eds., *Economic Development in the Republic of Korea: A Policy Perspective*, pp. 431–71. Honolulu: East-West Center.

Lee, Young Jo. 1990. "Legitimation, Accumulation, and Exclusionary

Authoritarianism: Political Economy of Rapid Industrialization in South Korea and Brazil." Ph.D. diss., Harvard University Press.

Leffler, Melvyn P. 1992. *A Preponderance of Power: National Security, the Truman Administration, and the Cold War.* Stanford, Calif.: Stanford University Press.

———. 1994. "The Interpretive Wars over the Cold War, 1945–1960." In Gordon Martel, ed., *American Foreign Relations Reconsidered, 1890–1993*, pp. 106–24. London: Routledge.

Leipziger, D. M., D. Dollar, A. F. Shorrocks, and S. Y. Song. 1992. *The Distribution of Income and Wealth in Korea.* Washington, D.C.: World Bank.

Lent, John A. 1990. *The Asian Film Industry.* Austin: University of Texas Press.

Lewin, Tamar. 1990. "South Korea Slows Export of Babies for Adoption." *New York Times,* February 12, A15.

Lewis, John P. 1955. *Reconstruction and Development in South Korea.* Washington, D.C.: National Planning Association.

Lewis, Linda. 1988. "The 'Kwangju Incident' Observed: An Anthropological Perspective on Civil Uprisings." In Donald N. Clark, ed., *The Kwangju Uprising: Shadows over the Regime in South Korea,* pp. 15–27. Boulder, Colo.: Westview Press.

Lewis, W. Arthur. 1955. *The Theory of Economic Growth.* London: George Allen & Unwin.

———. 1966. *Development Planning: The Essentials of Economic Policy.* London: George Allen & Unwin.

———. [1949] 1969. *The Principles of Economic Planning.* 3d ed. London: George Allen & Unwin.

———. 1978. *The Evolution of the International Economic Order.* Princeton, N.J.: Princeton University Press.

Lie, John. 1990a. "Is Korean Management Just Like Japanese Management?" *Management International Review* 30: 113–18.

———. 1990b. "South Korean Development: The Elusive Reality of Conflicts and Contradictions." *Pacific Affairs* 63: 367–72.

———. 1991a. "The Prospect for Economic Democracy in South Korea." *Economic and Industrial Democracy* 12: 501–13.

———. 1991b. "Democratization and Its Discontents: Origins of the Present Crisis in South Korea." *Monthly Review* 42(9): 38–52.

———. 1991c. "The State, Industrialization and Agricultural Sufficiency: The Case of South Korea." *Development Policy Review* 9: 37–51.

———. 1991d. "Rethinking the 'Miracle'—Economic Growth and Political Struggles in South Korea." *Bulletin of Concerned Asian Scholars* 22: 64–69.

————. 1992a. "The Political Economy of South Korean Development." *International Sociology* 7: 285–300.

————. 1992b. "The Concept of Mode of Exchange." *American Sociological Review* 57: 508–23.

————. 1995. "The Transformation of Sexual Work in Twentieth-Century Korea." *Gender & Society* 9: 310–27.

————. 1996a. "From Agrarian Patriarchy to Patriarchal Capitalism." In Valentine M. Moghadam, ed., *Patriarchy and Development: Women's Positions at the End of the Twentieth Century*, pp. 34–55. Oxford: Clarendon Press.

————. 1996b. "The Confucian Ethic in South Korea? A Critique." *Kyŏngje yŏn'gu* (Hanyang University) 17: 177–92.

Liebau, Eberhard. 1987. "Labor-management Relations in the Republic of Korea." In Il SaKong, ed., *Human Resources and Social Development Issues*, pp. 64–107. Seoul: Korea Development Institute.

Lim, Hy-Sop. 1982. "Acceptance of American Culture in Korea: Patterns of Cultural Contact and Korean Perception of American Culture." In Sungjoo Han, ed., *After One Hundred Years: Continuity and Change in Korean-American Relations*, pp. 28–40. Seoul: Asiatic Research Center, Korea University.

Lim, Hyun-Chin. 1985. *Dependent Development in Korea, 1963–1979*. Seoul: Seoul National University Press.

Lim, Hyun-Chin, and Woon-Seon Paek. 1987. "State Autonomy in Modern Korea: Institutional Possibility and Structural Limits." *Korea Journal* 27(11): 19–32.

Lim, Youngil. 1973. "Gains and Costs of Postwar Industrialization in South Korea." Occasional Paper Series, Center for Korean Studies, University of Hawaii.

————. 1981. *Government Policy and Private Enterprise: Korean Experience in Industrialization*. Berkeley: Institute of East Asian Studies, University of California.

Lipton, Michael. 1977. *Why Poor People Stay Poor*. Cambridge, Mass.: Harvard University Press.

List, Friedrich. [1885] 1966. *The National System of Political Economy*. Trans. Sampson S. Lloyd. New York: Augustus M. Kelley.

————. [1837] 1983. *The Natural System of Political Economy*. Trans. and ed. W. O. Henderson. London: Frank Cass.

Lockwood, Christopher. 1988. "Division of the Spoils." *Economist*, May 21.

Lone, Stewart, and Gavan McCormack. 1993. *Korea Since 1850*. Melbourne, Australia: Longman Cheshire.

Lord, Mary. 1987. "Chun's Option: To Crush or Concede." *U.S. News & World Report*, June 29, pp. 26–28.

Louie, Miriam Ching Yoon. 1995. "*Minjung* Feminism: Korean Women's Movement for Gender and Class Liberation." *Women's Studies International Forum* 18: 417–30.

Lovell, John P. 1970. "Politics and Military in South Korea." In Lovell, ed., *The Military and Politics in Five Developing Nations*, pp. 143–202. Kensington, Md.: American Institute for Research.

———. 1975. "The Military and Politics in Postwar Korea." In Edward Reynolds Wright, ed., *Korean Politics in Transition*, pp. 153–99. Seattle: University of Washington Press.

Lowenthal, Abraham F., ed. 1975. *The Peruvian Experiment: Continuity and Change Under Military Rule*. Princeton, N.J.: Princeton University Press.

Luedde-Neurath, Richard. 1986. *Import Controls and Export-Oriented Development: A Reassessment of the South Korean Case*. Boulder, Colo.: Westview Press.

———. 1988. "State Intervention and Export-oriented Development in South Korea." In Gordon White, ed., *Developmental States in East Asia*, pp. 68–112. Houndmills, U.K.: Macmillan.

Luttwak, Edward. 1968. *Coup d'Etat: A Practical Handbook*. London: Allen Lane.

Lyons, Gene M. 1961. *Military Policy and Economic Aid: The Korean Case, 1950–1953*. Columbus: Ohio State University Press.

Mabe Yōichi. 1986. *Kankoku keizairyoku no yomikata*. Tokyo: Nihon Jitsugyō Shuppansha.

Macdonald, Donald Stone. 1990. *The Koreans: Contemporary Politics and Society*. 2d ed. Boulder, Colo.: Westview Press.

———. 1992. *U.S. Korean Relations from Liberation to Self-Reliance: The Twenty-Year Record*. Boulder, Colo.: Westview Press.

MacEwan, Arthur. 1990. *Debt and Disorder: International Economic Instability and U.S. Imperial Decline*. New York: Monthly Review Press.

MacGaffey, Janet. 1991. *The Real Economy of Zaire: The Contribution of Smuggling and Other Unofficial Activities to National Wealth*. Philadelphia: University of Pennsylvania Press.

Maddison, Angus. 1995. *Monitoring the World Economy, 1820–1922*. Paris: OECD.

Maeda Yasuhiro. 1988. *Daitenkanki no Chōsen hantō*. Tokyo: Kyōikusha.

Mallaby, Sebastian. 1995. "The House That Park Built." *Economist*, June 3.

Mardon, Russell. 1990. "The State and the Effective Control of Foreign Capital: The Case of South Korea." *World Politics* 43: 111–38.

Martin, James R. 1973. "Institutionalization and Professionalization of the Republic of Korea Army: The Impact of United States Military Assistance through Development of a Military School System." Ph.D. diss., Harvard University.

Mason, Edward S. 1982. "Stages of Economic Growth Revisited." In Charles P. Kindleberger and Guido di Tella, eds., *Economics in the Long View*, vol. 1, *Models and Methodology*, pp. 116–40. New York: New York University Press.

Mason, Edward S., Mahn Je Kim, Dwight H. Perkins, Kwang Suk Kim, and David C. Cole. 1980. *The Economic and Social Modernization of the Republic of Korea*. Cambridge, Mass.: Council on East Asian Studies, Harvard University.

Masumi Junnosuke. 1993. *Hikaku seiji III: Higashi Ajia to Nihon*. Tokyo: Tokyo Daigaku Shuppankai.

Mathews, Tom. 1980. "Chon 'Koreanizes' Democracy." *Newsweek*, August 25, pp. 43–44.

Matray, James Irving, ed. 1991. *Historical Dictionary of the Korean War*. Westport, Conn.: Greenwood Press.

Maxfield, Sylvia. 1990. *Governing Capital: International Finance and Mexican Politics*. Ithaca, N.Y.: Cornell University Press.

McBeth, John, and Mark Clifford. 1988. "Now, the Peaceful Invasion." *Far Eastern Economic Review*, September 8, pp. 51–54.

McCann, David R. 1979. "Arirang: The National Folksong of Korea." In David R. McCann, John Middleton, and Edward J. Schultz, eds., *Studies on Korea in Transition*, pp. 43–56. Honolulu: Center for Korean Studies, University of Hawaii.

McCormack, Gavan. 1978a. "The South Korean Economy: GNP versus the People." In Gavan McCormack and Mark Selden, eds., *Korea, North and South: The Deepening Crisis*, pp. 91–111. New York: Monthly Review Press.

———. 1978b. "Japan and South Korea, 1965–1975: Ten Years of 'Normalisation.'" In Gavan McCormack and Mark Selden, eds., *Korea, North and South: The Deepening Crisis*, pp. 171–87. New York: Monthly Review Press.

———. 1978c. "Britain, Europe and Korea." In Gavan McCormack and Mark Selden, eds., *Korea, North and South: The Deepening Crisis*, pp. 188–98. New York: Monthly Review Press.

McCormick, Thomas J. 1989. *America's Half-Century: United States Foreign Policy in the Cold War*. Baltimore, Md.: Johns Hopkins University Press.

McCune, George M. 1950. *Korea Today*. Cambridge, Mass.: Harvard University Press.

McCune, Shannon. 1956. *Korea's Heritage: A Regional and Social Geography*. Rutland, Vt.: Charles E. Tuttle.

————. 1966. *Korea: Land of Broken Calm*. Princeton, N.J.: D. Van Nostrand.

McGinn, Noel F., Donald R. Snodgrass, Yung Bong Kim, Shin-Bok Kim, and Quee-Young Kim. 1980. *Education and Development in Korea*. Cambridge, Mass.: Council on East Asian Studies, Harvard University.

McGleish, Weyland. 1977. "Letter from Seoul." *America*, February 5, pp. 99–101.

McNamara, Dennis L. 1990. *The Colonial Origins of Korean Enterprise, 1910–1945*. Cambridge: Cambridge University Press.

Meade, E. Grant. 1951. *American Military Government in Korea*. New York: King's Crown Press.

Merrill, John. 1983. "Internal Warfare in Korea, 1948–1950: The Local Setting of the Korean War." In Bruce Cumings, ed., *Child of Conflict: The Korean-American Relationships, 1943–1953*, pp. 133–62. Seattle: University of Washington Press.

————. 1989. *Korea: The Peninsular Origins of the War*. Newark: University of Delaware Press.

Michell, Tony [A. Michell]. 1982. "South Korea: Vision of the Future for Labour Surplus Economies." In Manfred Bienefeld and Martin Godfrey, eds., *The Struggle for Development: National Strategies in an International Context*, pp. 189–216. Chichester, U.K.: John Wiley & Sons.

————. 1984. "Administrative Traditions and Economic Decision-making in South Korea." *IDS Bulletin* 15: 32–37.

————. 1988. *From a Developing to a Newly Industrialised Country: The Republic of Korea, 1961–82*. Paris: International Labour Office.

————. 1989. "Control of the Economy During the Korean War: The 1952 Co-ordination Agreement and Its Consequences." In James Cotton and Ian Neary, eds., *The Korean War in History*, pp. 151–62. Atlantic Highlands, N.J.: Humanities Press International.

Mies, Maria. 1986. *Patriarchy and Accumulation on a World Scale: Women in the International Division of Labour*. London: Zed.

Mills, C. Wright. 1959. *The Sociological Imagination*. London: Oxford University Press.

Mills, Edwin S., and Byung-Nak Song. 1979. *Urbanization and Urban Problems*. Cambridge, Mass.: Council on East Asian Studies, Harvard University.

Min, Yŏng-bin, ed. [1960] 1993. *The April Heroes*. Seoul: Sisayŏngosa.

Minard, Lawrence. 1985. "The Fragile Miracle on the Han." *Forbes*, February 11, pp. 38–41.

Ministry of Culture and Information. N.d. *Threat and Response:*

Questions and Answers about the Proposed Special Measures Law on National Defense. Seoul: Ministry of Culture and Information.

Ministry of Public Information, Republic of Korea. 1965. *Korean Economy: Progress and Prospect*. Seoul: Ministry of Public Information.

Ministry of Reconstruction, Republic of Korea. 1958. *Development of the Korean Economy*. Seoul: Ministry of Reconstruction.

———. 1959. *Korea's Continuing Development*. Seoul: Ministry of Reconstruction.

Mitchell, Bernard, and John Ravenhill. 1995. "Beyond Product Cycles and Flying Geese: Regionalization, Hierarchy, and the Industrialization of East Asia." *World Politics* 47: 171–209.

Mitchell, C. Clyde. 1948. "Land Management and Tenancy Reform in Korea Against a Background of United States Army Occupation, 1945–1948." Ph.D. diss., Harvard University.

———. 1949. "Land Reform in South Korea." *Pacific Affairs* 22: 144–54.

———. 1951. *Korea: Second Failure in Asia*. Washington, D.C.: Public Affairs Institute.

Mitchell, Timothy. [1989] 1991. *Colonising Egypt*. Berkeley: University of California Press.

Miyata Setsuko. 1985. *Chōsen minshū to "kōminka" seisaku*. Tokyo: Miraisha.

Moffitt. Michael. 1983. *The World's Money: International Banking from Bretton Woods to the Brink of Insolvency*. New York: Simon & Schuster.

Moon, Chung-In. 1988. "The Demise of a Developmentalist State? Neoconservative Reforms and Political Consequences in South Korea." *Journal of Developing Societies* 4: 67–84.

———. 1995. "Globalization: Challenges and Strategies." *Korea Focus* 3(3): 62–77.

Moon, Pal Yong. 1982. "Problems in Organizing Joint Utilization of Farm Machinery in Korea's Smallholder System." In Chi-ming Hou and Tzong-shian Yu, eds., *Agricultural Development in China, Japan and Korea*, pp. 195–228. Taipei: Academia Sinica.

———. 1991a. "A Positive-Grain Price Policy (1969) and Agricultural Development." In Lee-Jay Cho and Yoon Hyung Kim, eds., *Economic Development in the Republic of Korea: A Policy Perspective*, pp. 371–404. Honolulu: East-West Center.

———. 1991b. "The Saemaul (New Community) Movement (1971)." In Lee-Jay Cho and Yoon Hyung Kim, eds., *Economic Development in the Republic of Korea: A Policy Perspective*, pp. 405–27. Honolulu: East-West Center.

Moon, Tong Hwan (Stephen). 1982. "Korean Minjung Theology: An

Introduction." In Wonmo Dong, ed., *Korean-American Relations at Crossroads*, pp. 12–34. Princeton Junction, N.J.: Association of Korean Christian Scholars in North America.

Moore, Barrington, Jr. 1966. *Social Origins of Dictatorship and Democracy: Lord and Peasant in the Making of the Modern World.* Boston: Beacon Press.

Moore, Mick. 1984. "Mobilization and Disillusion in Rural Korea: The Saemaul Movement in Retrospect." *Pacific Affairs* 57: 577–98.

———. 1988. "Economic Growth and the Rise of Civil Society: Agriculture in Taiwan and South Korea." In Gordon White, ed., *Developmental States in East Asia*, pp. 113–52. Houndmills, U.K.: Macmillan.

Moran, Theodore H. 1974. *Multinational Corporations and the Politics of Dependence: Copper in Chile.* Princeton, N.J.: Princeton University Press.

Morley, James W. 1965. *Japan and Korea: America's Allies in the Pacific.* New York: Walker.

Morrow, Robert B., and Kenneth H. Sherper. 1970. *Land Reform in South Korea.* Washington, D.C.: U.S. Agency for International Development.

Mullins, Mark R. 1994. "The Empire Strikes Back: Korean Pentecostal Mission to Japan." In Karla Poewe, ed., *Charismatic Christianity as a Global Culture*, pp. 87–102. Columbia: University of South Carolina Press.

Mydans, Seth. 1995. "Vietnam Speaks English with an Eager Accent." *New York Times*, May 7, E16.

Nakagawa Nobuo. 1988. *Chōsen hantō wa dōnaruka.* Tokyo: Miraisha.

———. 1990. *Gekidō no Chōsen hantō.* Tokyo: Ryokufū Shuppan.

Nakane Chie. 1973. "Kankoku sobyō: hito to hito no majiwari." In *Kankoku nōson no kazoku to saigi*, pp. 183–87. Tokyo: Tokyo Daigaku Shuppankai.

Nam, Chang-Hee. 1995. "South Korea's Big Business Clientelism in Democratic Reform." *Asian Survey* 35: 357–66.

Nam, Joo-Hong. 1986. *America's Commitment to South Korea: The First Decade of the Nixon Doctrine.* Cambridge: Cambridge University Press.

Nam, Koon Woo. 1989. *South Korean Politics: The Search for Political Consensus and Stability.* Lanham, Md.: University Press of America.

Nam, Sang-Woo, and Chung H. Lee. 1995. "Korea." In Stephan Haggard and Chung H. Lee, eds., *Financial Systems and Economic Policy in Developing Countries*, pp. 31–55. Ithaca, N.Y.: Cornell University Press.

Nara Chŏngch'aek Yŏn'guhoe, ed. 1993. *Han'guk sahoe undong ŭi hyŏksin ŭl wihayŏ*. Seoul: Paeksan Sŏdang.

Nathan (Robert R.) Associates. 1952. *Preliminary Report on Economic Reconstruction of Korea*. Washington, D.C.: Robert R. Nathan Associates.

————. 1954. *An Economic Programme for Korean Reconstruction*. Washington, D.C.: Robert R. Nathan Associates.

Naya, Seiji. 1971. "The Vietnam War and Some Aspects of Its Economic Impact on Asian Countries." *Developing Economies* 9: 31–57.

Neff, Robert, and Laxmi Nakarmi. 1991. "Asia's Next Powerhouse: An All-But-Unified Korea?" *Business Week*, October 14, p. 63.

Nishina Kenichi and Noda Kyōmi. 1989. *Kankoku kōgai repōto: genpatsu kara rōsai made*. Tokyo: Shinkansha.

Nodongbu. 1988. *1987-yŏn yŏrŭm ŭi nosa pun'gyu p'yŏngga pogosŏ*. Seoul: Nodongbu.

Nomura Sōgō Kenkyūsho, ed. 1988. *Sekai ni hiyaku suru Kankoku sangyō: sono pawā no gensen o saguru*. Tokyo: Nomura Sōgō Kenkyūsho.

Norman, E. H. 1940. *Japan's Emergence as a Modern State*. New York: Institute of Pacific Relations.

North, James. 1986. "Korea's Conscience." *New Republic*, November 3, pp. 15–18.

North, Liisa, and Tanya Korovkin. 1981. *The Peruvian Revolution and the Officers in Power, 1967–1976*. Montreal: Centre for Developing Area Studies, McGill University.

Nurkse, Ragnar. 1962. *Equilibrium and Growth in the World Economy*. Ed. Gottfried Haberler and Robert M. Stern. Cambridge, Mass.: Harvard University Press.

O Sŏng. 1989. *Chosŏn hugi sangin yŏn'gu*. Seoul: Iljogak.

Odell, John S. 1982. *U.S. International Monetary Policy: Markets, Power, and Ideas as Sources of Change*. Princeton, N.J.: Princeton University Press.

O'Donnell, Guillermo A. 1979. *Modernization and Bureaucratic-Authoritarianism: Studies in South American Politics*. Berkeley: Institute of International Studies, University of California.

Office of Administrative Coordination for the Prime Minister, Republic of Korea. 1981. *Evaluation Report of the Fourth Year Program: The Fourth Five-Year Economic Development Plan*. Seoul: Office of Administrative Coordination for the Prime Minister, Republic of Korea.

Office of Economic Analysis and Reporting, U.S. Aid for International Development. 1972. *Survey of the Korean Hardwood Ply-*

wood Industry and International Plywood Markets. Seoul: Office of Economic Analysis and Reporting, U.S. Aid for International Development.

Office of the President. 1975. *Saemaul*. Seoul: Office of the President, Republic of Korea.

Office of Public Information. 1955. *Where Korea Stands*. Seoul: Office of Public Information, Republic of Korea.

Ogle, George E. 1977. *Liberty to the Captives: The Struggle Against Oppression in South Korea*. Atlanta: John Knox Press.

———. 1990. *South Korea: Dissent within the Economic Miracle*. London: Zed.

Oh, John Kie-chiang. 1968. *Korea: Democracy on Trial*. Ithaca, N.Y.: Cornell University Press.

———. 1996. "The 1995 Local Elections in Korea." In Robert G. Rich Jr., ed., *Korea's Economy 1996*, pp. 22–29. Washington, D.C.: Korea Economic Institute of America.

Oh, Suek Hong. 1982. "The Counter-corruption Campaign of the Korean Government (1975–1977)." In Bun Woong Kim and Wha Joon Rho, eds., *Korean Public Bureaucracy*, pp. 322–44. Seoul: Kyobo Publishing.

Oh, Sun Joo. 1983. "The Living Conditions of Female Workers in Korea." *Korea Observer* 14: 185–200.

Okai Teruo. 1976. *Kankoku 15-nen no shuyakutachi*. Tokyo: Asahi Sonorama.

Oliver, Robert T. 1993. *A History of the Korean People in Modern Times, 1800 to the Present*. Newark: University of Delaware Press.

Oregon Advisory Group in Korea. 1961. *A Report on the University of Oregon Advisory Mission to the Korean Economic Development Council*. Eugene: School of Business Administration, University of Oregon.

Osgood, Cornelius. 1951. *The Koreans and Their Culture*. New York: Ronald Press.

Otsuka, Keijiro. 1993. "Land Tenure and Rural Poverty." In M. G. Quibria, ed., *Rural Poverty in Asia: Priority Issues and Policy Options*, pp. 260–86. Hong Kong: Oxford University Press.

Oxman, Stephen A., Otto Triffterer, and Francisco B. Cruz. 1987. *South Korea: Human Rights in the Emerging Politics*. N.p.: International Commission of Jurists.

Ozawa, Terutomo. 1979. *Multinationalism, Japanese Style: The Political Economy of Outward Dependency*. Princeton, N.J.: Princeton University Press.

Packenham, Robert A. 1973. *Liberal America and the Third World:*

Political Development Ideas in Foreign Aid and Social Science. Princeton, N.J.: Princeton University Press.

————. 1992. *The Dependency Movement: Scholarship and Politics in Development Studies.* Cambridge, Mass.: Harvard University Press.

Paddock, William, and Elizabeth Paddock. 1973. *We Don't Know How: An Independent Audit of What They Call Success in Foreign Assistance.* Ames: Iowa State University Press.

Paik, Nak-chung. 1993. "The Idea of a Korean National Literature Then and Now." *positions* 1: 553–80.

Pak, Chi-Yong. 1980. *Political Opposition in Korea, 1945–1960.* Seoul: Seoul National University Press.

Pak Hyŏn-ch'ae. 1978. *Minjung kwa kyŏngje.* Seoul: Chongŭsa.

————. 1983. *Han'guk kyŏngje wa nongŏp.* Seoul: Kkach'i.

————. 1984. "Han'guk chabonjuŭi chŏn'gae ŭi chedan'gye wa kŭ kujojŏk t'ŭkching." In Pak et al., *Han'guk sahoe ŭi chaeinsik 1,* pp. 19–50. Seoul: Hanul.

————. 1988. *Minjok kyŏngje wa minjung undong.* Seoul: Ch'angjak kwa Pip'yŏngsa.

Pak Hyŏn-ch'ae and Cho Hŭi-yŏn, eds. 1989. *Han'guk sahoe kusŏngch'e nonjaeng.* 2 vols. Seoul: Chuksan.

Pak Hyŏn-ch'ae et al. 1985. *Han'guk chabonjuŭi wa nodong munje.* Seoul: Tolbegae.

Pak Il. 1992. *Kankoku no NIES-ka no kunō: keizai kaihatsu to minshuka no jirenma.* Tokyo: Dōbunkan.

Pak, Ki Hyuk. 1956. "Economic Analysis of Land Reform in the Republic of Korea with Special Reference to an Agricultural Economic Survey, 1954–1955." Ph.D. diss., University of Illinois at Urbana-Champaign.

Pak, Ki Hyuk, and Kee Chun Han. 1969. *An Analysis of Food Consumption in the Republic of Korea.* Seoul: Yonsei University.

Pak, Ki Hyuk, with Sidney D. Gamble. 1975. *The Changing Korean Village.* Seoul: Shin-Hung Press.

Pak Kŭn-ho. 1993. *Kankoku no keizai hatten to Betonamu sensō.* Tokyo: Ochanomizu Shobō.

Pak Kyŏng-sik. 1973. *Nihon teikokushugi no Chōsen shihai.* 2 vols. Tokyo: Aoki Shoten.

Pak Se-gil. 1989. *Tasi ssŭnŭn Han'guk hyŏndaesa 2: hyujŏn esŏ 10–26 kkaji.* Seoul: Tolbegae.

————. 1992. *Tasi ssŭnŭn Han'guk hyŏndaesa 3: 1980-nyŏn esŏ 90-nyŏndaech'o kkaji.* Seoul: Tolbegae.

Pak T'ae-sun and Kim Tong-ch'un. 1991. *1960-nyŏndae ŭi sahoe undong.* Seoul: Kkach'i.

Pak Wŏn-sun. 1989. *Kukka poanpŏp yŏn'gu 1: kukka poanpŏp pyŏnch'ŏnsa.* Seoul: Yŏksa Pip'yŏngsa.

Palais, James B. 1975. *Politics and Policy in Traditional Korea.* Cambridge, Mass.: Harvard University Press.

———. 1986. "Human Rights in the Republic of Korea." In Asia Watch, ed., *Human Rights in Korea,* pp. 1–339. Washington, D.C.: Asia Watch.

———. 1996. *Confucian Statecraft and Korean Institutions: Yu Hyŏngwŏn and the Late Chosŏn Dynasty.* Seattle: University of Washington Press.

Palley, Marian Lief. 1990. "Women's Status in South Korea: Tradition and Change." *Asian Survey* 30: 1136–53.

Parente, William J. 1974. "Korea: Time to Dissent." *America,* November 23, pp. 319–21.

Park, Anna Y.M. 1992. "South Korea: Mass Retrenchment vs Labour Shortage." *Asian Women Workers Newsletter* 11(2): 14–16.

Park, Chong Kee. 1991. "The 1966 Tax Administration Reform, Tax Law Reforms, and Government Saving." In Lee-Jay Cho and Yoon Hyung Kim, eds., *Economic Development in the Republic of Korea: A Policy Perspective,* pp. 247–72. Honolulu: East-West Center.

Park, Chung Hee. 1962. *Our Nation's Path.* Seoul: Dong-A.

———. [1962] 1970. *The Country, the Revolution and I.* 2d ed. Seoul: Hollym.

———. 1971. *To Build a Nation.* Washington, D.C.: Acropolis Books.

———. 1979a. *Korea Reborn: A Model for Development.* Englewood Cliffs, N.J.: Prentice-Hall.

———. 1979b. *Saemaul: Korea's New Community Movement.* Seoul: Korea Textbook Company.

Park, Eul Yong. 1984. "An Analysis of the Trade Behavior of American and Japanese Manufacturing Firms in Korea." In Karl Moskowitz, ed., *From Patron to Partner,* pp. 19–37. Lexington, Mass.: Lexington Books.

———. 1985. "Foreign Economic Policies and Economic Development." In Youngnok Koo and Sungjoo Han, eds., *The Foreign Policy of the Republic of Korea,* pp. 106–36. New York: Columbia University Press.

Park, Jae Kyu. 1985. "Korea and the Third World." In Youngnok Koo and Sungjoo Han, eds., *The Foreign Policy of the Republic of Korea,* pp. 219–61. New York: Columbia University Press.

Park, No-Yong. 1961. "Should We Impose Democracy on Korea?" *Current History,* December, pp. 341–65.

Park, Seong Ho. 1969. "Export Expansion and Import Substitution in the Economic Development of Korea, 1955–1965." Ph.D. diss., American University.

Park, Young June. 1974. "Land Reform in South Korea." Ph.D. diss., Temple University.

Park, Young-Ki. 1974. *Labor and Industrial Relations in Korea: System and Practice.* Seoul: Institute for Labor and Management, Sogang University.

Park, Yung Chul. 1994. "Korea: Development and Structural Change of the Financial System." In Hugh T. Patrick and Yung Chul Park, eds., *The Financial Development of Japan, Korea, and Taiwan: Growth, Repression, and Liberalization,* pp. 129–87. New York: Oxford University Press.

Park, Yung Chul, and Dong Won Kim. 1994. "Korea: Development and Structural Change of the Banking System." In Hugh T. Patrick and Yung Chul Park, eds., *The Financial Development of Japan, Korea, and Taiwan: Growth, Repression, and Liberalization,* pp. 188–221. New York: Oxford University Press.

Pastor, Robert A. 1980. *Congress and the Politics of U.S. Foreign Economic Policy, 1929–1976.* Berkeley: University of California Press.

Payer, Cheryl. 1974. *The Debt Trap: The International Monetary Fund and the Third World.* New York: Monthly Review Press.

———. 1982. *The World Bank: A Critical Analysis.* New York: Monthly Review Press.

———. 1991. *Lent and Lost: Foreign Credit and Third World Development.* London: Zed.

Perlmutter, Amos. 1977. *The Military and Politics in Modern Times: On Professionals, Praetorians, and Revolutionary Soldiers.* New Haven, Conn.: Yale University Press.

Polanyi, Michael. 1959. *The Study of Man.* Chicago: University of Chicago Press.

Portway, Donald. 1953. *Korea: Land of the Morning Calm.* London: Harrap.

Pred, Allan. 1992. "Outside(rs) In and Inside(rs) Out: South Korean Capital Encounters Organized Labor in a California Industrial Suburb." In Allan Pred and Michael John Watts, *Reworking Modernity: Capitalisms and Symbolic Discontent,* pp. 155–91. New Brunswick, N.J.: Rutgers University Press.

Preston, Samuel H. 1988. "Urban Growth in Developing Countries: A Demographic Reappraisal." In Josef Gugler, ed., *The Urbanization of the Third World,* pp. 11–31. Oxford: Oxford University Press.

Prosterman, Roy L., and Jeffrey M. Riedinger. 1987. *Land Reform and*

Democratic Development. Baltimore, Md.: Johns Hopkins University Press.

Pye, Lucian W. 1985. *Asian Power and Politics: The Cultural Dimensions of Authority.* Cambridge, Mass.: Harvard University Press.

Pyŏn Hyŏng-yun and Kim Tae-hwan, eds. 1980. *Che-3 segye ŭi kyŏngje paljŏn.* Seoul: Kkach'i.

Quijano, Aníbal. 1971. *Nationalism and Capitalism in Peru: A Study in Neo-Imperialism.* Special issue of *Monthly Review* 23(3).

Rabinow, Paul. 1989. *French Modern: Norms and Forms of the Social Environment.* Cambridge, Mass.: MIT Press.

Reeve, W. D. 1963. *The Republic of Korea: A Political and Economic Study.* London: Oxford University Press.

Republic of Korea. 1962. *Summary of the First Five-Year Economic Plan, 1962–1966.* Seoul: Republic of Korea.

———. 1966. *The Second Five-Year Economic Development Plan, 1967–1971.* Seoul: Republic of Korea.

———. 1971. *The Third Five-Year Economic Development Plan, 1972–1976.* Seoul: Republic of Korea.

———. 1976. *The Fourth Five-Year Economic Development Plan, 1977–1981.* Seoul: Republic of Korea.

Reynolds, L. G. 1983. "The Spread of Economic Growth to the Third World: 1850–1980." *Journal of Economic Literature* 21: 941–80.

Rhee, Jong-Chan. 1994. *The State and Industry in South Korea: The Limits of the Authoritarian State.* London: Routledge.

Richards, Alan, and John Waterbury. 1990. *A Political Economy of the Middle East: State, Class, and Economic Development.* Boulder, Colo.: Westview Press.

Robertson, A. F. 1984. *People and the State: An Anthropology of Planned Development.* Cambridge: Cambridge University Press.

Robinson, Joan. [1962] 1964. *Economic Philosophy.* Harmondsworth, U.K.: Penguin.

———. 1965. "Korean Miracle." *Monthly Review* 16(9): 541–49.

———. 1974. *Reflections on the Theory of International Trade.* Manchester: Manchester University Press.

Robinson, Michael Edson. 1988. *Cultural Nationalism in Colonial Korea, 1920–1925.* Seattle: University of Washington Press.

———. 1993. "Enduring Anxieties: Cultural Nationalism and Modern East Asia." In Harumi Befu, ed., *Cultural Nationalism in East Asia: Representation and Identity,* pp. 167–86. Berkeley: Institute of East Asian Studies, University of California.

Rodgers, Ronald A. 1993. "Industrial Relations Policies and Practices in the Republic of Korea in a Time of Rapid Change: The Influence of American-Invested and Japanese-Invested Transnational Corporations." Ph.D. diss., University of Wisconsin, Madison.

Roh, Tae Woo. 1990. *Korea: A Nation Transformed: Selected Speeches*. Oxford: Pergamon.

Rostow, W. W. [1960] 1971. *The Stages of Economic Growth: A Non-Communist Manifesto*. 2d ed. Cambridge: Cambridge University Press.

Rowan, Roy. 1977. "There's Also Some Good News about South Korea." *Fortune*, September, pp. 170–76.

Sakurai Hiroshi. 1976. *Kankoku nōchi kaikaku no saikentō*. Tokyo: Ajia Keizai Kenkyūsho.

———. [1979] 1991. "Kankoku inasaku seisanryoku no shindankai to sono kōzō." In Taniura Takao, ed., *Chōsen hantō*, pp. 147–72. Tokyo: Ajia Keizai Kenkyūsho.

Sandbrook, Richard. 1993. *The Politics of Africa's Economic Recovery*. Cambridge: Cambridge University Press.

Sandbrook, Richard, with Judith Barker. 1985. *The Politics of Africa's Economic Stagnation*. Cambridge: Cambridge University Press.

Satterwhite, David H. 1994. "The Politics of Economic Development: Coup, State, and the Republic of Korea's First Five-Year Economic Development Plan (1962–1966)." Ph.D. diss., University of Washington.

Scalapino, Robert A., and Chong-Sik Lee. 1972. *Communism in Korea: Part I*. Berkeley: University of California Press.

Scott, John. 1982. *The Upper Classes: Property and Privilege in Britain*. London: Macmillan.

Secretariat, Supreme Council for National Reconstruction. 1961. *Military Revolution in Korea*. Seoul: Secretariat, Supreme Council for National Reconstruction, Republic of Korea.

Sen, Amartya K. 1981. *Poverty and Famines*. Oxford: Clarendon Press.

Seok, Hyunho. 1982. "Migration Differentials and Socioeconomic Structure in Korea." In Yunshik Chang, Tai-Hwan Kwon, and Peter J. Donaldson, eds., *Society in Transition with Special Reference to Korea*, pp. 101–30. Seoul: Seoul National University Press.

Seoul Kyŏngje Sinmun, ed. 1992. *Han'guk ŭi inmaek*. Seoul: Han'guk Ilbo.

Shapiro, Michael. 1990. *The Shadow in the Sun: A Korean Year of Love and Sorrow*. New York: Atlantic Monthly Press.

Shaplen, Robert. 1972. "New Chapter in Korea-II." *New Yorker*, December 2, pp. 128–55.

———. 1976. "Letter from South Korea." *New Yorker*, January 26, pp. 64–81.

———. 1978. "Letter from South Korea." *New Yorker*, November 13, pp. 173–222.

———. 1980. "Letter from South Korea." *New Yorker*, November 17, pp. 174–207.

Shaw, Edward S. 1973. *Financial Deepening in Economic Development.* New York: Oxford University Press.

Sherry, Michael S. 1995. *In the Shadow of War: The United States Since the 1930s.* New Haven, Conn.: Yale University Press.

Shim, Jae Hoon, and Andrew Sherry. 1995. "Absolute Power." *Far Eastern Economic Review*, November 30, pp. 71–72.

Shimizu Toshiyuki. 1987. "Park Chung Hee ishin taisei to rōdō tōsei no tenkai." 3 parts. *Hokudai Hōgaku Ronshū* 36: 1747–1780; 37: 469–519; 38: 275–93.

Shin, Dong-Ho. 1993. "Economic Growth and Environmental Problems in South Korea: The Role of Government." In Michael C. Howard, ed., *Asia's Environmental Crisis*, pp. 235–56. Boulder, Colo.: Westview Press.

Shin, Gi-Wook. 1990. "Defensive Struggles or Forward-Looking Efforts: Tenancy Disputes in Colonial Korea." *Journal of Korean Studies* 7: 3–33.

Shorrock, Tim. 1996. "Debacle in Kwangju." *Nation*, December 9, pp. 19–22.

Sin Tu-bŏm. 1993. *Kankoku seiji no genzai: Minshuka e no dainamikusu.* Tokyo: Yūhikaku.

Sin Yong-ha. 1987. *Han'guk kŭndae sahoe sasangsa yŏn'gu.* Seoul: Iljisa.

———. 1990. *Han'guk hyŏndaesa wa minjok munje.* Seoul: Munhak kwa Chisŏngsa.

Sin Yu-gŭn. 1984. *Han'guk kiŏp ŭi t'uksŏng kwa kwaje.* Seoul: Seoul Taehakkyo Ch'ulp'anbu.

Smith, Lee. 1984. "Korea's Challenge to Japan." *Fortune*, February 6, pp. 94–104.

Sŏ, Kiwŏn. [1963] 1990. "The Heir." Trans. Uchang Kim. In Peter Lee, ed., *Modern Korean Literature: An Anthology*, pp. 169–83. Honolulu: University of Hawaii Press.

Sŏ Kwan-mo. 1984. *Hyŏndae sahoe ŭi kyegŭp kusŏng kwa kyegŭp punhwa.* Seoul: Hanul.

Sochurek, Howard. 1969. "South Korea: Success Story in Asia." *National Geographic*, March, pp. 301–45.

Sohn, Hak-Kyu. 1989. *Authoritarianism and Opposition in South Korea.* London: Routledge.

Sohn, Jae Souk. 1968. "Political Dominance and Political Failure: The Role of the Military in the Republic of Korea." In *The Military In-*

tervenes: Case Studies in Political Development, pp. 103–21. New York: Russell Sage Foundation.

Sŏl Tong-hun. 1992. "Kukche nodongnyŏk idong kwa Han'gungnae oegugin nodongja." In Han'guk Sahoesa Yŏn'guhoe, ed., *Han'guk ŭi chiyŏk munje wa nodong kyegŭp*, pp. 231–325. Seoul: Munhak kwa Chisŏngsa.

Solzhenitsyn, Alexander. 1974. *The Gulag Archipelago*. Vol. 1. Trans. Thomas Whitney. New York: Harper & Row.

Son, Dug-Soo. 1983. "The Change of Rural Community and Rural Poor Women." In Christian Institute for the Study of Justice and Development, ed., *My Mother's Name Is Worry: A Preliminary Report of the Study on Poor Women in Korea*, pp. 85–153. Seoul: Christian Institute for the Study of Justice and Development.

Song, Byung-Nak. 1990. *The Rise of the Korean Economy*. Hong Kong: Oxford University Press.

Song Chŏng-nam. 1985. "Han'guk nodong undong kwa chisigin ŭi yŏkhal." In Kim Kŭm-su et al., *Han'guk nodong undongnon*, pp. 177–96. Seoul: Miraesa.

Sonu, Hwi. 1980. "Thoughts of Home." Trans. Marshall R. Pihl. In David R. McCann, ed., *Black Crane 2: An Anthology of Korean Literature*, pp. 24–36. Ithaca, N.Y.: China-Japan Program, Cornell University.

Sorensen, Clark W. 1988. *Over the Mountains Are Mountains: Korean Peasant Households and Their Adaptations to Rapid Industrialization*. Seattle: University of Washington Press.

Sŏuldae Sahoehakkwa Sahoe Paljŏn Yŏn'guhoe. 1988. *Nongmin ch'ŭngbunhae wa nongmin undong*. Seoul: Miraesa.

Spencer, Robert F. 1988. *Yŏgong: Factory Girl*. Seoul: Royal Asiatic Society, Korea Branch.

Stallings, Barbara. 1990. "The Role of Foreign Capital in Economic Development." In Gary Gereffi and Donald L. Wyman, eds., *Manufacturing Miracles: Paths of Industrialization in Latin America and East Asia*, pp. 55–89. Princeton, N.J.: Princeton University Press.

Standish, Isolde. 1994. "Korean Cinema and the New Realism: Text and Context." In Wimal Dissanayake, ed., *Colonialism and Nationalism in Asian Cinema*, pp. 65–89. Bloomington: Indiana University Press.

Steinberg, David I., Sung-Hwan Ban, W. Donald Bowles, and Maureen A. Lewis. 1984. *Korean Agricultural Services: The Invisible Hand in the Iron Glove. Market and Nonmarket Forces in Korean Rural Development*. Washington, D.C.: U.S. Agency for International Development.

Steinmo, Sven. 1993. *Taxation and Democracy: Swedish, British, and*

American Approaches to Financing the Modern State. New Haven, Conn.: Yale University Press.

Stendhal. [1830] 1991. *The Red and the Black*. Trans. Catherine Slater. Oxford: Oxford University Press.

Stepan, Alfred. 1978. *The State and Society: Peru in Comparative Perspective*. Princeton, N.J.: Princeton University Press.

Stephens, Bernard. 1988. "Labor Resurgence in South Korea." *Nation*, November 19, pp. 193–96.

Stopford, John M., and Susan Strange. 1991. *Rival States, Rival Firms: Competition for World Market Shares*. Cambridge: Cambridge University Press.

Streeten, Paul. 1987. *What Price Food? Agricultural Price Policies in Developing Countries*. Houndmills, U.K.: Macmillan.

Stueck, William. 1995. *The Korean War: An International History*. Princeton, N.J.: Princeton University Press.

Suh, Bong Kyun. 1972. *The Strategy for Agricultural Development in Korea*. Seoul: Samhwa.

Suh, Dae-Sook. 1988. *Kim Il Sung: The North Korean Leader*. New York: Columbia University Press.

Suh, David Kwang-Sun. 1990. "Forty Years of Korean Protestant Churches." In Christian Institute for the Study of Justice and Development, ed., *Korean Church*, pp. 22–46. Seoul: Christian Institute for the Study of Justice and Development.

Suh, Sang-Chul. 1978. *Growth and Structural Changes in the Korean Economy, 1910–1940*. Cambridge, Mass.: Council on East Asian Studies, Harvard University.

Suh, Sang-Mok. 1992. "The Economy in Historical Perspective." In Vittorio Corbo and Sang-Mok Suh, eds., *Structural Adjustment in a Newly Industrialized Country: The Korean Experience*, pp. 6–34. Baltimore, Md.: Johns Hopkins University Press.

Suh, Suk Tai. 1975. *Import Substitution and Economic Development in Korea*. Seoul: Korea Development Institute.

Sumiya Mikio. 1976. *Kankoku no keizai*. Tokyo: Iwanami Shoten.

Tacitus. [97–98] 1970. "Agricola." In Tacitus, *Agricola, Germania, Dialogus*. Loeb Classical Library.

Tai, Hung-Chao. 1974. *Land Reform and Politics: A Comparative Analysis*. Berkeley: University of California Press.

Takasaki Sōji. 1993. *"Hannichi kanjō": Kankoku, Chōsenjin to Nihonjin*. Tokyo: Kōdansha.

Takizawa Hideki. 1984. *Kankoku minzokushugiron josetsu*. Tokyo: Kage Shobō.

———. 1988. *Kankoku shakai no tenkan*. Tokyo: Ochanomizu Shobō.

———. 1992a. *Kankoku no keizai hatten to shakai kōzō.* Tokyo: Ochanomizu Shobō.

———. 1992b. *Kankoku e no samazama na tabi.* Tokyo: Kage Shobō.

Tamura Tetsuo. 1984. *Gekidō Seoul 1500 nichi: Chun Doo Hwan seiken e no michi.* Tokyo: Seikō Shobō.

Tanaka Akira. 1988. *Kankoku no "minzoku" to "hannichi."* Tokyo: Asahi Shinbunsha.

Taniura Takao. 1989. *Kankoku no kōgyōka to kaihatsu taisei.* Tokyo: Ajia Keizai Kenkyūsho.

Tanzer, Andrew. 1988. "Samsung: South Korea Marches to Its Own Drummer." *Forbes,* May 16, pp. 84–89.

Tax, Sol. 1953. *Penny Capitalism: A Guatemalan Indian Economy.* Washington, D.C.: Smithonian Institution.

Taylor, Eugene. 1953. "South Korea's Job of Reconstruction." *New York Times Magazine,* June 14, pp. 10–11.

Theobald, Robin. 1990. *Corruption, Development and Underdevelopment.* Durham, N.C.: Duke University Press.

Thompson, E. P. [1967] 1991. "Time, Work-Discipline and Industrial Capitalism." In Thompson, *Customs in Common: Studies in Traditional Popular Culture,* pp. 352–403. New York: New Press.

Thompson, F.M.L. 1994. "Business and Landed Élites in the Nineteenth Century." In Thompson, ed., *Landowners, Capitalists, and Entrepreneurs: Essays for Sir John Habakkuk,* pp. 139–70. Oxford: Clarendon Press.

Thompson, Kenneth W. 1981. *Cold War Theories.* Vol. 1, *World Polarization, 1943–1953.* Baton Rouge: Louisiana State University Press.

T.K. 1976. *Letters from South Korea.* Ed. Sekai, trans. David L. Swain. New York: IDOC/North America.

T. K. Sei. 1974. *Kankoku kara no tsūshin.* Ed. Sekai Henshūbu. Tokyo: Iwanami Shoten.

Toffler, Alvin. 1970. *Future Shock.* New York: Random House.

Tto Hana ŭi Munhwa, ed. 1988. *Chibae munhwa, namsŏng munhwa.* Seoul: Ch'ŏngha.

———. 1990. *Chubu, kŭ makhim kwa t'ŭim.* Seoul: Tto Hana ŭi Munhwa.

Tu, Wei-ming. 1991. "The Search for Roots in Industrial East Asia: The Case of the Confucian Revival." In Martin E. Marty and R. Scott Appleby, eds., *Fundamentalisms Observed,* pp. 740–81. Chicago: University of Chicago Press.

Turner, John E., Vicki L. Hesli, Dong Suh Bark, and Hoon Yu. 1993. *Villages Astir: Community Development, Tradition, and Change in Korea.* Westport, Conn.: Praeger.

Twitchell, James B. 1992. *Carnival Culture: The Trashing of Taste in America*. New York: Columbia University Press.

United Nations Development Programme. 1994. *Human Development Report 1994*. New York: Oxford University Press.

Unno Fukuju. 1995. *Kankoku heigō*. Tokyo: Iwanami Shoten.

U.S. Department of State. 1961. "Mr. Bowles Responds to Request for U.S. Views on Korean Economy." *Department of State Bulletin*, June 12, pp. 930–33.

Valdés, Juan Gabriel. 1989. *La Escuela de Chicago: Operación Chile*. Buenos Aires: Grupo Editorial Zeta.

Van der Wee, Herman. [1984] 1986. *Prosperity and Upheaval: The World Economy, 1945–1980*. Trans. Robin Hogg and Max R. Hall. Berkeley: University of California Press.

Vogel, Ezra F. 1991. *The Four Little Dragons: The Spread of Industrialization in East Asia*. Cambridge, Mass.: Harvard University Press.

Wachtel, Howard M. 1986. *The Money Mandarins: The Making of a Supranational Economic Order*. New York: Pantheon.

Wada Haruki. 1995. *Chōsen sensō*. Tokyo: Iwanami Shoten.

Wade, L. L. 1980. "South Korean Political Culture: An Interpretation of Survey Data." *Journal of Korean Studies* 2: 1–45.

Wade, L. L., and B. S. Kim. 1978. *Economic Development of South Korea: The Political Economy of Success*. New York: Praeger.

Wade, Robert. 1982. *Irrigation and Agricultural Politics in South Korea*. Boulder, Colo.: Westview Press.

———. 1990. *Governing the Market: Economic Theory and the Role of Government in East Asian Industrialization*. Princeton, N.J.: Princeton University Press.

Walker, Martin. [1993] 1994. *The Cold War: A History*. New York: Henry Holt.

Wang, In Keun. 1986. *Rural Development Studies: Korea and Developing Countries*. Seoul: Seoul National University Press.

Warnberg, Tim. 1987. "The Kwangju Uprising: An Inside View." *Korean Studies* 11: 33–57.

Watanabe Toshio. 1982. *Gendai Kankoku keizai bunseki: kaihatsu keizaigaku to gendai Ajia*. Tokyo: Keisō Shobō.

———. 1986. *Kankoku: Venchā kyapitarizumu*. Tokyo: Kōdansha.

Watanabe Toshio and Fukagawa Yukiko. 1988. *Gonengo no Kankoku: Nihon o ou seichō kokka no kinmirai*. Tokyo: PHP Kenkyūsho.

Waterston, Albert. 1965. *Development Planning: Lessons of Experience*. Baltimore, Md.: Johns Hopkins University Press.

Watts, William. 1982. *The United States and Asia: Changing Attitudes and Policies*. Lexington, Mass.: Lexington Books.

Weber, Max. [1968] 1978. *Economy and Society: An Outline of Interpretive Sociology*. 2 vols. Ed. Guenther Roth and Claus Wittich. Berkeley: University of California Press.

Weems, Clarence Norwood. 1960. *Korea: Dilemma of Underdeveloped Country*. New York: Foreign Policy Association.

Wellons, Philip A. 1987. *Passing the Buck: Banks, Governments and Third World Debt*. Boston: Harvard Business School Press.

Wells, Kenneth M., ed. 1995. *South Korea's Minjung Movement: The Culture and Politics of Dissidence*. Honolulu: University of Hawaii Press.

West, James M., and Edward J. Baker. 1988. "The 1987 Constitution Reforms in South Korea: Electoral Processes and Judicial Independence." *Harvard Human Rights Yearbook* 1: 135–77.

Westphal, Larry E., Yung W. Rhee, Linsu Kim, and Alice Amsden. 1984. *Exports of Capital Goods and Related Services from the Republic of Korea*. Washington, D.C.: World Bank.

Westphal, Larry E., Yung W. Rhee, and Gary Pursell. 1979. "Foreign Influences on Korean Industrial Development." *Oxford Bulletin of Economics and Statistics* 41: 359–88.

Whang, In Joung. 1968. "Elites and Economic Programs: A Study of Changing Leadership for Economic Development in Korea, 1955–1967." Ph.D. diss., University of Pittsburgh.

———. 1981. *Management of Rural Change in Korea: The Saemaul Undong*. Seoul: Seoul National University Press.

White, Lawrence J. 1974. *Industrial Concentration and Economic Power in Pakistan*. Princeton, N.J.: Princeton University Press.

White, Margaret B., and Herbert D. White, eds. 1973. *The Power of People: Community Action in Korea*. Tokyo: Urban Industrial Mission, East Asian Christian Conference.

Wideman, Bernie. 1974. "The Plight of the South Korean Peasant." In Frank Baldwin, ed., *Without Parallel: The American-Korean Relationship Since 1945*, pp. 271–317. New York: Pantheon.

Winchester, Simon. 1988. *Korea: A Walk Through the Land of Miracles*. New York: Prentice-Hall.

Wolf, Charles, Jr. 1962. "Economic Planning in Korea." *Asian Survey* 2(10): 22–28.

Woo, Jung-en. 1991. *Race to the Swift: State and Finance in Korean Industrialization*. New York: Columbia University Press.

Wood, Robert E. 1986. *From Marshall Plan to Debt Crisis: Foreign Aid and Developmental Choices in the World Economy*. Berkeley: University of California Press.

World Bank. 1990. *World Development Report 1990*. New York: Oxford University Press.

————. 1993. *The East Asia Miracle: Economic Growth and Public Policy.* New York: Oxford University Press.

Worsley, Peter. [1964] 1970. *The Third World.* 2d ed. Chicago: University of Chicago Press.

Yang, Sung Chul. 1981. *Korea and Two Regimes: Kim Il Sung and Park Chung Hee.* Cambridge, Mass.: Schenkman.

Yi Chin-gyŏng. 1986. *Sahoe kusŏngch'eron kwa sahoekwahak pangbŏmnon.* Seoul: Ach'im.

Yi, Eunhee Kim. 1993. "From Gentry to the Middle Class: The Transformation of Family, Community, and Gender in Korea." Ph.D. diss., University of Chicago.

Yi Hŭng-t'ak. 1992. "Han'guk chŏnjaeng kwa ch'ulsannyŏk sujun ŭi pyŏnhwa." In Han'guk Sahoehakhoe, ed., *Han'guk chŏnjaeng kwa Han'guk sahoe pyŏndong,* pp. 23–59. Seoul: P'ulbit.

Yi Hyo-jae, Pak Hye-in, Pak Suk-cha, Yun Hyŏng-suk, Pak Min-ja, and An Chŏng-nam. 1991. *Chabonjuŭi sijanggyŏngje wa honin.* Seoul: Tto Hana ŭi Munhwa.

Yi Ki-ung. 1992. "Hugi chabonjuŭi wa sahoejuŭijŏk simin sahoeron." In Han'guk Sanŏpsahoe Yŏn'guhoe, ed., *Han'guk sanŏp sahoe ŭi hyŏnsil kwa chŏnmang,* pp. 115–91. Seoul: Munhak kwa Chisŏngsa.

Yi, Munyol. [1987] 1995. *Our Twisted Hero.* Trans. Kevin O'Rourke. Seoul: Minumsa.

Yi, Pŏm-sŏn. [1959] 1973. "A Stray Bullet." Trans. Marshall R. Pihl. In Marshall R. Pihl, ed., *Listening to Korea: A Korean Anthology,* pp. 127–54. New York: Praeger.

Yi Sun-ae, ed. 1989. *Bundan kokufuku to Kankoku josei kaihō undō: 1970-nendai o chūshin ni.* Tokyo: Ochanomizu Shobō.

Yi Tae-gŭn. 1987. *Han'guk chŏnjaeng kwa 1950-nyŏndae ŭi chabon ch'ukchok.* Seoul: Kkach'i.

————. 1990. "Kaihōgo kizokujitsugyōtai no jittai to sono shori katei." Trans. Kimura Mitsuhiko. In Nakamura Satoru, Kajimura Hideki, An Pyŏng-sik, and Yi Tae-gŭn, eds., *Chōsen kindai no keizai kōzō,* pp. 405–32. Tokyo: Nihon Hyōronsha.

Yi Tae-gŭn and Chŏng Un-yŏng, eds. 1984. *Han'guk chabonjuŭiron.* Seoul: Kkach'i.

Yi T'ae-jin. 1986. *Han'guk sahoesa yŏn'gu.* Seoul: Chisik Sanŏpsa.

————. 1989. *Chosŏn yugyo sahoesaron.* Seoul: Chisik Sanŏpsa.

Yi Uk-chŏng. 1994. "Kungnae Panggŭlladesi nodongjadŭl saengwhal silt'ae wa chŏgŭng chŏllyake kwanhan sarye yŏn'gu." Master's thesis, Seoul National University.

Yi Yŏng-hŭi. 1974. *Chŏnhwan sidae ŭi nolli.* Seoul: Ch'angjak kwa Pip'yŏngsa.

Yi Yŏng-u. 1991. "Urugwai raundŭ wa Han'guk kyŏngje chaep'yŏn."

In Yang U-jin et al., *Han'guk chabonjuŭi punsŏk*, pp. 269–313. Seoul: Ilbit.

Yi, Young-Suk. 1990. "Liberal Protestant Leaders Working for Social Change: South Korea, 1957–1984." Ph.D. diss., University of Oregon.

Yim, Louise. 1951. *My Forty Year Fight for Korea.* New York: A. A. Wyn.

Yoffie, David B. 1983. *Power and Protectionism: Strategies of the Newly Industrializing Countries.* New York: Columbia University Press.

Yŏm Hong-ch'ŏl, ed. 1980. *Che-3 segye wa chongsok iron.* Seoul: Han'gilsa.

———. 1983. *Chongsok ŭi kŭkpok.* Seoul: P'ulbit.

Yoon, Dae-Kyu. 1990. *Law and Political Authority in South Korea.* Boulder, Colo.: Westview Press.

Yoon, Jeong-Ro. 1989. "The State and Private Capital in Korea: The Political Economy of the Semiconductor Industry, 1965–1987." Ph.D. diss., Harvard University.

———[Yun Chŏng-no]. 1992. "Kwahak esŏ ŭi posang ch'egye." In Han'guk Sanŏpsahoe Yŏn'guhoe, ed., *Han'guk sanŏp sahoe ŭi hyŏnsil kwa chŏnmang*, pp. 67–88. Seoul: Munhak kwa Chisŏngsa.

Yŏsŏng Han'guk Sahoe Yŏn'guhoe, ed. 1990. *Han'guk kajongnon.* Seoul: Kkach'i.

Young, Crawford. 1994. *The African Colonial State in Comparative Perspective.* New Haven, Conn.: Yale University Press.

Young, Marilyn B. 1991. *The Vietnam Wars, 1945–1990.* New York: HarperCollins.

Yu, Eui-Young. 1982. "Seoul: Dynastic Capital to Metropolis." In Yunshik Chang, Tai-Hwan Kwon, and Peter J. Donaldson, eds., *Society in Transition with Special Reference to Korea*, pp. 79–100. Seoul: Seoul National University Press.

———. 1990. "Regionalism in the South Korean Job Market: An Analysis of Regional-Origin Inequality Among Migrants in Seoul." *Pacific Affairs* 63: 24–39.

Yu In-ho. 1979. *Nongŏp kyŏngje ŭi silsang kwa hŏsang.* Seoul: P'yŏngminsa.

———. 1982. *Minjung kyŏngjeron.* Seoul: P'yŏngminsa.

Yu, In Ho, and Byung Tae Kim. N.d. *The Economic Plight of Korean Farmers.* Seoul: Christian Institute for the Study of Justice and Development.

Yu Mun-mu. 1993. "Chabonjuŭi wa taejung munhwa." In Im Hŭi-sŏp and Pak Kil-sŏng, eds., *Onŭl ŭi Han'guk sahoe*, pp. 83–105. Seoul: Nanam.

Yu Tong-sik. 1987. *Kankoku no Kirisutokyō*. Tokyo: Tokyo Daigaku Shuppankai.

Yun, Heung-gil. [1977] 1989. "The Man Who Was Left as Nine Pairs of Shoes." Trans. Bruce Fulton and Ju-Chan Fulton. In Yun, *The House of Twilight*, ed. Martin Holman, pp. 96–147. London: Readers International.

Yun Kyŏng-ch'ŏl. 1986. *Bundango no Kankoku seiji*. Tokyo: Bokutakusha.

Yun Sŏk-nam and Cho Chu-hyŏn, eds. 1993. *Kyŏlhon iranŭn ideollogi*. Seoul: Hyŏnsil Munhak Yŏn'gu.

Zanzi, A. W. 1954. *Economic Reconstruction Problems in South Korea*. New York: Institute of Pacific Relations.

Zeon, Young-cheol. 1973. "The Politics of Land Reform in South Korea." Ph.D. diss., University of Missouri.

Zysman, John. 1983. *Governments, Markets, and Growth: Financial Systems and the Politics of Industrial Change*. Ithaca, N.Y.: Cornell University Press.

Index

In this index an "f" after a number indicates a separate reference on the next page, and an "ff" indicates separate references on the next two pages. A continuous discussion over two or more pages is indicated by a span of page numbers, e.g., "57–59." *Passim* is used for a cluster of references in close but not consecutive sequence.

Library of Congress Cataloging-in-Publication Data

Lie, John.
Han unbound : the political economy of South Korea / John Lie.
        p.   cm.
Includes bibliographical references and index.
ISBN: 978-0-8047-3055-6   ISBN: 978-0-8047-4015-9
    1. Korea (South)—Economic conditions—1948–1960.
    2. Korea (South)—Economic conditions—1960–   3. Korea
(South)—Politics and government—1948–1960.   4. Korea
(South)—Politics and government—1960–   I. Title.
HC467.L5   1998
330.95195'043 — dc21   97-34019
                                                            CIP
                                                            Rev.

Original printing 1998

Last figure below indicates year of this printing:
07   06   05   04   03   02   01   00